THE GLOBAL IN THE LOCAL

THE GLOBAL IN THE LOCAL

A CENTURY OF WAR, COMMERCE, AND TECHNOLOGY IN CHINA

XIN ZHANG

Harvard University Press

CAMBRIDGE, MASSACHUSETTS

LONDON, ENGLAND

2023

Printed in the United States of America

First printing

LIBRARY OF CONGRESS CATALOGING-IN-PUBLICATION DATA

Names: Zhang, Xin, 1956– author.
Title: The global in the local : a century of war, commerce, and technology in China / Xin Zhang.
Description: Cambridge, Massachusetts : Harvard University Press, 2023. | Includes bibliographical references and index.
Identifiers: LCCN 2022032511 | ISBN 9780674278387 (hardcover)
Subjects: LCSH: Globalization—China—Zhenjiang Xian—History. | Opium trade—China—Zhenjiang Shi—History. | Steam-navigation—China—Zhenjiang Shi—History. | Zhenjiang Shi (China)—History. | Zhenjiang Shi (China)—Commerce.
Classification: LCC DS797.56.Z546 Z43 2023 | DDC 951/.136—dc23/eng/20220815
LC record available at https://lccn.loc.gov/2022032511

For my beloved daughter, Lucie Eda Zhang

CONTENTS

ACKNOWLEDGMENTS

IT WAS QUITE A JOURNEY TO BRING this book from its inception to fruition. While my first book addressed rural societies in Henan, this covers urban communities in the lower Yangtze, delving into a range of topics spanning war to commerce to technology. It required fresh research, new contacts in China, and examination of never-before-seen materials. This ambitious project proved to be more challenging than I had anticipated, but I was very fortunate to have a few fine scholars guiding me every step of the way.

My endeavor began with conversations with the following scholars, whose advice and encouragement laid the foundation for the project: Jian Chen, Parks M. Coble, Huaiyin Li, Hanchao Lu, William T. Rowe, R. Keith Schoppa, Qin Shao, Brett Sheehan, Di Wang, R. Bin Wong, Ping Yao, and Wen-hsin Yeh. Bryna Goodman suggested I visit the national archives in England, France, and Japan, which allowed me to gather valuable materials from non-Chinese sources. Henrietta Harrison recommended a list of books and articles to me when I was conceiving the project. Anne Reinhardt sent me chapters of her manuscript before they were published. Ritika Prasad, a specialist in Indian history, also sent me copies of several chapters before her book was available.

While conducting fieldwork in China, I received support from Ma Junya, who helped me gain access to the Second Historical Archives of

China and Nanjing University's special collection. As I traveled to each local archive in the lower Yangtze, I met several individuals who assisted me in getting access and internal government documents. My contacts in Zhenjiang provided me with unpublished materials not even available to researchers in China, let alone someone from the United States. To protect their identities, I will not mention their names but I always remember them in my heart. In the United States, I visited the Library of Congress and university libraries at Harvard, Stanford, Chicago, Columbia, and Berkeley. The staff at Berkeley's Center for Chinese Studies copied many of the materials in its special collection for me.

I am especially grateful to the following people, whose unwavering support has been crucial: Kenneth Pomeranz, Elizabeth J. Perry, William C. Kirby, and Prasenjit Duara. To them all, I owe my deepest gratitude. I could write long paragraphs about what each one of them has done for me to enable this book to be published, but I will try to summarize here. As a leading scholar of global history, Kenneth Pomeranz has always been a source of inspiration and guidance. Elizabeth J. Perry provided a reading list as I began the project. William C. Kirby lent a helping hand every time I needed it. Prasenjit Duara generously spent valuable time on me.

My thanks also go to Stephen Halsey, whose knowledge about China has greatly broadened my own view, and J. Megan Greene, who offered moral support. These acknowledgments won't be complete without mentioning Kathleen McDermott, executive editor for history at Harvard University Press. From the start, Kathleen recognized the value of my work, and she continued to advocate for me over the years. Her persistence made it possible for this book to be published by Harvard University Press. For that, I will always be grateful.

Of course, I would not have been able to persevere through these years without the support of my family. My affectionate wife, Guangming Yang, has always been by my side and never doubted my ability to finish this book. My daughter, Lucie Eda Zhang—to whom this book is dedicated—has shown me endless love and confidence in many ways. And Jenaveve, my German shepherd, has brought me more joy than she will ever know.

I consider myself very privileged to have a family that regards my work as a priority.

In addition, I owe my gratitude to Indiana University for its support of the production of this book through a generous grant from its Presidential Arts and Humanities Program.

THE GLOBAL IN THE LOCAL

Introduction

UNDERSTANDING GLOBAL CHANGES IN CHINA

AN IMPORTANT QUESTION for students of Chinese history is how to ascertain changes in China in the global context that produced the rise of modern imperialism, intensified economic integration, and the spread of mechanized technology from Europe and North America during the nineteenth and early twentieth centuries. The difficulty in answering this question derives from the fact that some of the changes were entangled with the aspirations for global dominance of the industrialized countries in Europe, North America, and, later, Japan. Based on successful military campaigns against the Qing dynasty, these countries deeply penetrated Chinese society, subjugating most Chinese people to their economic interests and imperial ambitions. Still, during the same period, aided by mechanized technology, China embarked on a transformation that extended its economic linkages to the rest of the globe.

Because this segment of Chinese history is interwoven with those industrialized countries, it has been a challenge for us to ferret out the changes in China that reflected a deeper level of global transition beneath the surface while also observing the changes that followed the country's specific historical trajectory. We have been confronted with this challenge since the inception of China studies as an academic field in the United States, and it is therefore helpful to explore the scholarship on the three components of this study—the Opium War, trade, and technology—over the past decades.

Until the late 1970s, Chinese historians were under the influence of the Eurocentric and teleological view of global change inherent in the "grand narrative" of the rise of the West. Much of the early work rested on the assumption that China had to depend on stimuli from countries in Europe and North America to modernize. After the late 1970s until the early 1990s, China studies were focused on internal changes, ignoring much of the Chinese history related to global changes, a trend that continued especially after Paul Cohen highlighted a "China-centered approach."

Regarding the Opium War, aside from European imperialism, attention focused on how the Qing dynasty—and its "Middle Kingdom" mindset—interacted with the West while treating the opium trade as part of its tributary system. As many US scholars had by the late 1960s moved their investigation to the question of how China attempted to strengthen itself after defeat, still framing it as China's response to the West, Frederic Wakeman's 1966 *Strangers at the Gate* was a sharp departure.[1] For the first time, a work examined the war's effect on local society, especially as a cause for the Taiping Rebellion. By highlighting the social and economic changes after the war that underlay rural disorder, secret society activities, and widespread discontent, Wakeman not only brought attention to the interconnectedness between the war and local society, but also paid specific attention to the merchants, gentry, and villagers deeply impacted by the changes.[2]

Soon thereafter, the rise of social history saw historians in the United States not only moving away from such previously popular subjects as regime change, political figures, and leading intellectuals, but also focusing on local societies. Social historians set out to rediscover societies locale by locale, which eventually led to a much better understanding of the world. However, by design, social history was not disposed to address the "big questions" (as Lynn Hunt calls them) as global changes.[3] In China studies, social history had already started to take hold in the late 1970s and early 1980s. Paul Cohen's advocacy of a "China-centered approach" coincided with the gradual opening of local archives in China. Between the late 1970s and early 1990s, the field saw many significant achievements in social and economic history and local society. However, most scholars shied away from topics like the Opium War, to avoid an association with a Western-centric view of Chinese history.[4] New cultural history sparked a great deal of interest among historians on China in the 1990s, but none of the resulting studies targeted the war directly.[5]

As part of postcolonial discourse, some historians on China saw in the Opium War an opportunity to reexamine issues of Western imperialism. However, they paid little attention to the people in the local society.[6] There has been renewed interest in the Opium War after James Hevia's work, and there is a clear trend toward using personal records such as memoirs, personal correspondence, and private journals to tell the story.[7] Aided by these new sources, scholars have addressed the significant role of various individuals in the war. Several studies present a Chinese perspective in which individual character and morals mattered as much as the diplomatic missteps and military weakness of the Qing dynasty. Others relate the war to the cultural context in which the British interacted with China, from gift exchange to etiquette practices.[8] Despite their contributions, these studies concentrated exclusively on Qing officials or individuals like European travelers and missionaries. Recently, more and more historians have begun to study the experiences of ordinary people in other wars. A study of people's experiences in the Opium War will thus enable us to better grasp the meaning of the war as a tool of modern imperialism.[9]

While the influence of social history resulted in a loss of scholarly interest in the Opium War, work on the Chinese commercial system benefited from it. Nevertheless, the focus was not on the transformation of the system or people's experiences as China was confronting immense pressure from global changes; it was the structure of China's commercial system that received the most consideration from researchers like G. William Skinner, who argued that, due to insurmountable geographical barriers, most trade activities were conducted macroregionally, within each macroregion rather than between them. Skinner insists there was only a limited amount of transregional trade activity between macroregions before the end of the nineteenth century, albeit a great deal existed along the Yangtze River. A national level of market integration only surfaced when modern technology was available, after the Treaty of Shimonoseki in 1895.[10]

Its immense popularity notwithstanding, Skinner's model received criticism for the lack of attention to "human agency." One of the critics was William Rowe, who argued for the power of the social network that allowed trade groups to link with one another across macroregions, an argument buttressed not only by American scholars but also by leading researchers in China. Some have shown that what Skinner considered a discrete macroregion was part of a much larger trade zone stretching to South Asia; others have pointed out the existence of crossregional trade activities. Recently, a growing number of historians have begun to realize that localities in China were not bounded territories; there were already significant translocal activities during the period. But these studies are not targeting questions regarding the transformation of the commercial system during intense global changes in the late nineteenth and early twentieth centuries.[11]

As some Chinese historians debated the structure of China's commercial system, a group of scholars attempted to answer questions related to China's commercial transition from the perspective of "Western penetration" of China, through a focus on the treaty ports. Most concluded that the Western infiltration of the ports had little impact on the native Chinese economy, especially in rural, interior China. Later, Thomas Rawski supported that conclusion. After Rawski, more research was devoted to treaty ports, but the new studies did not address China's commercial transformation amid global changes.[12]

Alongside the treaty-port conversation, there was discussion among several Japanese scholars who study "intra-Asia trade" and shed light on how Chinese treaty ports connected to the commercial networks of Asia, with links into the country's interior. Kaoru Sugihara considers the growth of "intra-Asian trade" the result of Asian producers and merchants who responded to trade opportunities, not the consequence of Western penetration, especially after the Dutch and English East India companies, as well as the Qing rulers, relaxed restrictions on trade.[13] Takeshi Hamashita showed that the intrusion of the Euro-American economy did not alter the regional trade system; rather, it lost itself within the system. He discovered not only the connection between traditional Chinese tributary system and the global changes that led to the creation of treaty ports in Asia, but also the way trade in East Asia was linked through the treaty ports, the hinterland of open ports, and coastal regions.[14] One important question was: When in the nineteenth century did the major transition in China's trade system occur? Whereas Skinner and Rowe both deem the 1880s the beginning of that transition, Hamashita marks the mid-nineteenth century as the turning point. The difference comes from the fact that they have looked at two different aspects of long-distance trade: one within the territories of Chinese dynasties (transregional trade) and the other, the extension of the former to the rest of Asia.[15]

Another central issue revolves around the size of the cities that have been studied. Research interest has been slanted toward large cities, not the medium or small-sized cities that provide the crucial link between large cities and the vast countryside. Among the large cities that received attention, Shanghai tops the list, with more studies than all other cities combined. After Shanghai, one finds work on Beijing and Guangdong; Nanjing; and Hong Kong, Tianjin, and Macau. Medium or small cities have received much less attention; a shortlist includes places such as Nantong and Yangzhou.[16]

Still, in studies of large cities, there are plenty of considerations about the life of ordinary people. Similarly, many works about other large cities have devoted attention to the people's lives.[17] Yet, when it comes to medium or small cities, research about ordinary people is lacking. The only few excellent works have come from scholars like Qin Shao, Antonia Finnane, Elisabeth Köll, and Hanchao Lu. We need to discover how medium or small cities served as the crucial linkage between the large cities and China's vast countryside. We shall find out how people in local society played a role as facilitators in the transformation while confronting various circumstances brought about by global changes.[18]

Now we turn to the scholarship on China's experiences with technological changes. Historians used to examine Chinese technology by using Western science as the benchmark, treating technology as part of science. Only recently did we begin to recognize the Chinese identity in scientific development as we started to separate technology from science. By doing so, we began to discover how the advancement of China's technology impacted people's lives.

The quest for knowledge about China's development of science and technology began in the early twentieth century among European thinkers with a "failure narrative" about China's inability to develop capitalism and a scientific revolution as Western European countries had. During the 1950s and 1960s, some pointed specifically to Confucian orthodoxy as the probable cause. Quite a few scholars of Chinese science were shadowed for decades by the same assumption that Chinese civilization prevented the development of modern science and technology.[19]

To some degree, the ascent of social history impacted the field of Chinese science and technology. In the early 1980s, social historians adopting the "China-centered approach" began to use different methods for answering earlier questions, relying mainly on Chinese sources.[20] Under the influence of postcolonialism, the 1990s became a decade of dynamic changes in the study of the Chinese history of science and technology that witnessed multiple ongoing trends and diversification of research approaches. For instance, Francesca Bray broke new ground by discovering the role of women in material production, with an approach developed by gender studies within social history.[21]

Another major shift in the field was just on the horizon when Benjamin Elman published his article "'Universal Science' versus 'Chinese Science.'" Then Elman's book *On Their Own Terms* challenged the "Chinese acceptance" literature by suggesting that though benefiting from Western learning, the Chinese produced scientific knowledge "on their own terms." In *A Cultural History of Modern Science in China* a year later, Elman further criticizes the way the exchange of scientific knowledge between China and Europe was perceived in the past.[22] Not only did Elman enhance awareness of the interactive nature of exchange between the Chinese and Europeans on science, but his work also led to a new search for China's own identity in science and technology.[23]

Studies started to move away from transmission and reception questions into Chinese technology, paying attention to general-purpose technologies related to everyday life.[24] Rather than subjugating it under a broader category of science, Francesca Bray treats technology as a viable subject matter in itself, and has examined the differences in gender roles in Chinese technology through the daily experiences of ordinary people plowing, weaving, and managing the domestic sphere.[25]

Meanwhile, as historians returned to subjects related to countries in the North Atlantic, they started to reexamine China's experiences with Western technology, including studies on railroads and steamships. Steamship studies were conducted as far back as the early 1960s and 1970s, but because most were framed within Western imperialism in China, their appeal diminished long ago.[26] But Anne Reinhardt has examined the Chinese experience with steamships from a new perspective. She sheds light on the question of "China's particular experience with Western domination and its legacies in the late nineteenth and early twentieth centuries" from the perspective of how the steamship network itself played a role in semi-colonializing Chinese society.[27]

More and more studies on China's involvement with Western technology have come out recently. Despite their undeniable contribution, however, most of the research is not aimed at telling the story of people's experiences with the technology.[28] We need studies about how the Chinese met Western technology when it arrived as part of global changes. Specifically, we need to know not only how local government dealt with various local issues caused by the appearance of the new technology, but also, and more importantly, how people negotiated the technology, how they struggled to cope with circumstances arising from the use of the technology, and how their efforts to take advantage of the technology to better their lives inadvertently contributed to China's technological transformation.

ZHENJIANG AS CASE STUDY

To fill in the gaps in our understanding of how China transformed itself during the nineteenth and early twentieth centuries and to meet the challenge Chinese historians have been facing for decades, I use the case study of Zhenjiang, a medium-sized city 153 miles west of Shanghai. Situated at the crossroads of the Yangtze River and the Grand Canal, it was also part of the most prosperous region in the country, the lower Yangtze.[29]

In many ways, Zhenjiang's experiences give us a unique opportunity to ascertain how Chinese society interacted with three global changes: the rise of modern imperialism, intensified economic integration, and the spread of mechanized technology from Europe and North America during the nineteenth and early twentieth centuries. Zhenjiang was one of the few inland places invaded by the British army during the Opium War, although it was not on the east coast, where most invasions took place. Because it was one of the main connecting points for trade groups north and south of the Yangtze River, it was at the center of China's commercial transformation. The city was among the first to see the arrival of steamship technology brought to China by the industrialized countries during the war and their economic expansion. By concentrating on Zhenjiang, therefore, we will be able to peek into how local society negotiated global changes during the nineteenth and early twentieth centuries, a crucial period of modern Chinese history.[30]

First, I apply the definition of "local" to Zhenjiang with the following observations regarding what constituted "local communities" in the urban context and the scope of local activities in the late nineteenth and early twentieth centuries. Dictionaries typically define "local" as "a particular place" for "neighborhoods or communities," or "a restricted area" such as "a small city, town, or district." Some see local as the opposite of global in a stratified world layered like a cake; others consider the local parts of the global as stars in a galaxy. Meanwhile, "local" often has a spatial dimension for delimiting human activities within a specific territory or a geographic distance. This perception can sometimes lead us to overlook the fact that most human activities are not constrained by a given territory, including those at the local level.

Although the city of Zhenjiang, especially the area within the city wall, may fit the definition of "local" administratively, local communities in the urban context were very different from those in rural areas. In the early nineteenth century, the city (not unlike other cities of similar size), consisted of neighborhoods (*jiefang* 街坊) divided by streets. Most residents in those neighborhoods were much like villagers, with little sense of being urban. Growth meant that by the late nineteenth century the city was full of newcomers, many of whom were small storeowners, business brokers, and artisans, as well as sojourners like merchants, boatmen, and laborers, so that the city was fragmented into small communities or ethnic enclaves. These communities came together and turned the city into what Henri Lefebvre called "lived spaces," as people from different communities met in common areas like teahouses or joined one another in city rituals like festivals or other street celebrations. Therefore, I see localities in China not as bounded territories. Besides, there were already significant translocal activities in Chinese society during the period under investigation.[31]

Second, an important change in Chinese society during the late nineteenth and early twentieth centuries was the increasing mobility of the general population after the arrival of the steamboat and, later, the train. Because of this, not only did cities grow to include their adjacent suburbs, but also the area where residents conducted their activities, marketing or otherwise, largely spread along the Yangtze River. This resulted in the expansion of both translocal networks and the scope of local activities that extended far beyond their base communities.[32]

These observations lead us to revise the way we measure the scope of local activity during the period, given that what differentiates "local" activity from "regional" or "national" is no longer the area covered by these activities but the scale on which, as well as the degree to which, the activities were organized. In other words, as long as the activities were not organized at the regional level, even if people from several localities participated, they should still be considered local activities. In this book, therefore, I recognize "local activities" undertaken beyond those neighborhoods.

In addition, we also need to reconsider definitions of the term "people" for the study of Zhenjiang. In recent years, it has become common among historians of China to study Chinese local society with bifurcated categories of "elite" versus "non-elite" by relying on criteria like wealth, power, and prestige. As historian Chris Bayly points out in his discussion of the issue of rural movement in India in subaltern studies, it is rather difficult (as well as problematic) to apply such categories to individuals whose social position is hard to determine. As Bayly notes, "every subaltern was an elite to someone lower than him." Similarly, I also have found it difficult to use these bifurcated categories for a wide range of individuals such as smaller shop owners, petty brokers, and artisans who made up a large portion of the population in Zhenjiang. For example, it would be rather arbitrary to categorize big brokers as "elite" but smaller ones as "non-elite," because the line between them is usually blurred. Furthermore, the bifurcated categorization seems to be more useful when we investigate the power structure of local society than when we are analyzing local society's negotiation with global changes. For practical purposes, therefore, I will use the term "people" in this study to include a broad spectrum of individuals from street beggars to small steamboat-business owners.[33]

The book is organized in three parts. In Part I, I investigate how the Opium War, as the embodiment of modern imperialism, hastened historical changes in China by bringing Chinese local society into direct negotiation with global changes. I want to find out how a war that was forced upon China brought the invader and the invaded, from different parts of the globe and carrying distinctive cultural backgrounds, into a negative form of contact with each other. My goal is to show not only how Chinese soldiers, including Manchu and Han, and British military men became part of the "negotiation," but also how ordinary people in China, including women and children, were drawn into experiences that led to the tragedy of mass suicide. I intend to discover, above the atrocities and destruction, how the war enabled the people of Zhenjiang as well as the British soldiers there to gain firsthand knowledge of each other, albeit not without a great deal of misperception and misinterpretation.

For this part of the study, I rely on "transnational memories" from both sides of the war, British as well as Chinese. Historian Akira Iriye has described the significance of relying on what he called "transnational memory" when studying transnational history. He notes how, in the examples of the films *Flag of My Father* and *Letters from Iwo Jima,* through the "parallel stories" of soldiers from the United States and Japan, the characters' "common humanity comes out quite clearly, suggesting that the experiences of fighting a deadly battle could also reveal what the soldiers on both sides shared. That would be conducive to generating a sense of transnational memory." This book similarly uses personal memoirs and diaries from British officers (none were available from ordinary British soldiers) and personal journals from Chinese contemporaries.[34]

In Part II, I scrutinize how Chinese local society's negotiation with global changes unfolded in the economic arena in the second half of the nineteenth century. I investigate Zhenjiang's participation in the global economic transition during which Shanghai rose as an economic center of the country, not only engendering the transformation of China's commercial system of transregional trade but also extending China's economic connection with other Asian countries and the rest of the globe. To discern Zhenjiang's experiences in the transition, I take a close look at the city's role as a brokerage town for merchants north and south of the Yangtze River, many of whom were agents of major commercial networks in the country and traded with the rest of Asia. I examine how Zhenjiang reoriented itself within this urban context to become part of the Shanghai commercial network that existed transnationally between China and Japan. My examination will first target brokers then traditional financial institutions to identity the "building blocks" of the new day-to-day business practices that surfaced during the late nineteenth century and enabled the local communities in Zhenjiang to become active participants in global economic transition.[35]

Part III examines Chinese local society's negotiation with global changes after the arrival of one of the world's major new technologies from Europe and North America: steam navigation. I show how steamship technology enhanced the global and local nexus, making people face specific sets of new challenges in everyday life. I investigate how local communities coped with the challenges of this new and foreign technology by not only adopting it but also leveraging its tremendous opportunities for their own benefit. I first consider how local entrepreneurs circumvented obstacles from within Chinese society when using steamboats on the inner waterways. I then focus on the efforts of people in local communities to grapple with the various challenges this new technology introduced to everyday life. Some challenges resulted from boat accidents, the settlements of which often involved higher levels of authority as well as foreign consulates. I underscore that people in Chinese society were capable of taking charge of their lives amid global technological changes even as their lack of knowledge regarding the technology created a great deal of confusion and puzzlement.

One thing I note in this study is the role of the state when Chinese local society was negotiating global changes. For example, when Zhenjiang was under British invasion, the reaction of state officials—both those sent by the dynasty and those in local administration—had a significant effect on the response of local communities. Following the outbreak of the Opium War, the Qing state signed a series of unequal treaties with the industrialized countries. Not only were these treaties largely responsible for subjugating Chinese local society to economic penetration by these countries, but they also led China into joining a transnational commercial system directly linked to countries in the North Atlantic. After China was introduced to steamship technology, state participation in the adoption of this technology—during each period of the Qing dynasty, the warlords, and the Nationalist government—influenced the way people negotiated with the technology. This book thus joins other studies in confirming the undeniable role of the state in global and local interaction.[36]

I have written the book as a narrative history characterized by Clifford Geertz's term "thick description," an approach that aims to present human experiences during historical change.[37] My goal is to reach a balance between "conceptual narrative"—"the concepts and explanations that we construct as social researchers"—and "ontological narrative"—the stories told by "social actors." Believing that the significance of historical research lies in the combination of micro and macro analyses, I pay a significant amount of attention to specifics before I reach my conclusion on a grand scale.[38]

CHINA AND GLOBAL CHANGE BEFORE THE NINETEENTH CENTURY

To gain insight into how Chinese local society negotiated global changes in the nineteenth and early twentieth centuries, it is instructive first to examine China's role in global changes before the nineteenth century. With the continuous expansion of external linkages with different parts of the world, China was already characterized by increasing interconnectedness before the nineteenth century.

Our understanding of long-term global changes and China's role in them before the nineteenth century is closely associated with the discussion of "world systems." According to analysts, several world systems existed before the sixteenth century. For some scholars, these were found in Europe, Russia, and the Ottoman Empire. There were also three world-economies between the Middle East and the Far East—Islamic, Indian, and Chinese—that could be considered as a whole the fourth system. For others, the systems revolved around the Indian Ocean, the areas centered on China, and the Mediterranean-European zones. Despite the fact that each analyst has a different way of discerning what amounts to a world system, scholars seem to agree that China was the hub of a large world economy before the sixteenth century.[39]

One reason is that the Silk Road was the main connection for the entire world (excluding the Americas). After the Han dynasty opened access to the Tarim Basin and the Gansu Corridor, the Silk Road became one of the chief avenues for China proper to be linked to Europe, Persia, the Indian subcontinent, and Arabia. Along the road, Buddhism was spread in the first and second centuries CE. Goods were sold from Peking to Rome, or Daqin (大秦, the Chinese name for Rome or, rather, Syria), through Kashgar, although most of that trade was conducted through middlemen like merchants from South Asia, Central Asia, and the Middle East. Ideas, as well as diseases, were also passed from one place to another by merchants, travelers, monks, pilgrims, and missionaries.[40]

Sea routes were another way of connecting different parts of the world. Asia was one of the earliest places in the world that saw seafaring activities, and China was a country among the most advanced in shipbuilding technology. Through the sea route, China was able to reach Java, India, Somalia, Arabia, Egypt, Persia, and Europe (via an overland route in Egypt).

The maritime trade in the Indian Ocean that allowed Asia, Europe, Africa, the Middle East, and India to meet emerged around the seventh century. After the rise of Islam, the area between the eastern Mediterranean and Persia had a relatively stable environment in terms of religion and political authority, giving merchants the opportunity to conduct trade. At the same time, merchants from the Indian subcontinent also brought products like cotton and silk to the Red Sea, the Persian Gulf, and east coast of Africa. That coincided with China's economic prosperity during the Tang dynasty (618–907 CE). Through trade networks in South and Southeast Asia, Chinese merchants became active in trade around 900 CE with goods like porcelain and silk that were highly prized by many, including Europeans. The Tang and Song dynasties very much depended on the income from maritime trade, including trade with places within Asia.[41]

The Mongol Empire, which spanned the thirteenth and fourteenth centuries, including its conquering of China and establishing the Yuan dynasty (1279–1368), did not cut off connections between different parts of the world. On the contrary, it enhanced them by offering a vast territory stretching from China to Hungary and from northern Russia to Tibet under a single Mongol rule. Though the Mongol rulers harshly treated the people they conquered, they brought to their territories not only the Pax Mongolica (Mongol Peace) but also a unified trading system along with a postal system. Because of this, trade routes along Central Asia were revived, which allowed Arab traders to access China proper and ultimately settle in the Muslim community in Quanzhou (presently the largest city in Fujian Province). They reached the rest of China from the coastal areas until the Mongol rulers set up trade bureaus to contain their activities within that area.[42]

Under the Mongol Empire, maritime trade flourished, and through it Chinese merchants brought to the world market goods like silk, porcelain, copper coinage, and silver bullion. Like previous dynasties, the Yuan dynasty treated the profit from maritime trade as an important source of revenue.[43]

Based on this, one group of scholars emphasizes the Mongol Empire's significance in the worldwide changes toward globality. For example, sociologist Janet L. Abu-Lughod believes that a premodern world system emerged in the thirteenth century, within which Asia Minor was connected with China over the land route while Egypt was connected with India, Malaysia, and China through the sea route. In agreement with Abu-Lughod, Martin Wolf considers the Mongol conquest of Eurasia in the thirteenth century one of two milestones in the rise of a global consciousness, with the other one being European voyages of discovery in the fifteenth and sixteenth centuries. Economist Ronald Findlay even suggests that the establishment of the Mongol Empire across the central Eurasian land mass was the beginning of the world moving toward globality.[44]

Not long after the Yuan dynasty in China—part of the Greater Mongol Empire—had ended, the Ming emperor, Zhu Yuanzhang, banned maritime activities (in 1371) while adopting a new policy to restrict private trade and monopolize the maritime trade under the tributary system. After Zhu died, the next emperor, Zhu Di, toward the end of Zheng He's maritime missions in 1433, declared it shameful to earn profits from trade and started restricting China's contact with foreign countries on the sea. Between the Ming and the Qing dynasties, the maritime trade ban was lifted and reimposed numerous times, limiting China's ability to compete against the European influence in South and Southeast Asia. Coincidentally, just about half a century after the Ming dynasty suspended its treasure ships that once traveled along the Indian Ocean trade routes and reached Arabia as well as East Africa, Christopher Columbus arrived in America (in 1492), and Vasco da Gama successfully journeyed around the Cape of Good Hope (in 1497).

Before these events, Muslim traders were the ones who linked Southeast Asia with India, the Persian Gulf, and the Red Sea. With the help of Sufist teaching, they converted much of western Indonesia to Islam. The expansion of cash crops like pepper in western Java, Sumatra, and Borneo, as well as mining in the Malay Peninsula, gave Muslims the opportunity to strengthen their hold on Southeast Asia and work with the Chinese and Indians in maritime trade.[45]

Following Vasco da Gama, the Portuguese arrived at the Indian Ocean and successfully defeated the Muslims to gain access to the entire area between the Indian Ocean and the South China Sea. Afterward, however, all European countries, including Portugal itself, competed against one another for access to, and in some cases dominance over, places like Melaka, Sumatra, Siam, the Philippines, Taiwan, and Japan.[46]

Meanwhile, while da Gama's voyage opened the sea route between Europe and Asia, Columbus's voyage led to what American historian

Alfred Crosby termed the "Columbian Exchange," in which the transfer of plants, diseases, populations, animals, technology, and culture occurred between Afro-Eurasia and America. Likewise, in 1521, Ferdinand Magellan sailed across the Pacific during his circumnavigation of the entire world, which led to what another American historian, John McNeill, called the "Magellan Exchange," or the transfer of different species across the Pacific. It is undeniable, however, that da Gama's journey enabled European countries including Portugal, Spain, the Netherlands, and England access to China through the footholds they established in Southeast Asia. These European ventures led eighteenth-century theoretician Adam Smith to call Columbus's voyage to America and da Gama's passage to the East Indies by the Cape of Good Hope "the most important events recorded in the history of mankind."[47] Since Smith, it has been accepted by many that the sixteenth century saw the emergence of changes on a global scale. Some divide these changes into three phases—archaic, proto, and modern—and stress the significance of these events in the rise of globality starting with the archaic phase. In their view, the events of the sixteenth century triggered the early process of globalization.[48]

By focusing on the exchange between Europe and Asia instead, others suggest that da Gama's journey created the "Eurasia maritime world," generating an interchange of ideas, philosophies, and cultural products between Europe and Asia. Some individuals, noting that after the Spaniards conquered Manila (Philippines), the place became the crucial link between Asian, European, and American markets, argue for the precise year of 1571 to be the date for the formation of global consciousness.[49]

From the perspective of global commerce, however, economic historians Kevin H. O'Rourke and Jeffrey G. Williamson argue that the world first began to see global changes in the nineteenth century, when a sudden drop in transport costs allowed the prices of commodities in Europe and Asia to equalize. Because events like Columbus's discovery of America and Vasco da Gama's reaching Southeast Asia had only a limited impact on commodity prices, they are seen as contributing little to the formation of global commerce.[50]

Nevertheless, from China's standpoint, events of the sixteenth century enhanced China's significance in the world by allowing it to be connected all the way to America, thus providing it the opportunity to play a major role in the evolving global commerce through being a center of the emerging system of intercontinental trade. Of course, this was possible only because China did not isolate itself from the rest of the world after the Ming dynasty canceled its treasure voyages.

For a long while, there existed the perception that China had shut its door to the outside world after the Ming dynasty's withdrawal from treasure ship journeys because of a "superiority complex" combined with xenophobia. Some even extrapolated that China's self-imposed isolation was the main reason the country did not live up to its potential in scientific as well as economic advancements.[51] This perception was based on the common assumption that China's overland trade declined once the expansion of maritime activities of countries like Portugal, Spain, the Netherlands, and England intensified maritime trade in the Indian Ocean and the South China Sea, decreasing the importance of the overland link between China and other parts of the world in the process. This assumption was reinforced by studies showing that not long after the thirteenth century, the connection between China and Italy was broken when merchants from the east and west no longer met at the Black Sea. This assumption persisted in spite of an early study that found that during the period of Emperor Zhu Di's restriction on maritime trade, China's overland ties with places like Central Asia continued because the Ming rulers allowed merchants from Central Asia to enter China. Meanwhile, the Ming dynasty sent many missions to Samarkand, Tashkent, Bukhara, and as far as Persia.[52]

In recent years, growing numbers of researchers have argued that China continued as an active participant in global commerce as the Europeans arrived in Asia. One of the reasons the Ming dynasty's restrictions failed to isolate China was that while the dynasty attempted to restrict private participation in maritime trade, it allowed overland trade to continue. Instead of ending the Silk Road or replacing it with the maritime route, the long-distance trade from the early fifteenth century to the nineteenth century not only endured but also strengthened from time to time. For instance, tobacco produced in the Bay of Bengal, the Arabian Sea, or the eastern Mediterranean was transported overland between Eurasia and China. Some was smuggled into Russia and Mongolia, and some was brought to the Eastern Turkestani territories, later known as Xinjiang.[53]

Meanwhile, even after China officially ended its maritime trade, the country continued to have contact with other parts of Asia and, through them, with the rest of the world, partially because merchants took advantage of the dynasty's tributary system to circumvent the trade restriction. A significant number of studies have addressed the Chinese tributary system since John Fairbank and S. Y. Teng's early paper appeared. An important focus of the research in the last decade or so has been on the system of the Qing dynasty. As a result, most of us discarded previous notions about the Qing basing its relationship with its neighbors mainly on one system after the new research showed, for example, that the Qing dynasty used various methods to deal with the Russians and Muslims for control of Upper Manchuria, Inner and Outer Mongolia, Qinghai, Tibet, and Xinjiang. And at the same time, it also used strategies ranging from violent repression to economic incentives to force people in those areas into submission. Because of these studies, many scholars became aware that the system had already started to decline before the end of the Ming dynasty, partially because of the European intrusion into the tributary states, a trend that continued during the Qing dynasty.[54]

Despite the decline of the tributary system, however, Chinese merchants continued to rely on the overseas networks that existed largely among the tribute states to trade with merchants from other parts of Asia. At the same time, most of these places became sites of indirect trade with European traders through intermediaries, which was the main reason the Chinese remained connected with the outside world. These networks spread all over the East and Southeast Asia in Korea, Japan, the Ryukyu Islands, Annan (Vietnam), Champa (central and southern Vietnam), Siam (Thailand), Burma (Myanmar), Nepal, and Taiwan (not a tribute state). Through these networks, Chinese merchants developed a complex trading system to link themselves to countries around the world.[55]

Inside China, merchants operated within their networks in the coastal regions of south and southeast China in places such as Haicheng (in Liaoning), Guangdong, and Amoy (in Fujian). From the coastal areas, they connected with overseas Chinese merchants in East and Southeast Asia.

Their trade activities thus contributed to the economic development of East and Southeast Asia, like helping the growth of commercial ports in Nagasaki and Kyushu and maintaining the prosperity of Macao, Manila, Banten, Batavia, Ayudhya, Melaka, and Taiwan (after Chinese settlement there).[56]

Chinese merchants were equally active in North Asia. While the Manchu Qing dynasty didn't succeed in subordinating Mongols within the tributary system, Chinese merchants of Han origin "gradually established intricate commercial networks covering most of the Mongolian plateau," causing the traditional Mongolian nomadic society to decline during the seventeenth and eighteenth centuries. By relying on their networking power, Chinese merchants forced some Mongol nobles into subservience.[57]

As a result of the networking activities of Chinese merchants, the tributary system became the foundation upon which the Asian trade networks that centered on China and extended from North Asia to Southeast Asia could rise in East Asia in the nineteenth century. Therefore, rather than becoming isolated, China continued to be well connected with the rest of the globe even after the Ming dynasty adopted a restrictive trade policy.[58]

To find out China's role in the emerging global commerce, we may take a closer look at the rising intercontinental commerce and the global silver exchange after the sixteenth century. Here we find a description of how increased intercontinental commerce appeared after the end of the fifteenth century and coincided with China's economic development during the Ming dynasty: because sea routes were safer and faster than overland routes, they allowed various commodities to flow among the continents of Eurasia, Africa, and America. Therefore, not long after the end of the fifteenth century, there was an exponential increase of goods—in addition to a large number of slaves from Africa—from Southeast Asia (spices), India (cotton fabrics), Africa (gold), the Americas (silver, furs, sugar, and tobacco), and China (silk and porcelain).

This new development in global commerce later met with the increase of the production of goods in China in the seventeenth century, many of which were targeted for overseas markets. At the same time, the Pearl River Delta in China became the export center that traded ceramics, silks, and other luxury goods for markets in Asia, the Middle East, and Europe. The decision by Emperor Qianlong to designate Canton (in 1759) as the only trading port for foreigners did not alter China's position in the global market.[59]

Alongside increasing intercontinental commerce, there emerged a new global financial system based on the worldwide adoption of silver as its currency. As Adam Smith noted, starting in the sixteenth century, silver from Mexico and Bolivia flooded Western European countries, creating the most significant economic changes in Western Europe since Columbus's sighting of the Americas. What Smith observed was an important change in the global economy—the silver exchange—that encompassed Eurasia, Africa, and America between the sixteenth and mid-eighteenth centuries.[60]

China dominated this emerging global economy. That was because the world's silver bullion continued to flow into China during the Ming dynasty's monetization and commercialization. For instance, a significant amount of Spanish Carolus dollars entered China's market from the Philippine islands after Spain annexed the Philippines.[61]

On the other hand, through various changes, China was able to hold one of the largest silver reserves in the world by the eighteenth century. Contributing to this were the Ming dynasty's decision to use silver as tax payment after the dynasty's failure to use paper money; the large population that created a huge demand for silver; and the surge of China's overseas trade when the trade ban was relaxed, as well as through the tributary system. These changes overvalued silver in China relative to the rest of the world, creating a flow of silver mined in places like Spanish America and Japan into China through Nagasaki, Taiwan, Indochina, India, Cape Horn, Manila-Acapulco, Russia, the Ottoman Empire, and sites along the Silk Road.[62]

China's ability to provide the global market with prized products like silk, tea, and porcelain also resulted in the inflow of silver from other parts of Asia, Europe, and the Americas. Therefore, through the silver exchange, China participated in the Euro-American-Asian trade that shaped global commerce starting as early as the sixteenth century.[63]

China could continue to play a significant role in global commerce up to the nineteenth century because, unlike European countries, it was able to quickly recover from major crises. A remarkable historical phenomenon appearing in the seventeenth century was the increasing similarity in economic, as well as political, changes in different parts of the world to form discernable global patterns. One such change was a series of events known as "the crisis of the seventeenth century." During the mid-seventeenth century, Eurasia experienced renewed Malthusian pressures and environmental disasters, which first arose in the fourteenth century and were accompanied by a crisis of authority that led to the collapse of large states, from Stuart England to Ottoman Turkey to the Ming dynasty in China.[64]

Despite the various reasons for this global scale of change, China quickly recovered. One reason was that the Qing dynasty took a proactive stance in empire building in the seventeenth and eighteenth centuries, albeit often yielding to the interests of its multiethnic constituencies. For instance, the dynasty relied on its skillful rulership rather than resorting to Sinification. Promoting empire building in Central Asia and Xinjiang in the eighteenth and nineteenth centuries, the Qing resorted to policies that protected the interests of the local ethnic Uyghur group. Furthermore, contrary to what some have assumed, the Qianlong emperor was capable of catering to the needs of his multiethnic subjects to maintain unity. The result was that China under Qianlong became one of the world's most populous, politically stable, and multiethnic countries.[65]

In any sense, the Qing dynasty was "by no means the inward-looking and hermetic 'Celestial Empire' that Westerners once believed it to be." It wasted no time in engaging in territorial expansion, even after the dynasty had already created a state twice the size of its predecessor. In China's northwest, the Qing dynasty competed against Muscovite Russia and Mongolian Zunghars for control of Eurasia. Its success in territorial expansion transformed powerful relations in Eurasia, where China and Russia were the only remaining dominant countries and contributed to global changes in what historians have seen as the reversal of the seventeenth-century crisis: countries caught up in the previous crisis began to consolidate power, embarking on state building and territorial expansion along border areas. By the mid-eighteenth century, China finally became one of the world's largest empires. The Qing dynasty later applied the knowledge it gained from Eurasia to deal with "British" India after the mid-eighteenth century. Through these efforts, the dynasty continued to interact with the outside world, albeit with limited understanding.[66]

During this period, the Qing dynasty restored China's trading relations with countries like Korea and Japan. And the Qing dynasty, being a consumerist dynasty, took an "open door" approach, reaching out to sea to get the consumer goods needed to meet its internal demand.[67]

As we can see, not only was China well connected with the rest of the world throughout its history prior to the nineteenth century, albeit through indirect channels with places like Europe, but it also played a significant role in the global financial system beginning in the sixteenth century. The country maintained that role through state building and territorial consolidation in the eighteenth century.

◆

At the beginning of the nineteenth century, however, changes around the globe were destined to alter the way China connected to the rest of the world, and these global changes coalesced with local changes in China. A detailed description of what occurred in Zhenjiang will help us understand one of the most important yet difficult questions about Chinese history in the period under discussion: How do we comprehend the changes in China in a global context within which we see the rise of modern imperialism, the hastening of economic integration, and the spread of mechanized technology from Europe and North America to many parts of the world during the nineteenth and early twentieth centuries?

PART ONE

WAR AS A NEGATIVE FORM OF LIAISON

ONE OF THE MOST OBVIOUS CHANGES in China in the early nineteenth century was the emergence of industrialized countries from Europe and North America seeking global dominance after the rise of modern imperialism. As a result, China expanded and made more direct connections with these countries, albeit reluctantly and with insufficient knowledge of them. Meanwhile, a combination of factors, including differences in cultural traditions and worldviews, led to a series of confrontations between China and those countries, resulting in the Opium War that commenced with the British invasion of China.

Among scholars who study war as a primary form of human conflict, some consider war part of the global process, believing it has shrunk the world and contributed to a greater awareness of the world as one interconnected whole. According to political scientists Halvard Buhaug and Nils P. Gleditsch, war is an opportunity for negative interaction. By dividing human interactions into two types, positive and negative, they argue that war is the negative exchange of value or information between different sides. Tarak Barkawi, who specializes in the history of warfare, explains how this type of negative interaction takes place during war: "In and through war . . . people on both sides come to an intensified awareness of one another, reconstruct images of self and other, initiate and react to each other's moves." Based on this understanding, Barkawi suggests that "to be at war is to be interconnected with the enemy."[1]

What can the Opium War tell us about Chinese local society's negotiation with modern imperialism, beyond the confrontations, military and cultural, inside and outside the battlefield, and between the invader and the invaded—the ordinary people in local society? For answers, I will illustrate in this part not only how each side in the war prepared, engaged, and participated in the fight against its adversary, but also how the Chinese people reacted to the European soldiers during the battle of Zhenjiang.

Not only did this kind of "negotiation" incur a heavy price in human suffering, but the war itself, as a way of connecting those who came from different cultural and historical backgrounds, enhanced previous misperceptions of each side regarding the other. In this way, the Opium War was a negative form of liaison for both invader and invaded.

1

Place, History, and People

BEFORE WE EXAMINE THE WAR ITSELF, it is necessary to take a brief look at Zhenjiang and its people and history. Not only was Zhenjiang a place of historical significance, but life there was also vibrant and peaceful until it was destroyed under modern imperialism. We begin with Zhenjiang's first appearance as a ferry port.

Zhenjiang is located in what is currently Jiangsu Province, in the southwest corner. Transregional trade led to its emergence, along with other cities along the Yangtze River, especially its lower reaches. By the mid-nineteenth century, Zhenjiang, like Yangzhou and Nantong, had grown considerably, although most were still small or medium-sized.[1] The Yangtze River runs across China from today's Qinghai Province in the west to Shanghai in the east. It is the world's third-longest river, after the Nile in Africa and the Amazon in South America. The upper river goes from its source on the Tibetan plateau to Yichang (in Hubei); the middle runs between Yichang and Hukou (in Jiangxi); and the lower section flows eastward from Hukou to the Pacific Ocean. Despite the fact that the name "Yangtze River" is widely known in the West, most Chinese call it Changjiang (长江, Long River).[2]

Zhenjiang was part of the lower Yangtze region, historically the country's most prosperous, which began to develop circa 220 CE, at the end of the Eastern Han dynasty. During the Song dynasty, around 1127 CE, it became a social, economic, and cultural hub. In the ensuing centuries, it was not only the most populated region, but also the one where "urbanization was most conspicuous." The region remained the most commercialized in the country throughout the late imperial period.[3]

In China, people usually call the lower Yangtze region "Jiangnan" (江南, south of the river). In 1645, the Qing dynasty established Jiangnan Province, and in 1665 divided it into two: Anhui and Jiangsu. Since then, the name has referred to an area roughly coinciding with the present-day cities of Nanjing, Zhenjiang, Changzhou, Wuxi, Suzhou, Shanghai, Jiaxing, Huzhou, and Hangzhou.[4]

A large part of the region's population came from the north through three migrations that occurred between the Eastern Han and Northern Song dynasties. These did more than merely augment the population; they infused new lifestyles, agricultural practices, and other cultural elements into the culture. For instance, migrants facilitated the transformation of farming methods from extensive cultivation (*cufang gengzuo* 粗放耕作) to intensive (*jinggeng xizuo* 精耕细作), an improvement that significantly boosted rice production.[5]

In spring and autumn, the lower Yangtze River east of Zhenjiang was shaped like a tilted V, with a wide opening toward the East China Sea. The V converged where the river met the sea, and thus was called "the Gate of the Sea" (*haimen* 海门). Around 1300 CE, silt from the upper stream started to narrow the opening and gradually pushed the mouth of the sea eastward.[6]

During the Western Zhou dynasty, what is today Zhenjiang was a garrison set up by a branch of the royal family of the Zhou dynasty. Between the Qin and Western Han dynasties, the only connection between the north and south lower Yangtze River was a ferry crossing between a place called Jingkou (京口) on the south side and Guangling (广陵) on the north. Jingkou thus became a destination for travelers, especially those going north to south. During the Three Kingdoms period, Sun Quan, one of the three power contenders, built a fortress in front of the Beigu Mountain in Jingkou that resembled the shape of a metal vessel. It is believed that this fortress was the predecessor of the modern city of Zhenjiang.[7]

Zhenjiang's significance was greatly enhanced when the Sui dynasty built the Grand Canal. The second emperor, Sui Yangdi, had several reasons for building the canal, one of which was to allow him to tour the south. But the more important motivation was to transport tribute grains from the south, which was more economically developed than the north, to the new nation's capital, Luoyang. These considerations prompted his decision to dredge the existing canals, add more sections, and ultimately link the entire canal from modern-day Beijing to Hangzhou.[8]

The Grand Canal had four main parts, excluding a separate canal connecting Changan with the Yellow River. Jingkou was the entry point to one of the four, the Jiangnan Canal (江南河), which could accommodate boats up to 200 *chi* long, 50 *chi* wide, and 45 *chi* tall (with one *chi* equaling 1.21875 feet). Because the Grand Canal linked the country's five major rivers—the Hai, Yellow, Huai, Yangtze, and Qiantang—Zhenjiang instantly became part of the most extensive network of waterways in the country, especially given that it was situated at the crossroad of the Yangtze River and Grand Canal. *Caoyun* (漕运, transport of tribute grains to the dynastic capital) helped Zhenjiang become a busy city on the Yangtze River.[9]

THE RISE OF ZHENJIANG AND GRAIN TRANSPORT

Although tribute grains were already transported by river every spring and autumn, it was not until the construction of the Grand Canal that most tribute grains were shipped to the dynastic capitals through waterways. During the Sui and early Tang dynasties, Zhenjiang became the second major transshipment center for *caoyun*. *Caoyun* declined by the end of the Tang dynasty, however, and temporarily ceased to operate during the Five Dynasties and Ten Kingdoms period due to the division among regional military governors.[10]

The Northern Song dynasty soon revived *caoyun* by inheriting the shipping method from the Tang dynasty and reorganizing transportation routes to rely heavily on the rivers and the canal. After that, tribute grains along with other commercial goods were shipped from the lower Yangtze region to the national capital, Bianjing (汴京, modern-day Kaifeng), through the Grand Canal. With this new transport system, tribute grains from the southeast were first gathered at various locations south of the Yangtze River to be carried via the Grand Canal to the north. Although Zhenjiang was not a gathering site at the time, it was the point of transition for *caoyun* boats from Jiangnan to the northern section of the Grand Canal. Zhenjiang thus became a busy place for *caoyun*, so much so that a separate channel had to be built to relieve some of the traffic congestion caused by boats entering the Grand Canal from the city.[11]

Near the end of the Northern Song dynasty, the disruption of the Grand Canal north of the Yangtze River created by the war between the Song and Jin (a Jurchen tribe in northeast China) caused Yangzhou to lose much of its significance in *caoyun*. That inadvertently enhanced Zhenjiang's role in *caoyun*, however, especially when the Southern Song dynasty began relying heavily on the Jiangnan Canal to transport goods to the capital, Linan (临安, modern-day Hangzhou). After the dynasty reorganized the waterway transportation and centered it on the new capital, the Jiangnan Canal became the crucial link between Linan and the upper-lower Yangtze region. Zhenjiang thus emerged as one of the most prosperous cities along the lower Yangtze River.[12]

The Yuan dynasty established its capital in Dadu (大都, modern-day Beijing), which eliminated the need to transport tribute grains to Kaifeng or Luoyang, the original purpose of the Grand Canal. The dynasty rerouted the canal directly from the southeast to the northeast instead of from the southeast to the northwest. Over the years, however, the Huitong River became shallower, with several sections completely clogged with silt, so the dynasty opened a sea route for *caoyun* that went through the Yellow Sea and the Bohai Sea to the capital. The opening of the sea route significantly reduced the importance of Zhenjiang in *caoyun*.[13]

When the Ming dynasty banned maritime trade, Zhenjiang could have returned to its previous glory, had *caoyun* and the north-south trade on the Grand Canal been resumed. Instead, Emperor Ming Taizu moved the capital to Yingtianfu (应天府, modern-day Nanjing), making the shipping of tribute grains through the canal unnecessary, and activities along the canal were greatly reduced. In addition, the physical deterioration of the canals led long-distance traders to choose other routes. Both factors delayed the reemergence of Zhenjiang.[14]

The situation changed when Emperor Ming Chengzu moved the capital to Shuntianfu (顺天府, modern-day Beijing) and made one of his top priorities the shipping of tribute grains from the south to the new capital. The emperor contemplated continuing the previous dynasty's method of combining the sea route with the Grand Canal but disregarded the idea because of Japanese piracy and the dangers of sea travel. The only alternative seemed to be reconstruction of the Grand Canal.[15]

As soon as the Grand Canal again became the main route for *caoyun*, the sea route was completely abandoned, and later dynasties also actively maintained the canal. This resulted in many years of undisrupted canal service, despite the fact that the Yellow River frequently changed course after accumulating tremendous amounts of silt and had banks that deteriorated.[16]

Throughout these changes, Zhenjiang regained its previous status in the *caoyun* system. Because the crossing between Zhenjiang and Guazhou (on the other side of the Yangtze River) was safer and more convenient than other locales, most transporting junks went through it until many years later, when the water level at this crossing became too low. Soon, Zhenjiang would play a major role as a north-south connection in China's transregional trade during the mid-Ming commercialization.[17]

LINKING NORTH AND SOUTH IN TRANSREGIONAL TRADE

When the Ming dynasty banned maritime trade, the country was already en route to large-scale commercialization that lasted well into the nineteenth century. Based on the early economic expansion in the Song dynasty, this commercialization was characterized by a new trade system heavily reliant on long-distance trade and simultaneously involving multiple regions for the exchange of staples as well as luxury goods. The rise of the system benefited from the following changes: improving conditions for transportation, the influx of silver from abroad, the emergence of a textile industry, and the loosening of governmental control of the market. It also changed the peasant economy from self-sufficient to market dependent. For Zhenjiang, this offered the opportunity to become a crucial link between north and south in transregional trade.[18]

How this commercialization occurred and gradually affected Zhenjiang is summarized in what follows. At the core of this economic change lay the specialization of agricultural production: the rise of cash crop farming. According to one estimate, 40 to 70 percent of peasants in Guangdong had already committed their farm production to sugarcane by the mid-Ming. In northern China, cotton growing occupied 20 to 30 percent of farmland, replacing grain. The region became one of the best cotton producers in the entire empire, second only to Jiangnan. By the eighteenth century, fruit and tobacco became the main cash crops in Guangdong and Fujian. What epitomized this commercial transformation, however, was Jiangnan's silk and cotton production.[19]

Jiangnan was previously a rice-growing region. After the economic center moved from north to south China during the Tang dynasty, Jiangnan remained the most important dynastic base for tribute grains. Rice from Jiangnan was shipped to the capital mostly through the Grand Canal. That all changed after the mid-Ming, when Jiangnan gradually lost its dominance in rice production, although Suzhou continued to be the national center for the rice trade. Instead, the region ultimately had to import rice from Sichuan, Hunan, Anhui, and Jiangxi to meet demand, despite the fact that tribute grains continued to be shipped from there to the capital. One reason for this stands out: the specialization of agricultural production in cash crops, sufficient incentive for most farmers to switch from rice to silk and cotton products.[20]

This change in Jiangnan created social and economic reverberations across the country. The accumulation of wealth, and especially the huge demand for silk and cotton products, made it more profitable to produce them than to grow rice in Jiangnan. In response to high market demand for silk, farmers in the area turned to growing mulberry. With the high profits generated, they acquired fertilizer, high-quality silk cocoons, mulberry seedlings, and charcoal for silkworm raising and reeling, to improve production. Jiangnan soon became a center of silk and cotton production. Along with this, a textile industry emerged in Jiangnan. The transition resulted in the uprooting of an exclusively rice-growing agricultural base in Jiangnan.[21]

Meanwhile, however, the intensification of cash crop production, coupled with population growth, transformed Jiangnan into an importer of rice from places like Sichuan, Hunan, and Jiangxi, all located in the upper and middle Yangtze River regions. Both the Ming and Qing dynasties seemed to have a good understanding of this change and encouraged rice distribution from those regions to Jiangnan. This new agricultural production led to the transformation of long-distance trade to accommodate the need for rice from Jiangnan, which had more mouths to feed than anywhere else in the country.[22]

The direct consequence was the emergence in the mid-Qing of rice transshipment hubs such as Chongqing, Hankou, Jiujiang, and Wuhu on the Yangtze River. These cities served as regional gathering centers and linkages for the provinces of Sichuan, Hubei, Hunan, Jiangxi, and Anhui to Jiangsu, Zhejiang, Guangdong, and Fujian.[23] As a benefit of this development, Zhenjiang first became a rice-gathering hub for northern Jiangsu, then gradually turned into the connection between Jiangnan and the upper and middle Yangtze. Almost all the rice coming out of the upper and middle Yangtze and headed for Jiangnan arrived at Zhenjiang before it entered the Grand Canal to arrive at Suzhou through the Jiangnan Canal. In the Qing dynasty, Fujian and Guangdong purchased large quantities of rice from the upper and middle Yangtze in the Suzhou market, and most came through Zhenjiang.[24]

An important reason why Zhenjiang was able to play such an important role in the rice trade derived from the economic development of the upper and middle Yangtze regions during the early Qing. The upper Yangtze was historically known for producing abundant quantities of rice. Its major city, Chengdu, was the so-called heaven's storehouse (*tian fu zhi guo* 天府之国), although the city was not on the Yangtze and was connected to the river through the Min River. The upper Yangtze, however, became almost unreachable before the Qing, not only because it was hard to access on foot, but also because of the dangers posed in traveling down the Chuan River, the main pass to the middle and lower Yangtze. Because of this, Sichuan remained mostly detached from the country's major commercial centers, transporting only small amounts of products such as tea and silk.[25]

Since the beginning of the Qing, the dynasty made strenuous efforts to rejuvenate the upper Yangtze's economy. Through government subsidies and encouraging migration, the upper Yangtze experienced an economic resurgence that lasted into the nineteenth century. Migration not only substantially increased the amount of land registered during the first half of the eighteenth century but also introduced advanced farming techniques that significantly raised crop yields and increased the number of commodities. The upper Yangtze thus became a full participant in transregional trade. Rice, sugar, and salt from along the tributaries of the Chuan River were gathered at Yibin, Luzhou, and Chongqing for transportation down the Yangtze. By the late eighteenth century, the upper Yangtze region became "better integrated into the national economy than any other peripheral region."[26]

When this took place, the middle Yangtze economy also started to grow. The region was deeply impacted by the Manchu invasion at the end of the Ming, resulting in the abandonment of many sections. At the beginning of the Qing, however, the dynasty encouraged people to migrate into the highlands of the Yangtze and Han River areas to take up residence on the deserted land. Although this was not wholly successful, the region's economy received a boost nonetheless. For instance, the mountainous area of southern Shaanxi and hilly northern Hubei began to grow, bringing the Han River back to life. The region soon became one of the major rice-supplying locations that were reintegrated into the national grain market.[27]

The lower Yangtze River was the primary transportation route to Jiangnan, although there were river routes for interior trade in the middle Yangtze region: the Gan River, Xiang River, and West River. Goods like grains, wood, cotton, silk, tea, and rice, in particular, were shipped eastward via the Yangtze River.[28]

This flow of goods from the upper and middle Yangtze regions to Jiangnan and vice versa helped Zhenjiang emerge from obscurity to prominence. During the late Ming and most of the Qing periods, large quantities of commodities other than tribute grains passed through the city, some of which were sold to merchants from different parts of the country. For example, a large portion of the cotton used in Jiangnan that came from the north was shipped through Zhenjiang. Silk products from Suzhou, Hangzhou, and Huzhou passed through Zhenjiang for frontier trading in Xinjiang. Timber from Sichuan, Hunan, Yunnan, and Guizhou was also transported down the Yangtze River to Zhenjiang and then to Suzhou. Thus, even before the nineteenth century, Zhenjiang had become a north-south link in transregional trade.[29]

A VIBRANT CITY IN THE EARLY NINETEENTH CENTURY

In the early nineteenth century, before the city was invaded by the British, there were four markets inside Zhenjiang's city wall, one of which was the city center. The largest was at the city's south gate, adjacent to the Grand Canal, and it was the busiest market because most goods were brought there through the canal. The second market was in the west corner of the city. The third was a little different, along the bank of the small Guan River (关河), which ran through the city, connecting the Yangtze River with the Grand Canal. Because of that, the area around the market was crammed with stores, restaurants, and street vendors. There was an archway, so the area was dubbed the "four decorated archways" (*sipailou* 四牌楼). The city center was connected to a business section consisting of five commercial streets, nicknamed the "five streets."[30]

A large number of stores in the markets sold staples such as paper, oil lamps, traditional medicine, grains, liquor, vinegar, sesame oil, nails, and silk. Aside from that, there were shops that catered to small businesses, offering printing supplies, house construction materials, woven goods, and dye. The streets were naturally segregated into separate quarters, each housing particular specialties such as fishnet repair and carpentry. The streets were often named after those specialties.[31] There also were street performers. Some locations had stages for local operas, some of which were located in the temple areas. There were shows on the stages constantly, not only during festivals but also for weddings and family celebrations. Vegetable oil lamps set up for the shows provided lighting after dark.[32]

The city's residential areas consisted of nineteen *fang* (坊, residential lanes), eleven streets, and ninety-five small streets (巷), many of which were separate from the markets.[33] Residential houses were usually made of wood, with a tile roof, and usually had three rooms, one with natural lighting and two without. Larger houses often had three large rooms plus two smaller bedrooms and a gatehouse.[34]

There were private gardens in the city, usually owned by the families of Qing officials or wealthy individuals. The grandest was "the dream of river stream" (*mengxiyuan* 梦溪园), named for the small stream that ran through it, a tributary of the river running through the city. The garden was ten *mu* (亩, equal to 1.65 acres), with a pagoda, small lake, and beautiful homes.[35]

Other popular locations included Buddhist temples such as the most prominent Taoist temple, *ganlusi* (甘露寺), and Chinese-style mosques used by the Hui people (回族). The streets that had temples were usually named after them. Aside from that, there were also temple-looking buildings for the academies of classical learning (书院) occupied by the local literati.[36]

As to the population in Zhenjiang, there were around 150,000 people living in the city and the outskirts between 1736 and 1795, during the reign of Emperor Qianlong. That number continued to increase until the early 1850s, when the Taiping rebels took over the city and most of the territories in Jiangsu province, then decreased to around 100,000. After the rebellion, the population gradually reached about 120,000, with 70,000 living inside the city wall at the beginning of the twentieth century. After the railroad appeared in Jiangsu in 1906, the population declined again. Only when the Jiangsu provincial government relocated itself to Zhenjiang in 1929 did the city see a steady increase in population. That lasted well into the late 1940s, as the provincial government remained in Zhenjiang during the period.

Most residents were of Han (汉) origin, and many descended from migrants from the Central Plain (中原), such as Henan. There were large families in the city, the largest of which was the Zhao family. The Mao family was the most prosperous. There were also people of Mongol, Uyghur (维吾尔), Khitan (契丹), and Hui (回回) origin, who had come from North China and Northwest China during the Yuan dynasty. The Hui were Muslim and built several mosques in the city. Therefore, some of the streets were named Baba Xiang (爸爸巷), Dababa Xiang (大爸爸巷), and Qingzhensi Xiang (清真寺巷) because they featured the living quarters of the Hui.[37]

Among the city residents, there were several loosely formed groups representing similar pursuits, the most well-known of which were the poets. One such group consisted of about fifty-one poets, all female, who printed their poems. There were also artists who developed distinctive styles in painting. Some were holders of state-conferred degrees.[38]

Aside from these groups, there was a voluntary organization, Zhenjiang Lifesaving Society (京口救生会), which not only rescued people from drowning but also supported those who had lost family members or became orphans because of water-related accidents. Through the years, the organization was supported by local businesses and won the approval of local authorities. It used donations to buy land and build houses to support its mission. The organization was usually headed by members of the local elite, but sometimes by retired officials. In one case, a Qing official took early retirement to lead the organization. After he passed away, his son took over. When the son passed the national examination and took an official position himself, he transferred the responsibility to other family members. As a rule, when members of the organization passed away, the organization carved their names on a monument in recognition of their contributions to the city.[39]

THE INCEPTION OF THE OPIUM WAR

The Opium War that started in 1839, when the British fired the first shot on Chinese soil, was, by all accounts, the beginning of the end of peaceful times in Zhenjiang. Not only did the British army damage the city's physical infrastructure when it invaded, but the war also caused suffering among all residents, be they laborers, shop clerks, or artisans. Although the reason for the war has always been a matter of debate, many would agree that among the causes were the attempts of the Chinese to rein in their declining tax revenue due to the influx of opium and the outflow of silver, and the determination of the British to access China at all costs.

The Chinese side of events unfolded when Qing dynasty emperor Daoguang noticed in the memorials sent to him by various officials the shortage of tax revenue and the rise of rebellion in the south. Several of these communications indicated that opium smoking and smuggling were wreaking havoc in the countryside, causing trouble for the dynasty. Opium smoking had long been a problem. By the early nineteenth century, foreign traders used clippers to deliver opium to Lintin Island (伶仃島) in the Pearl River estuary near Hong Kong, to be smuggled into China from the south. In the northwest, Muslim merchants brought opium to China through Xinjiang, where opium crops were also planted, as they were in Shaanxi and Gansu. Very soon, the cheaper opium produced in Malwa in west-central India overwhelmed the market in China, creating a shortage of silver across the country.[40]

The outflow of silver surfaced as early as the last years of Emperor Jiaqing's reign (1796–1820). By 1826, six years after Emperor Daoguang succeeded Jiaqing, the flow of silver out of the country had already cost China the dominant position in the global silver exchange that it had held through most of the eighteenth century. That resulted in a shortage of silver in circulation in general and in the dwindling of the dynasty's revenue due to the lack of silver for tax payments.[41]

Upon the recommendation of a group of officials, Emperor Daoguang sent Commissioner Lin Zexu to Guangdong on January 6, 1839, to tackle the opium problem. Lin first worked with the governor-general of Guangdong and Guangxi, Deng Tingzheng (登廷桢), and the governor of Guangdong province, Yiliang (怡良), to get opium smuggling under control. By May 1839, most of the opium supply brought by the British had been stopped. Lin then focused on opium smokers by confiscating their opium and closing opium dens. On June 3, 1839, Lin gave the order to destroy the opium he had seized in the town of Humen (虎门, also known as Bogue in the West) in Guangdong, after Charles Elliot—then superintendent of trade in China—surrendered the opium to him on behalf of British traders.[42]

A cascade of events then ensued on the British side that culminated in war. One was the action of a group of British merchants sojourning in Canton, known as the Warlike Party, who saw an opportunity for the British to defeat China for economic gain. These individuals returned to

London to urge the British Parliament to launch a war. However, public opinion in Britain was mixed at first, but eventually turned in favor of war, which might have influenced Parliament's decision to provoke war. In addition, the ongoing clashes between British and Chinese culture no doubt also played a role. The differences were manifested in many exchanges between the two countries, including the argument over whether the British should practice the Chinese kowtowing custom.[43]

Between September and October of 1839, shortly after news arrived in London about Lin Zexu's ordering the destruction of the opium and curtailing foreign factories' access to China, the British cabinet sent an expedition to China. Then, in April 1840, the British government won its argument for war during the parliamentary debate. An expeditionary force was then formed in Macao in June under the command of Admiral George Elliot, a naval officer who was newly appointed the full plenipotentiary, with his cousin Charles Elliot as a deputy plenipotentiary. The expedition force comprised 16 warships with 540 mounted guns, 4 armed steamers, 27 transport ships, 1 troop ship, and 4,000 troops, which included soldiers from Indian regiments led by British officers.[44]

The first confrontation between the British and the Chinese armies commenced in June 1840. A month later, the British attacked Dinghai (定海) in Zhejiang and reached the Bei River (北河) near Tianjin. After that, Qishan (琦善), then governor-general of Guangdong and Guangxi (*Liangguang zongdu* 两广总督), held a negotiation in Guangdong with Captain Charles Elliot, who had recently replaced Admiral George Elliot as the first plenipotentiary. By January 1841, Elliot and Qishan signed the Chuanbi Convention (*Chuanbi caoyue* 穿鼻草约), which included the provision of Hong Kong's cessation. The deal failed to win final approval from either the British government or the Qing emperor.[45]

Despite Charles Elliot's efforts to obtain concessions from Qishan, however, the British foreign secretary, Lord Palmerston, still found the settlement unsatisfactory. Palmerston then replaced Elliot with General Henry Pottinger to command the expeditionary army. While waiting for Pottinger to arrive, Elliot proceeded to lead the attack on Humen, to take control of the Pearl River mouth, and to hold the city of Guangzhou for ransom. During this period, Chinese peasants on the outskirts of Guangzhou, in Sanyuanli (三元里), attacked the British soldiers during a rainstorm, leading to what Chinese historians widely consider the first victory of the Chinese against the British.[46]

A few months later, in August 1841, Pottinger arrived in Hong Kong with two military officers: Sir William Parker and Viscount Hugh Gough. Although each belonged to a different chain of command, they shared responsibility for the war against China. Over many conversations at the dinner table, the three developed a strategy against the Qing dynasty.[47]

Between August and October of that year, the British took control of Xiamen in Fujian and three other places in Zhejiang: Dinghai (for the second time), Zhenhai, and Ningbo. Soon after, in the spring of 1842, Pottinger received reinforcements of twenty-five more warships, fourteen steamships, and ten thousand soldiers. With these in place, the British launched another round of attacks on China's east coast, seizing Zhapu (乍浦) in Zhejiang, Wusong (吴淞) in Jiangsu, and Shanghai between May and June 1842.[48]

Right after that, Pottinger faced the dilemma of whether to proceed to Tianjin or the Yangtze River. His translator, John Robert Morrison, persuaded him to choose the Yangtze, reasoning that it was China's main artery for tax-grain transport. As Morrison stated, "As long we keep our finger on it . . . We shall have our own way." This argument was supported by Gough, who was also adamant about the need to control the river. By doing so, Gough reasoned, the British army could cut off the life support of the Chinese capital at the Grand Canal and deal a major blow to the ailing Qing dynasty. Both Morrison and Gough thus helped Pottinger decide on the Yangtze River, which made Zhenjiang the next target for the British military campaign.[49]

2
The Battle of Zhenjiang

ON JULY 21, 1842, before the signing of the Treaty of Nanjing, the British expeditionary force invaded Zhenjiang. According to the plan agreed upon by three British commanders, a British fleet left Shanghai to enter the Yangtze River and set sail for Zhenjiang on July 6, 1842. Within four days, it arrived at Jiangyin (江阴), sixty-six miles east of Zhenjiang.

The fleet consisted of eleven warships and four troopships, five steam frigates and five light-draught iron steamers, two survey schooners, and forty-eight transport boats. Among them was the infamous warship *Nemesis,* a long and narrow flat-bottomed warship built specifically for the war against China. It was made of iron and had a unique hull design that made it easy to maneuver against the wind and in the Yangtze River "mud flats and sandbars that accommodated only shallow draft vessels."[1] With them were Chinese collaborators, most of whom were from Guangdong, Fujian, and Zhejiang, with only a few coming from Jiangsu and Anhui. Many were salt traders familiar with carrying weapons to guard their merchandise against the pirates who preyed on people along the coast. They joined the British mainly for profit, as the British promised them that they could take whatever they wanted once they helped infiltrate a city.[2]

What was the purpose of this invasion? As one British officer revealed in his journal, it was to cut off the bloodline of the Qing dynasty, the tribute-grain transport route. For that purpose, however, the British committed more soldiers than in any previous battle against the Chinese army and were ready to invade Zhenjiang, bringing ordinary people into this conflict.[3]

DISPUTE OVER DEFENSE PLANS

Before examining other aspects of Chinese involvement in the battle, we shall first take a look at the way state officials, especially those at higher than local levels, responded to the challenge of preparing the defense. Emperor Daoguang made these officials responsible for protecting the areas along the lower Yangtze River and preventing the British from entering China's interior through the river crossing at Zhenjiang. Because they had neither the experience nor the skill to prevail against any foreign army, let alone one with industrialized military technology and steam-powered warships, they had little idea about how to fulfill these staggering responsibilities.

Before the British left Xiamen (in Fujian), and when the news about the British attempt to reach the Yangtze River arrived in Zhenjiang, it triggered wrangling among different levels of Qing officials, as well as between the officials and local gentry, about how to best defend the river. Discussions ranged from how to prevent the British from penetrating inland through the river crossing at Zhenjiang, between Guazhou and Jingkou, to the best strategy for combat if the British did arrive there. There was active involvement in war preparations by the Qing emperor all the way down to local officials.

This started between Yuqian (裕谦) and Yilibu (伊里布), both of whom were responsible for guarding the area along the lower Yangtze River. As governor of Liangjiang (Jiangsu, Jiangxi, and Anhui), Yuqian received an appointment as commissioner for the defense of Zhejiang and reclaiming Dinghai after Dinghai fell into enemy hands. Yilibu was a commissioner appointed by the emperor to be responsible for protecting Zhejiang.

The main issue under debate was whether or not to close the river port at Zhenjiang to prevent the Chinese collaborators from infiltrating inland through the river crossing. Since Yilibu saw no evidence of the enemy entering the Yangtze River, he suggested to the emperor that closing the port would be an imposition on the merchants traveling the north-south route through the river crossing. His idea was to sink rock-filled boats at the entrance of the Yangtze River to block the British as well as their Chinese collaborators from entering altogether.[4]

Yuqian expressed a different view to the emperor. He noted that the river entrance was very shallow and filled with sand, so there was no need to worry about the British fleet entering the river. Besides, once the river was completely clogged, it would flood the farmland, causing the villagers to lose their harvests and perhaps even their lives. Furthermore, Yuqian considered it unnecessary to prevent the Chinese collaborators from coming to the lower Yangtze River to gather food supplies for the British because, as he understood the matter, the British did not eat grains, but only animals like chickens, cattle, and sheep.[5]

As for the Chinese collaborators, Yuqian recommended that the dynasty treat them with a combination of incentive and punishment. In his reasoning, those natives of coastal provinces were most likely assisting the enemy purely for profit. They were not against the dynasty. The emperor could entice them with a financial reward if they turned against the British or surrendered to the Qing dynasty. For a small number of their leaders, the emperor could offer a reward for their capture and severely punish them and their families.[6]

The exchange between Yuqian and Yilibu in front of the emperor finally ended with Yilibu withdrawing his plan and apologizing to the emperor that he was unaware of the possibility of flooding. Shortly after receiving Yilibu's apology, however, the emperor learned that Yuqian had died in Hangzhou (杭州, in Zhejiang) following his suicide attempt in Zhenhai during the British invasion.[7]

Having learned of Yuqian's death, Emperor Daoguang appointed Niu Jian (牛鉴) the next governor general of Jiangsu, Jiangxi, and Anhui (*liangjiang zongdu* 两江总督), to be in charge of creating a strong defense along the lower Yangtze River. Among those who also received appointments was Hailing (海龄), a lieutenant-general (*fu dutong* 副都统) who was put in charge of defending the city of Zhenjiang against a British invasion. The third person joining the defense effort was Qishen (齐慎), a provincial military commander in Sichuan (*Sichuan tidu* 四川提督) who was asked by the emperor to bring an army from Sichuan to assist in the defense of Zhenjiang after Wusong (吴淞) (part of Shanghai) fell into the hands of the British. Another round of discussion about what to do about the river crossing at Zhenjiang soon ensued in front of the emperor through memorials submitted to him by Niu Jian and Hailing, and later by Qishen.[8]

The conversation began with the emperor asking Niu Jian for his thoughts on how to prevent the enemy from infiltrating the Chinese interior through the river crossing. Niu Jian replied that he felt it unnecessary to be concerned about this, although he was acutely aware of the significance of the river crossing as the north-south connection for transporting tribute grains and government mail. For one thing, the lower Yangtze River, especially the section at the river crossing, was shallow, and only special Chinese boats such as sand boats were able to pass. Because of that, the British fleet would not be able to enter that section of the river, just as it had failed to get through Tongzhou (modern-day Nantong).[9]

Even if the British tried to get through the river, Niu Jian added, there were already plenty of soldiers guarding the area. The only concern should be if the Chinese collaborators infiltrated, because they could use Chinese boats to get through. Furthermore, Niu noted, these individuals were always with the British, who were very cautious about entering the Chinese interior. Niu saw no need to worry about the British taking control of the river crossing at Zhenjiang.[10]

Nevertheless, he suggested that, to be on the safe side, the emperor could order each province to gather tribute grains ahead of the regular schedule and have them shipped to Guazhou (across the Yangtze River from Zhenjiang) before the British had the opportunity to enter the Yangtze. Niu promised to carefully check every boat transporting tribute grains, to prevent the Chinese collaborators from entering the Yangtze River by disguising themselves as boatmen.[11]

The emperor then turned to Hailing, who had reported in a separate memorial that, having surveyed the area outside Zhenjiang, he realized that the part of the Yangtze River near Zhenjiang was indeed shallow and sandy, and the British would not be able to navigate it. There was only one location where the British could pass, but Hailing had already placed cannons on the hill overlooking it.[12] Shortly after the report was filed, however, Hailing told the emperor in a separate memorial that recent rain had elevated the water level at Zhenjiang, making it possible for the British to pass through. To prevent this, he had asked local officials to find people familiar with the river to form a group to destroy the British boats from below.[13]

Having read the memorial from Hailing, Emperor Daoguang saw Qishen's similar report about having placed soldiers at strategic locations at Zhenjiang and the river crossing. Qishen also mentioned that he had ordered local officials to gather people willing to fight against the British, especially those familiar with the river. He asked the emperor to offer them a good reward: If they could destroy a British boat, they should be allowed to take everything on the vessel as a reward. If they succeeded in burning the ship, they should be rewarded with silver.[14]

Although the discussion yielded minimal results, the emperor did accept Niu Jian's suggestion about collecting tribute grains ahead of schedule. By the time the British set sail to Zhenjiang, the emperor had already ordered most of the grain transported through the Grand Canal to the capital. Each shipment was heavily guarded by soldiers and local militia members to prevent theft by the Chinese collaborators.[15]

While Qing officials discussed the possibility of a British invasion, a similar debate surfaced between officials and members of the local gentry. The argument first centered on the strategy for attacking the British from the shore. It commenced when Yuqian arrived in Zhenhai and reported to the emperor that the rivers in Changzhou, Zhenjiang, and Yangzhou were too difficult to defend. He recommended creating a defense hold at Zhenhai.[16]

Having heard this, Bao Shichen (包世臣) wrote a letter criticizing Yuqian for not choosing to set up a defense line at Chui Mountain (Chuishan 圌山), twenty miles east of Zhenjiang, along the route between the Yangtze River and the city of Zhenjiang. Bao was a Juren-degree holder and one of the most respected and popular individuals in the city, largely because of his involvement in all kinds of charitable activities. When Zhenjiang faced the threat of British invasion, the local communities expected him to represent them. By the time Bao sent his letter to Yuqian, Yuqian had already left Zhenjiang; therefore, Bao asked local officials to forward the letter to Yuqian in Zhenhai. It took a while for the letter to reach Yuqian's office, and by the time it arrived, Yuqian had died.[17]

The letter to Yuqian was not the only one Bao sent to officials; he also wrote to Chen Qingxiang (陈庆祥), a newly appointed lieutenant-colonel (*canjiang* 参将) and an assistant to Hailing. Because Bao failed to reach the higher level of officials, he felt it necessary to talk to the lower-ranking Chen. In the letter, Bao recommended creating a cannon-based defense line on Chui Mountain and clogging the river there to stop the British warships from reaching shore. Because the river became much narrower closer to the mountain, he argued, cannon fire could easily reach the enemy ships. Bao also suggested destroying the British warships using boats set on fire.[18]

Chen Qingxiang showed the letter to Niu Jian, the newly appointed governor, and to Yijing (奕经), the emperor's nephew whom Emperor Daogung had just put in charge of gathering soldiers from the provinces outside Jiangsu to defend Zhenjiang. Both Chen Qingxiang and Niu Jian dismissed Bao's suggestion as unnecessary, given the soldiers already guarding the river by Chui Mountain.[19]

Rejected by two high-ranking officials, Bao decided to go a different route by sending letters to a prefectural-level official, Zhou Suo (周琐). Zhou, too, dismissed Bao's idea, saying that the British would never enter the river near Chui Mountain because they would get stuck in the shallow riverbank, leaving the Chinese ample opportunity to attack from shore.[20]

Later, Zhou Suo mentioned Bao's idea to Hailing. While agreeing with Zhou that the river pass in front of Chui Mountain was too narrow for British ships, Hailing told Zhou that even experienced Chinese boatmen would have trouble navigating it, let alone the British, who were not at all familiar with the river.[21] But after hearing that the British were approaching, Zhou hastily accepted Bao's second suggestion of sending boats with fire down the river to block the British fleet, as he realized that it was the only strategy being discussed. After gathering the chunks of wood, rocks, and fifty junks for the task, Zhou arranged a test run. Soon, the disappointing results were clear: as the junks burned, none floated down the river as intended. Nevertheless, Zhou decided to stay with the strategy.[22]

With war preparations underway, Hailing decided that sixteen-hundred soldiers were not sufficient to defend the city and sent several memorials to the emperor requesting more troops. After reading that the British had taken Dinghai and killed the chief military officer, Hailing expressed his shock in his memorial to the emperor over the speed of the British arrival and the fragility of the Chinese army. He asked the emperor to send Manchu soldiers from places like Zhili (直隶), Jilin (吉林), and Heilongjiang (黑龙江), all of which were in northeast China, to help protect Zhenjiang. He reasoned that these soldiers were better than the ones in Guangdong, Fujian, and Dinghai after those places had fallen to the British. Although Manchu soldiers were unfamiliar with water, he said, they could protect the city better than anyone.[23]

The emperor then asked Niu Jian and Liang Zhangju (梁章钜), governor of Jiangxi (*jiangxi xunfu* 江西巡抚), to secure more troops for Zhenjiang. He also assigned Chen Ankui (陈安魁), the chief commander of the provincial army in Xiamen, to assist Yijing in bringing two thousand soldiers from Zhejiang. Also under the emperor's order, a Manchu general, Dezhubu (德珠布), brought one thousand cavalry soldiers from Xi'an (in Shaanxi), and Qishen (齐慎) brought two thousand more soldiers from Zhejiang. They were joined by two thousand soldiers from Hubei, commanded by Liu Yunxiao (刘允孝), the provincial commander-in-chief of the Hubei Army.[24]

Above all, Hailing's effort led to the arrival of four hundred Manchu bannermen from Qingzhou (青州, in Shandong), widely considered China's bravest and most skilled soldiers. They were so well regarded that Dezhubu once mentioned in a memorial to the emperor that the dynasty would face the loss of a lifeline without these soldiers guarding Zhenjiang. Yijing assigned them to guard the cannon station, presumably the most strategic location outside the city. With reinforcements from other parts of the country, the total number of soldiers defending the city reached nine thousand.[25]

Hailing also gathered three hundred members of the local militia to join the defense effort but soon realized that his order to have boats built for attacking the British on the river had gone unheeded. Nor did the officials find people to form the militia. Even part of the city wall, which had collapsed due to heavy rain, was not repaired. With the help of local residents who donated materials and labor, the wall was finally repaired, but the rest of the plans were ignored.[26]

As preparations continued, there surfaced an argument for giving up the fight. As soon as Niu Jian arrived at Zhenjiang, he conveyed that recommendation to local officials and asked Zhou Suo to raise 120,000 taels of silver to ransom the city from the British. Although most wealthy residents agreed to follow his order, two of the most powerful families resisted, causing Niu Jian to give up the plan. As Niu Jian solicited ransom funds, ripples of panic spread across the city.[27]

PANIC WITHIN THE CITY

People in Zhenjiang reacted to the news of Shanghai's falling into the hands of the British with an uncontrollable "feeling of great fear" because they knew that, after taking Shanghai, the British were poised to invade. They had heard about British soldiers committing massacres, raping, and looting during their invasion of Zhapu and awaited their fate in utter despair. The situation was exacerbated by harsh Qing officials, which shows that the personal characters of state officials, including their views and judgments, played a significant role in how local communities coped with an impending crisis.[28]

Panic first took the form of a massive exodus. As most people tried to flee, local officials attempted to convince them that a suitable defense plan was in place. No one believed them. Large crowds gathered in front of the east gate of the city wall, where there were few guards, but they were thwarted by county government runners who yelled at them and were otherwise belligerent. Someone saw a woman give her belongings to a runner, after which the runner let her escape, and this caused a great deal of resentment. Meanwhile, there was a rumor that local officials had already moved their families out of the city, which fueled more outrage.[29]

Addressing the situation, Hailing ordered his soldiers to be on full alert for "traitors" (*hanjian* 汉奸)—spies for the British, including those sent by the Chinese collaborators. He thought many of those spies would travel down the Yangtze and try to sneak into Zhenjiang. The following incidents seem to confirm Hailing's suspicion.

Hailing's soldiers once stopped some boats carrying sugar from Chongming (崇明) and Haimen (海门), both of which were in Jiangsu. He suspected that Chinese collaborators were aboard and asked the soldiers to be vigilant. After that, Hailing's soldiers apprehended a man who identified himself as a merchant from Guangdong who had come to Zhenjiang to purchase rice. Although the man had a travel permit issued by officials in Guangdong, Hailing believed he could have been a spy.[30]

Then, inside the city, after Hailing arrested around one hundred people, he discovered that one of them was there to find out how many Chinese soldiers were in the city—intelligence clearly meant for the British. Right after that, Hailing also learned that, among the arrested, twelve had hidden weapons in their luggage. He determined that they were the spies and ordered them to be executed. Because of this incident, Hailing ordered the closing of the river port at Zhenjiang and prohibited traveling merchants from entering the city.[31]

Not long after, Hailing's suspicions resulted in a pattern of behavior that increased the desperation pervading the city. The behavior surfaced right after he heard that the Manchu bannermen soldiers in Zhapu failed to defeat the British troops, and none of their lives had been spared. He then ordered the soldiers to close the city's entry gates to prevent the Chinese collaborators from sneaking inside. Having placed the bannermen at the city gate close to the enemy's anticipated landing spot, he barricaded himself in a temple inside the city, with forty soldiers guarding him at night, after sending away his newlywed concubine and her family.[32]

The closing of the city gates led to chaos because there were more than ten thousand visitors, most of whom were farmers there to sell their goods, shop, or seek entertainment. Not only was there not enough food for this many additional people, but there was no place to board them. They had to stay on the street in the sweltering July heat.[33]

Prefect Xianglin (祥麟) pleaded with Hailing to allow the visitors to leave. Reluctantly, Hailing agreed, but ordered his soldiers to search everyone at the gate. The soldiers took advantage of the opportunity to harass people and fondle young women in front of the crowd, creating a scene that infuriated many. Worse, after only a few people had been allowed to exit, Hailing heard about the British advancement and changed his mind. The gates were closed again.[34]

The food shortage soon became another serious problem. The issue could be traced back to the time when officials ordered soldiers to amass food from the villagers on the outskirts of the city in preparation for battle. While the soldiers nearly depleted the remaining food supplies, there was still not enough food in the city to feed everyone within its walls.[35]

Hailing reduced the soldiers' rations. In response to mounting tension, some local officials tried to persuade Hailing to let them go out of the city to find food. After Hailing rejected the proposal, a group of soldiers protested in front of the city wall one night. Hailing ordered the Manchu bannermen to put on their armor and gather atop the wall, ready to fire. Some soldiers then started to loot the city. Some residents were so terrified that they stood atop the city wall, crying for help.[36]

When a local notable tried to bring about one thousand *dan* (fifty thousand kilograms) of rice through a city gate to help feed people, Hailing refused to let him in for fear he was spying for the British, and ordered execution on the spot for anyone who dared open the gate. He declared that those who disagreed with him were enemy collaborators and that the city had enough soldiers to kill them.[37] Tensions escalated to the point where people gathered at the city's primary market in a display of defiance. Hailing ordered his soldiers to be ready to fire upon the crowd. As anger continued to mount, Hailing accused all those present of being "traitors" (*hanjian* 汉奸) eager to surrender to the British.[38]

From that point on, Hailing's relationship with city residents deteriorated; he had become increasingly suspicious that a significant number of people in Zhenjiang were enemy collaborators. Hailing gave the order to shoot those gathered at the city wall, then forbade people to walk in pairs after dark, and detained anyone who did not speak with the local accent, regardless of whether they were traders, handymen, street beggars, or Buddhist monks.[39]

Under these orders, soldiers began to punish everyone suspected of being enemy collaborators, including some children. They executed detainees who confessed after harsh interrogation. The Parade Ground, where public executions were usually staged, thus became a place of torture and public humiliation. At one time, Hailing rounded up about 170 people, some of whom were beggars, for public execution. The only reason he did not go through with it was that he heard news of the approaching British. Even so, thirteen people had already lost their lives. An eyewitness later described how the bodies of the executed were cut into pieces. Among them was a monk whose body fat clogged a street drainage hole.[40]

The entire Parade Ground was filled with women and children crying out for mercy for their doomed family members. Seeing this, the prefect shed some tears. After intense persuasion by local officials, Hailing finally agreed to release those whose neighbors testified to their innocence, but ordered the soldiers to throw those lacking such testimonials off the city wall. As a result, many people died or were severely injured. A rumor quickly spread that Hailing resented ethnic Hans (*hanren* 汉人, hereafter Han Chinese) and targeted them specifically.[41]

Seeing that Hailing had exaggerated the possibility of Chinese collaborators infiltrating Zhenjiang, local officials like Zhuo Suo and Magistrate Qian Yangui (钱燕桂) began to question Hailing's actions of detaining and killing innocent people. Hailing insisted that he was only punishing the "enemy guides" (*koudao* 寇导) who spied for the British before their arrival. Zhou and Qian, realizing that Hailing would not listen to reason, let some of the captives go without asking permission. This enraged Hailing so much that he sent soldiers to search Zhou's and Qian's offices and detained seven of their staff. Later, when Zhou and Qian returned from a trip to manage military supplies and set up an office in a temple, Hailing refused to let them enter the city.[42]

No one except Zhou Suo and Qian Yangui dared speak up against Hailing, although some local officials disapproved of his actions. On the other hand, the only local official Hailing trusted was Prefect Xianglin, who not only was related to him by marriage but also never questioned his decisions. Thus, even before the arrival of the British, the city of

Zhenjiang was plunged into despair. To see how this would unfold when the British arrived, we shall now move to the British side of the story.[43]

APPROACHING OF THE BRITISH FLEET

The British left Jiangyin for Zhenjiang on July 12, 1842. Among the British army rank and file was the misperception that their mission was to teach the ancient Chinese dynasty how to interact with Western nations. They believed that the war was not waged for territorial gain, nor was it designed to incite rebellion against the dynasty. These beliefs, however, could not forestall the harsh reality that the war was meant for destruction.[44]

The British burned all junks along their way to Zhenjiang, even though salt merchants offered five hundred thousand taels of silver to spare their boats. As one British officer later declared in a celebratory tone, "The great object of the campaign of the Yang-tse-kiang [the Yangtze River] had thus been accomplished."[45] As they neared Zhenjiang, British troops encountered the first group of villagers, who had never before seen foreigners from Europe, let alone massive warships mounted with cannons. They turned out on the river bank by the thousands to gaze "with wonder and astonishment" as the fleet passed by, as if watching a spectacle. Many of them thought the red uniforms of the British were wings.[46]

Coincidentally, at that very moment, an eclipse of the sun occurred, which was perceived as a very unfavorable omen—something horrible was going to happen. It also strengthened the superstition that the British were something other than human, with connections to devils or demons, and would destroy everything in their path. Meanwhile, the eclipse facilitated the rumor that China would soon be conquered by a woman (most likely a reference to Queen Victoria) who was aided by the "red-haired Barbarians" (British soldiers) with ships that could easily master the Yangtze's tricky waves and currents. All of this fueled anguish over Zhenjiang's impending doom.[47]

The next day, as the two British warships anchored near Chui Mountain in advance of the fleet, the British troops had their first encounter with the Chinese soldiers defending Zhenjiang. After the British fired their cannon from the boat, wounding some, the Chinese soldiers immediately took shelter. They returned fire with a few cannon shots but failed to hit their targets, then scattered across the mountain. The British decided to move on.[48]

Around that time, about eighty fleeing Chinese soldiers arrived at a garrison fort on the mountain. They begged the guards to let them in to get medical treatment for their wounded, but the guards told them that Hailing specifically ordered them not to let anyone in. The soldiers were forced to leave without getting help.[49]

Three days after they left Jiangyin, the two British warships reached the river in front of Jiaoshan Island (焦山岛), three miles east of Zhenjiang city. In a display of their massive firepower, they fired several rounds of mortar shells at random targets. This volley was so loud that, as one Chinese eyewitness described, it seemed as if they were capable of pushing up the very waves of the Yangtze River. The warships and cannon fire created an intimidating presence.[50]

Some British soldiers reached the fort at the top of the hill on the island. As they started to climb over the wall, they heard a commotion. They discovered that several Chinese soldiers had jumped to their death from the top of the hill. Meanwhile, the local militia that had been assembled to guard the fort scattered, enabling the British to easily take control.[51] The cannon fire was heard loud and clear across Zhenjiang. As people ran for cover, looters ransacked some stores in the midst of the confusion. This included a group of local militiamen who broke into a county government office and stole money. Commander Liu Yunxiao immediately sent soldiers to apprehend the city's looters and executed one on the spot. Meanwhile, the British continued their march to the city.[52]

On July 20, 1842, the entire British fleet finally arrived at Golden Island (Jinshan 金山岛) outside of Zhenjiang. Before reaching the shore, the British saw a large raft full of pieces of wood slowly moving toward them, then being set on fire. The raft moved very slowly and the British soldiers pushed it away before it posed any threat. Obviously, this was a defensive strategy on the part of local officials.[53]

The British landed as soon as they reached the shore. The initial landing operation appeared chaotic, with some units reaching shore in the middle of the night, while at least two battalions missed their targeted locations entirely. Although the confusion opened a window of opportunity for the Chinese army to attack, no action was taken.[54]

The British soldiers were ordered not to harm the villagers or their farmland, in order to "conciliate the inhabitants." Instead of obeying, they set fire to houses and stole from the villagers wherever they went. In one case, British soldiers in search of food set fire to some hay and burned down the entire village. Elsewhere, they killed two villagers, later claiming self-defense. Others set fire to a Chinese temple, aware that Chinese soldiers were hiding inside. A British officer later confessed in his diary that the actions of his soldiers had led to "most disastrous consequences" for the Chinese.[55]

On the Chinese side, as soon as the British fleet arrived, both Qishen and Liu Yunxiao moved soldiers deep into two temples on Beigu Mountain (Beigu shan 北固山) overlooking the river bank. Hailing also posted a proclamation that the enemy had withdrawn to the other side of the river and advising people to wait for the Chinese soldiers to use their superior skills in close combat against the British, who were only familiar with battles at sea. But people across Zhenjiang realized—like those who watched from atop the city wall—that the British were advancing unabated.[56]

Just before the British launched their attack, one local member of the gentry, Yan Chongli (颜崇礼), approached, asking to see the British commander. Yan told the British that he represented the residents of Zhenjiang and Yangzhou in a plea for peace. A British officer accepted his gifts but refused to let Yan meet with the commander; instead, he took Yan to a Chinese collaborator with the surname of Guo (郭).

Guo told Yan that he used to be a Qing official, a magistrate in Ningbo province, but decided to work for the British. He attempted to convince Yan that the British had no intention of disturbing the peaceful lives of the Chinese people and that Zhenjiang and Yangzhou should rest assured that this would be the case. Their sole mission was to "avenge" (*shenyuan* 伸冤) ill treatment by the Qing dynasty before the war. The Qing dynasty deserved to be punished, since the Qing emperor never clearly stated a desire for either peace or war, and because officials like Yilibu did not show up themselves to beg for mercy from the British.

Guo showed Yan a list of Qing dynasty offenses against the British, which included causing the loss of opium as well as treating the British as its subjects. In addition, the British wanted parts of China to be open to foreign trade. Before Yan left, Guo promised that if the Chinese would not fire on the British, the British would not fire either. Later, when Zhou Suo reported to Emperor Daoguang about negotiations with the British, he recommended that the dynasty seek long-term peace because the enemy was too powerful to defeat.[57]

Despite all of the hullabaloo, rural villagers reacted to the British very differently than their urban counterparts. Many were curious but not alarmed or threatened. Some were so calm that they continued eating their rice as if nothing were out of the ordinary, even while in the path of cannon fire. Very soon, fierce fighting at the city gates ended their state of tranquility.[58]

ENEMY AT THE GATE

The British positioned themselves outside the city wall on July 21 as they prepared to invade Zhenjiang. The first round of battle took place outside the wall, where the Chinese army had set up several camps. As the Chinese overestimated their military strength vis-à-vis the opponent, they soon learned the miscalculation would cost them dearly.

The British army had nine thousand combatants, most of whom were British natives, along with a few Indian nationals. In addition, there were three thousand sailors, including some Africans and Malays, ready to join the battle when needed. There also was a large contingent of Chinese collaborators.[59] The British were equipped with Baker rifles and a musket rifle known as "Brown Bess" because of its color, all of which could reach about two hundred meters and be fired twice as fast as those used by the Chinese. The British cannons also were much more accurate than the Chinese versions. Even the British mortar shells were better designed, with advanced technology. Furthermore, each British warship was mounted with ten to twenty cannons, with the most powerful ones on the leading warship, *Nemesis.*[60]

FIG. 2.1 **The British outside the city wall.** Thomas Allom and James Stoddart, "West Gate of Ching-Keang Foo." Prints, Drawings and Watercolors from the Anne S. K. Brown Military Collection. Brown Digital Repository. Brown University Library.

The Chinese side had nine thousand soldiers in three types of military forces: the Manchu bannermen, the Green Standard Army (*Luying* 绿营), and the local militia. The Manchu bannermen were known to the British as Tatar and were distinctively Manchu natives. The Green Standard Army was made up of ethnically Han Chinese soldiers (hereafter, "Han soldiers") and was led by Chinese officials, mostly scholar-officials who lacked military knowledge or combat experience. The local militia was formed by people from the city and suburbs; it was headed by local officials and some members of the gentry.[61]

The Chinese cannons were nicknamed the "red barbarians' cannons" (*hongyi dapao* 红夷大炮) and were obtained from the Portuguese during the previous dynasty. Because they lacked advanced technology in cast iron, the Chinese were unable to build better models. The cannons were already obsolete; they would not fire when wet, and the shot only reached a short distance compared to the cannons used by the British.[62]

The primary weapons of Chinese foot soldiers were broadswords, spears, and bows and arrows. Only a few soldiers had access to a variation of a matchlock rifle known as a "fowling piece" (*niaotong* 鸟铳), developed in Europe in the early 1400s and in use until the 1700s. The Chinese got them from the Portuguese or seized them from Japanese pirates. The rifles usually had a range of around one hundred meters, half the distance of those used by the British. Though the rifles were woefully inadequate and obsolete, the Chinese continued to rely on them.[63]

These hindrances notwithstanding, the Chinese developed several practical methods to maneuver their weapons. For example, three soldiers carried a single rifle and the metal balls used as bullets, so that each bore one-third of the weight. They also devised a way of carrying the rifles and bullets with bamboo tubes and cotton belts that they fastened around their waists. Through these methods, they were able to load the rifles without putting the butts on the ground—as the Europeans did with this type of rifle—and fire them much quicker than the British, whose muskets were far more advanced.[64]

The battle started right after an incident on Beigu Mountain. The British commander had originally planned to wait for the Chinese to negotiate a surrender. Several days earlier, however, a monk at a temple on Beigu Mountain overheard two Chinese soldiers discussing the arrival of the British. The monk wanted to leave the temple but was stopped by the soldiers, who assured him he would be safe. They also confided in him that Hailing, who suspected monks of being enemy spies, had ordered all monks to be detained for questioning. The monk told his peers and fled with them. A Chinese collaborator heard about this incident when he followed General Hugh Gough to the top of the mountain to observe the city, and informed the British commander. The commander decided to launch the attack, with the self-righteous justification that this could save many Chinese from Qing officials like Hailing.[65]

As Hugh Gough prepared for attack, he found the city utterly still: No guards or troops were in sight; in fact, the only military presence was two entrenched camps set up by the Chinese army on the small hills to the south. Apparently, the Chinese commander had chosen the most convenient location to fight the battle. Gough thus decided to first attack the camps using the units that were by his side. Thus, the battle began outside the city wall.[66]

When the Chinese troops in the camps first saw the incoming British soldiers, they were alarmed because they knew they had overestimated the range of their own cannons. Instead, they proceeded with a ritual launched with a very loud yell, then fired their cannons, which failed to reach the British. The British immediately fired back, killing and wounding some Chinese soldiers. A large contingent of Chinese collaborators with all kinds of Chinese weapons charged the Chinese soldiers. They were about five hundred to six hundred people divided into two or three smaller groups led by someone whom they called "chief" (*Dazhangtou* 大丈头). Right behind them came the British. As the enemy advanced, the Chinese charged with broadswords and spears. A Chinese soldier saw a British officer directing the attack and aimed his cannon fire at him, hitting him.[67]

After British warships fired on the Chinese camps, the Chinese defense collapsed under heavy bombardment as soldiers abandoned their positions to scatter across the hill or hide in the bushes. Left behind were the sedan chairs used to carry Qing officials and a few loose horses presumably owned by the Chinese officers. After careful examination, the British commander determined that the Chinese officers had chosen the location to set up their camps because it was near a road that allowed them to escape in case of impending defeat.[68]

THE CITY UNDER ATTACK

As the battle raged outside the city, the British assault within the city commenced. During the battle, Chinese soldiers demonstrated bravery, for which the British later offered various interpretations. From the British standpoint, the soldiers were willing to fight only under coercion by their superiors. They soon realized, however, that there was more to the Chinese.

The battle at the city gates unfolded according to the British plan, as two British brigades appeared at the north gate, at the foothills of Beigu Mountain, to create the illusion that Britain's main focus was that gate,

FIG. 2.2 The Chinese bannermen fighting against the British soldiers.
Richard Simkin, "The 98th Regiment of Foot at the Attack on Chin-Kiang-Foo, 21st July, 1842." Prints, Drawings and Watercolors from the Anne S. K. Brown Military Collection. / Brown University Library / Wikimedia Commons.

while another column attacked the west gate at the southwest corner of the city. The British were told by some monks that the city was built on the south side of the mountain so that the north gate was not well fortified. The British speculated that the Chinese would assume the north gate was the main target, and thus developed this plan.[69]

The attack started with cannon fire from the two warships. Although Hugh Gough initially decided not to bombard the city with heavy artillery, he quickly changed his mind, given the onslaught of cannon fire from the Chinese. As the British units neared the north gate, they realized they were not facing ordinary Chinese soldiers—the enemies were the legendary and fierce Manchu bannermen.[70]

As the Manchu bannermen fired on the British with grapeshot, they were too occupied to notice that other British soldiers had advanced to the city wall. Using scaling ladders, and backed by their rifle firepower, the British managed to get on top of the wall to engage in hand-to-hand combat. During the fight, one Manchu bannerman managed to pull two British soldiers off the wall with him after being bayoneted several times. Eventually, the British prevailed after killing a large number of Chinese soldiers.[71]

At about the same time, the British brigade trying to open the west gate was joined by Hugh Gough. A unit of British soldiers advanced and tried to place explosives under the west gate as they were fired upon by Chinese soldiers from the top of the wall. The British took cover in a house on the side of the bridge that connected to the gate. Even under this heavy firepower, a British soldier managed to ignite the explosives. He quickly set up another explosion, after which the gate, which was buried under sandbags from inside, finally gave way. Three more British regiments arrived in time to storm through the massive hole in the city wall.[72]

FIG. 2.3 The British attacking the city. From Thomas Allom and G. N. Wright, *The Chinese Empire Illustrated* (London: London Printing and Publishing Company, 1858), 2:126 / Wikimedia Commons.

Inside the city walls, there were around 5,300 Chinese soldiers, many of whom were Han. Many engaged in hand-to-hand combat, demonstrating as much bravery as the Manchu bannermen. The British still advanced deep into the city, where they encountered more Han soldiers, who fired their rifles, then escaped. These soldiers had been placed there by Qishen and Liu Yunxiao.[73]

Breaching two of the city gates caused pandemonium among civilians desperate to leave. As Hailing walked toward the south gate, Prefect Xianglin followed and pleaded with him to let people exit there. Concerned that this would make him appear to be giving up, Hailing refused. Instead, he ordered his soldiers to fire into the large crowd gathered at the gate. Utterly bereft, Xianglin returned to his office to commit suicide, but his assistant stopped him.[74]

Seeing the dire situation, Intendant Zhou Suo and Magistrate Qian Yangui went with a large group of soldiers to Danyang County, about twenty miles south of Zhenjiang. They asked local officials to gather approximately one hundred junks to take them to Changzhou, another city in Jiangsu. The officials, unable to come up with enough junks in such a short time, instead lied to Zhou and Qian, telling them that the British had sent reconnaissance earlier and now were on their way to Danyang. Zhou and Qian decided to stay and fight, but the enemy never came.[75] While some Chinese officers and soldiers fled, a large number of soldiers, especially the Manchu bannermen, continued to fight. Those who were captured refused to eat and often attempted to kill themselves. Their bravery surprised the British, one of whom wrote in his diary that the Chinese soldiers showed "conspicuous gallantry."[76]

Some on the British side attributed the bravery of the Chinese to the stark warning they had received before the battle. Some British remembered finding bodies of Han soldiers at the north and west gates, seemingly left there before the battle as a warning to others. Each victim had either been mutilated or had his throat cut, and some had been killed by being struck in the head with a broadsword. The British surmised that these were the soldiers who wanted to run away and were therefore put to death.[77]

The British soon realized that there were two kinds of Chinese soldiers: Manchu bannermen and Han. While they had no clue about what made them different, they were certainly aware that only the Han ran away from battle. The Chinese side offered an explanation. Some believed that the entire Chinese army, woefully unprepared for battle, had underestimated its enemy. When some Han soldiers realized their enemy's prowess, they fled.[78]

Another explanation was offered by a local Chinese eyewitness, a member of the gentry, who contended that the Han soldiers considered both the British and the Manchu "barbarians" and therefore refused to participate in the war. To prove his point, he cited the example that, before the battle, the families of the Manchu bannermen were allowed to leave the city, but not the families of the Han soldiers. This caused tension to erupt between Manchus and Han Chinese. As a result, some Han soldiers set fires on the road around the city to block the Manchu bannermen, which eventually benefited the British.[79]

Above all, the fighting between the two sides in the battle of Zhenjiang tells only half of the story. The other half unfolded as soon as the British soldiers broke into the city: the direct contact between the British soldiers and the ordinary people of Zhenjiang, the invader and invaded.

3
The Invader and the Invaded

ONCE THE FIGHTING WAS OVER, the British noticed that bodies of women and children were strewn everywhere throughout the city. They soon realized that this was only the tip of a massive iceberg of suicides and mercy killings that had cost countless women and children their lives. During the invasion, the people of Zhenjiang suffered so profoundly that even the lead invader, the British commander Hugh Gough, felt "sick at heart of war and its fearful consequences." These tragic experiences reveal the very nature of the Opium War and its impact on Chinese society.[1]

There is no doubt, as nineteenth-century Prussian theoretician Carl von Clausewitz noted, that "war is a messy business." War involves the suffering of innocent people caught in the fighting, killing, and destruction. But what occurred in Zhenjiang also indicates that war is more than a form of destructive engagement by opposing forces. Aside from determining winners and losers, the negative interaction between the invader and invaded also results in calamitous consequences.[2]

As we are about to discover, the negative interaction between the British and the people of Zhenjiang produced dire consequences, including mass suicides and mercy killings. Beyond that, it also led to sharply contrasting interpretations of this self-destructive phenomenon from each side, owing to differences in historical backgrounds and cultural traditions of the explicators. These differences existed before the battle of Zhenjiang and were perpetuated long after. To decipher the deeper meanings and far-reaching implications of this tragedy in Chinese society, we shall now examine carefully how ordinary people in Zhenjiang "interacted" with the invader.

SUICIDE AS A SOCIAL PHENOMENON

According to historians studying European imperialism in other parts of the world, Native Americans and Africans resorted to suicide in their resistance against Europeans, in addition to "everyday forms of resistance" such as fleeing and hiding. Similarly, the people of Zhenjiang reacted to the British invasion with mass suicides and mercy killings. The following are merely a few examples among many the British military men witnessed firsthand and later recorded in diaries.[3]

British soldiers walking along the city wall saw two Chinese soldiers in the distance. Just as the British soldiers were about to open fire, they realized that women and children were clustered behind the pair. When the women saw the British, they pushed the children into a ditch filled with water and forcibly drowned them. After all the children were dead, the Chinese soldiers did the same to the women, then jumped into the water to drown themselves. "We were on the rampart," one British soldier remembered, "and too far off to interfere."[4]

On another occasion, several thirsty British soldiers came upon an enticing well. One took a drink and was delighted by the taste of the water, so his fellow soldiers joined him. The next day, they learned that the bodies of nine women and children lay at the bottom of that well. Other British soldiers found in a well the bodies of women who apparently had committed suicide by drowning. The women's jewelry and clothes indicated that they were well-to-do and most likely Manchu.[5]

Many British soldiers came upon the bodies of women—young and old—and children whose wounds looked deep. The throats of some had been slashed. When several British soldiers stepped into a house, for example, they found three women, presumably a mother and two daughters, with their throats cut from ear to ear and their heads placed atop their bodies. On the other side of the house, the soldiers found the bodies of two young girls—and a Chinese soldier hiding under them.[6] Similarly, another group of soldiers found an infant lying on the ground in a house, apparently left by the parents, who had committed suicide. They discovered the bodies of more than sixteen women and children there, poisoned or with their throats cut.[7]

In another house, a British soldier found several people gasping their dying breaths alongside others already dead. In one room, he came upon a disconsolate old man attending to two children whose spines had been severed. A girl was on the bed, blood gushing through the silk scarf around her neck. Nearby were an older woman whose body had been twisted as if from strangulation and a child who had been stabbed through the neck. Other women were also found, their faces distorted by anguish.[8]

The Qing official Hailing was among the suicides. The British troops sought him out immediately after entering the city, but they were too late to find him alive. Accounts on how he had ended his life differ. Some claim he jumped into a fire after killing his wife and children. Hailing's assistant told the British that, having realized the battle was lost, Hailing went into his house and ordered his assistant to gather various government documents and take them into another room. There, Hailing placed a pile of wood on top of the documents and sat in the middle of the pile, then ordered his assistant to set him on fire. His second son and daughter were prevented from killing themselves. Meanwhile, Prefect Xianglin jumped into a well but was rescued.[9]

To verify Hailing's death, the British went to view his partially burned body. At his home, they also found correspondence between Hailing and the emperor, in which Hailing expressed his strong sense of duty and determination to fight to the bitter end. The emperor scathingly criticized Hailing's inability to thwart the British movement toward Zhenjiang and warned of dire consequences if Hailing failed once more.[10]

Different reasons for the widespread suicides were given by those who witnessed the tragedies. There was no doubt on the Chinese side that the

British were responsible. As a member of the local literati noted in his personal journal, the British were the ones who cut the throats of many women and children. While considering the British culpable because they had started the war in the first place, a few others implied that some of these women, children, and elderly victims were killed by their family members.[11]

On the British side, however, the blame was placed entirely on the Chinese. The British claimed that the Manchu bannermen and Han soldiers were the ones who killed their own wives, sisters, and daughters. Some speculated that before the battle began, Chinese officials had asked the soldiers to die for the dynasty if necessary. The soldiers put their wives, sisters, and daughters to death before joining their superiors to fight the enemy or commit suicide themselves.[12]

As several British officers noted, they first became suspicious about the behavior of the Chinese soldiers during the battle when some Manchu bannermen threw down their weapons and took off their uniforms so they could disappear into the crowd of civilians. What puzzled the British was that those soldiers had demonstrated enormous courage in fighting and did not seem afraid of the enemy.[13] After finding the bodies of civilians, the British realized that the Manchu bannermen soldiers left to accomplish a more important mission: to put their family members to death. In other words, these Manchu soldiers decided to commit mercy killings of their families before the foreign invader could reach them.[14]

Some British considered the actions of those Chinese soldiers barbaric, whereas others thought of them as an attempt to preserve the honor and dignity of their families. As some in the latter group speculated, these soldiers must have thought that self-destruction was the only way out for their wives, sisters, and daughters, whose ultimate disgrace was inevitable. Since nothing was more humiliating than being physically violated by foreigners, it seemed only logical that Chinese women preferred to commit suicide and that Chinese soldiers killed their wives, sisters, and daughters. Interestingly, neither the Chinese nor the British mention anything in their diaries about whether or not the Chinese collaborators were responsible for some of the killings.[15]

Among the British who attempted an explanation, some compared Zhenjiang with Zhapu, where they had encountered a similar situation,

although with fewer cases of self-immolation. One British soldier remembered seeing women in Zhapu trying to drown themselves and bystanders pulling women and children out of a small pond while still alive. Another prevented an elderly woman in Zhapu from drowning her daughter, but as soon as he turned to leave, the woman ended her daughter's life and her own.[16]

Some British soldiers attempted to link the suicide phenomenon in Zhenjiang to the similar tradition in Japan, interpreting this as part of Asian culture. One mentioned that when a Japanese man failed to fulfill his duty, he often resorted to suicide by first bringing family members and close friends together for a feast, after which he gave away his belongings, as if preparing for an eternal journey, then committed suicide in front of the group. He would die in the midst of applause, a hero to his relatives and friends.[17]

Hypothesizing aside, a few British recognized fear as a leading factor in the suicides and mercy killings but considered the Qing officials, or even superstition, as their source—not the invasion or the soldiers' subsequent behavior. Some suggested that Qing officials instilled in their people the notion that foreigners were creatures of "monstrosity and savageness," and that if they did not commit suicide, they would experience extreme suffering before being killed. Regarding the influence of superstition, it was mentioned that people in Zhenjiang and Zhapu seemed to share feelings of inevitable doom, which gave the Chinese soldiers a sense of urgency in their gruesome deed.[18] Finally, some British soldiers found it deeply disturbing to witness the suicides, killings, and destruction of the city. One British officer jotted these words in his diary: "A heart would be hardly human that could feel unaffected by the retrospection, but the hardest heart of the oldest man . . . could not have gazed on this scene of woe unmoved."[19]

Meanwhile, the British offered another set of interpretations of Hailing's suicide in particular. First, according to one opinion, Hailing intended to set a good example by sacrificing himself to atone for his breach of duty, making it an act of despair rather than heroism. Another held that his suicide was a way to avoid severe punishment from the emperor. Some considered Hailing's suicide an act of courage, making him worthy of the equivalent to a noble title in Europe.[20]

A CITY IN RUINS

As both sides considered the phenomenon, chaos reigned in Zhenjiang with the burning of houses and widespread looting. One British soldier described "a terrible scene of ruin" after the fighting ended. The air was filled with the stench of decay and burning, and the sound of people wailing was heard all over the city. It seemed that the only creatures left alive in the streets were the starving stray dogs searching for food.[21]

Although some of the devastation was caused by the fires set by both British troops and Chinese soldiers—the former attempting to destroy Chinese arsenals and the latter trying to leave their enemy with a mere shell of a city—more came from large-scale looting in the city and its suburbs, which started with the first gunshot, as people scrambled to leave the city. The pillaging continued as the battle raged on and did not end until the entire city was completely depleted of valuables.[22] Revealingly, some British soldiers noted in their journals that they participated in looting. For instance, one soldier stumbled upon some valuables, including beautifully carved pieces of jade, and, sensing their value, took them. He later stole some joeys and batons, porcelain cups, and a mirror. When a British officer and his soldiers discovered a large quantity of silver hidden inside the residence of a high-ranking Chinese official, they took it all before setting fire to the house.[23]

On separate occasions, a British soldier took a gong from a temple with the intention of making a name for himself by donating it to a British museum. He replaced it with a cooking pot to humorously show that he was exchanging the gong for something equally valuable. A group of British soldiers searching for Manchu soldiers in Manchu homes absconded with everything of value. The Chinese looters who followed found little left behind. As a British officer confessed in his journal, plundering was rampant among British troops as a large number of valuables such as silver ingots and watches "found their way into the possession of the [British] soldiers."[24]

The fact that the British committed looting in Zhenjiang adds more evidence supporting a pattern of behavior among British soldiers throughout the Opium War, as demonstrated in Amoy, Beijing, and else-

where. The British were not the only plunderers in Zhenjiang, however. British and Chinese eyewitnesses have suggested that a significant number of Chinese were involved in ravaging the city.[25]

The Chinese looters appeared to have been very skilled. Some deliberately set fire to both ends of a street to allow them to begin their house-to-house rampages in the midpoint of the block. They also often bypassed items of lesser value for those worth more. When they were done, many escaped under cover of darkness through the southeast gate, which was not guarded by the British until the next day.[26] Once, a big crowd surrounded a county government depository, intent on robbing the place. They refused to leave even after the British showed up. Only when the British began to threaten severe punishment did they reluctantly depart.[27]

There were different kinds of Chinese looters. A large portion were Chinese collaborators—the former salt traders, pirates, and bandits—which somewhat affirmed the suspicions of several Qing officials that they had colluded with the British for the purpose of looting. Others came from other towns. A few were envious neighbors, disgruntled servants, or jealous relatives. Many took everything valuable that the British left behind, hauling it away on carts, if not on their shoulders, and smuggled their booty out by tying it into bundles that they lowered from the city wall with ropes.[28]

Eventually, everyone who wanted to benefit from the disorder, confusion, and misfortune of others joined in. On the Chinese side, there were locals and villagers, and on the British side, the Indians, other Europeans, Malays, and Africans, some of whom were crew members on the British ships. One British medic noted that, as he picked up wounded British soldiers, these crew members "deposit[ed] their loads of loot in the boats" alongside him.[29]

Some British officers attempted to prevent looting by arresting and publicly whipping looters, and they executed some Africans and Indians, leaving their bodies behind as a public warning. But they did nothing to British soldiers who were guilty. The British stationed some guards at the entrances to large residential areas, but this had little effect, given the sheer number of plunderers, which seemed to quickly multiply, with many carrying weapons.[30]

When it comes to the question of who did the most damage, both the British and Chinese pointed at the other side. According to the British, it was "gangs of Chinese plunderers" that took advantage of the lapse of authority and wreaked havoc. On the Chinese side, the British and their Chinese collaborators were seen as mainly responsible.[31]

THE INVADER AND THE INVADED IN DAILY CONTACT

Once the British invasion and the ensuing chaos ended, Hugh Gough wanted his troops to march on to Tianjin but was persuaded to remain. During this period, the British tried to force the people of Zhenjiang into submission. By deciding to stay, Gough unwittingly placed his soldiers in day-to-day contact with the people of Zhenjiang, giving each side the opportunity to observe and interact with the other much more closely than during the life-and-death struggle of battle. As the following instances show, despite the changes in the overall dynamic between the British and Chinese, deep suspicions of British evil intent remained, as did fear of the foreign invader.

Having decided to stay in Zhenjiang for a few days, Hugh Gough changed the tactics for how the locals should be treated. After the battle, the British caught one of Hailing's assistants and ordered him to draft a letter to the Qing officials, asking them to surrender. The letter claimed that the British had started the war because the emperor failed to meet their needs, implying that the war was against the emperor, not Chinese officials or the Chinese people. The British commander then ordered the British soldiers and Chinese collaborators to stop looting and burning houses.[32]

The British began to show leniency toward those fighting them. On one occasion, British soldiers released five Chinese men who tried to attack them, instead of having them executed as they usually would, because the Chinese men explained that they were prisoners convicted of only minor offenses and were coerced by Chinese officials to attack the British in exchange for their freedom. The British went to the city jail immediately after that and released all the prisoners.[33]

The British also changed the way they treated ordinary townspeople. When someone gave a Briton a copper coin instead of a silver dollar at a local market, the culprit was beaten, but let go. When an Indian soldier wounded a would-be robber, a British soldier separated the two. Later, not only was the money returned with additional compensation, but the Indian soldier was severely punished by a British officer. In a later incident, when a local resident robbed a British officer's son, the officer asked the Chinese prefect to deal with the situation. The prefect arrested the thief's uncle and pressured him to bring the perpetrator to the officer for punishment. Although the officer initially threatened to bombard the north gate if the uncle did not comply, he let the uncle go even though the robber was still at large.[34]

The British adopted friendly gestures in an attempt to win the hearts of people in Zhenjiang, such as giving more compensation than was needed to those who brought them food. They sometimes gave friendly townspeople posters that said, "Under the Protection of Great Britain" (*da ying hu zhao* 大英护照), to display at the front of their houses to discourage looters.[35]

When some townspeople asked Hugh Gough to appoint them neighborhood headmen (*lizhang* 里长), he not only obliged them gladly but also performed an installation ceremony in front of the drum tower, where such events typically took place. About twenty people received these coveted appointments. They treated the related documents as if they had been issued by the Qing emperor himself.[36] Furthermore, the British commander enlisted about three hundred local people as helpers. They were trained to use weapons and assigned to different units—and had their pigtails cut as required by the British.[37]

These efforts led some to soften their stance on the British. When a drunken British soldier was found collapsed outside the south gate, instead of killing him as they would have done previously, the Chinese informed the British so that they could return him to his camp. In return, after some townspeople helped carry a drunken soldier on a stretcher back to camp, the British rewarded them with several silver dollars. On a separate occasion, a group of Chinese came upon a wounded British soldier and delivered him to the British. A British officer observed that those same people steadfastly ignored the bodies of the slain Manchu bannermen or kicked them into a ditch.[38]

Through personal contacts, the British further witnessed the courage and skill of their military adversary as more and more injured Chinese soldiers were brought to the British for treatment. Some of the treatment involved the amputation of limbs; the Chinese soldiers endured the pain without anesthesia, earning praise from the British. On one occasion, when British soldiers tried to pull a cannon up a hill, they spent a considerable amount of time calculating the weight, measuring the distance, and discussing various methods, only to conclude the task was impossible. A group of perplexed Chinese onlookers were granted permission to try, and maneuvered the cannon onto the hill through the use of ropes and poles. The soldiers were pleasantly surprised.[39]

Likewise, these personal exchanges allowed the Chinese to observe the foreigners. As one local resident later described, close proximity made him realize that there were two kinds of foreigners: black and white. The white ones acted superior to the black ones, and each seemed to have different body parts. None used chopsticks when they ate, instead diving into meals of barbecued beef or mutton with their hands and leaving chicken raw.[40] The city's primary market reopened just days after the fighting ended. People once again appeared in the streets, as if, as one local gentry resentfully commented, "they never suffered under the British."[41]

Surprisingly, some local people—including women—began to show curiosity toward the British. When a British officer came into the city to return the courtesy of a Qing official's visit, people gathered around him. According to an eyewitness, "These people jammed the main street just like when the city was attacked by the British, but this time, women were dressed up. They either looked the foreigners directly in the eye or were looking from the higher points of the houses. They displayed no feelings of shame or anger toward the foreigners."[42]

This change in attitude made one British officer wonder if the Chinese would react very differently if the British invaded again, speculating that they would open the gates to them as if the British were there to save their lives and property rather than destroy both. This sentiment seemed to correspond to the one expressed by the British who invaded Ningbo.

After the invasion, some members of the rank and file also thought the Chinese would become more cooperative if given the chance to observe "the justice and moderation of the British army."[43]

Despite these changes, fear of the foreign invader was undeniably already deeply ingrained in the minds of many Chinese people, as exemplified in the following encounter. A British officer interested in the history of a pagoda sought the help of a monk at a nearby temple. Instead of talking to the foreigner, the monk was so frightened that his face contorted into an awkward grimace and tears poured down his cheeks. The officer later commented in his diary that "the emotion of fear must produce a different sensation in a Chinese from what it does in other people, for, when most afraid, they invariably laugh the heartiest."[44]

THE AFTERMATH OF THE BATTLE

The eight-day battle at Zhenjiang ended with relatively few casualties on the British side: 169 officers and soldiers were wounded or killed, not counting 60 who died from a cholera outbreak right after the battle was over. Partly in response to the disease, Hugh Gough decided to take most of his troops out of Zhenjiang on July 29 to head for Jiangnin (modern-day Nanjing), leaving some soldiers on Beigu Mountain.[45] Before their departure, however, the British demanded an indemnity of a large sum of silver dollars from the city. They then posted notes on the four city gates stating that they had left some of that money with Yilibu to be used for the city's recovery. Absurdly, the notes also urged people to go to Chui Mountain to purchase opium from the remaining British soldiers, promising discounted prices.[46]

As soon as the troops left, Emperor Daoguang ordered Qishen to install a sufficient defense to prevent the British from marching toward Jiangnin (Nanjing). Qishen later reported to the emperor that he had led his army to attack the British inside the city of Zhenjiang, killing one officer and eight hundred soldiers. After local officials in Zhenjiang informed the imperial court that they had no knowledge of this, Qishen ordered his subordinates to send reports to the court to convince the emperor that his report was credible.[47]

Qing officials outside Zhenjiang also started planning to take the city back from the remaining British troops. They first solicited support from salt merchants, asking them to persuade the boatmen transporting tribute grain to work in support of the plan. Next, some Manchu bannermen plotted to sneak back to the city to retrieve their lost weapons, but ended up just looting the city. Once Qing officials regained control of the city, they quickly put together a local militia with the help of some Han soldiers to stop the looting. Even the British helped by sending around one hundred soldiers to guard the city. All this finally drove the looters out of the city, and, a few days later, the British left Zhenjiang. Soon after, an investigation into Hailing's death was launched. At first, Emperor Daoguang instructed the newly appointed chief commander of the Hangzhou army, Qiying (耆英), to lead the case. Qiying was told that Hailing went into his home and hanged his wife and himself after handing over his official seal to his assistant. Upon reading the report, the emperor uttered, "It is a real pity."[48]

A few months later, a rumor surfaced that Hailing had been killed by a mob after his excessive use of force under the pretense of rooting out enemy spies. Zhou Suo reported this to the emperor, criticizing Hailing for creating chaos ahead of the British invasion. Zhou listed other examples of Hailing's wrongdoings, including closing the city gates, firing on innocent people, and killing those he suspected of collaborating with the enemy. In addition, Hailing abused his power by controlling all the money in the government treasury, making it impossible for other officials to draw funds for legitimate use.[49]

Upon receiving this report, the emperor asked Qiying to reinvestigate Hailing's death. Qiying later reported to the emperor that he was confident that Hailing had committed suicide, citing as evidence the fact that after the British occupied Zhenjiang, a group of Chinese soldiers sneaked back into the city and found Hailing's remains, along with a piece of his robe and his wife's bracelet. Qiying also stated that he had questioned 109 witnesses and they were unanimous on the matter.[50]

In Hailing's defense, Qiying stressed that Hailing had executed no more than thirteen people, a decision justified as an attempt to quell people's increasing agitation at not being allowed to leave the city. Hailing doubted their intentions and executed some to control the agitators.

Qiying recommended that the emperor compensate Hailing's family for its loss, based on the fact that Hailing had acted heroically when he ended his life. The emperor ultimately sided with Qiying, finding Zhou Suo guilty of reporting false information.[51]

Ultimately, the emperor punished almost all of the officials responsible for Zhenjiang's defense, except for Dezhubu and Qishen. Prefect Xianglin and a good number of lower-ranking army officers were reassigned to minor duties. A military officer who tried to escape during the battle was shackled and put on public display for a month. A memorial temple was built for the brave Manchu bannermen from Qingzhou, marking the final note of the British invasion of Zhenjiang.[52]

◆

The war brought Chinese local society into "negotiation" with modern imperialism, making it an exclusively negative form of liaison that led to a tragic outcome for the Chinese people. This tragedy derived from a combination of global and local factors, the leading one being the nature of war itself. As an exercise in modern imperialism, the war was intended for destruction, despite the British attempt to justify its cause.

But there were other contributing factors. One was the deep suspicion held by the local population toward all foreigners. The suspicion was intensified by the circumstances surrounding the local communities facing the foreign invasion, including Qing officials' way of managing the stressful situation and the superstition that the British were inhuman. When those circumstances were compounded with the people's shared historical memory of wartime atrocities, an acute feeling of fear resulted. That feeling became utter despair at the news of the suffering of people in Zhapu at the hands of the British, generating mass suicides and mercy killings by civilians and Chinese soldiers alike.

Among those victimized by the war, a considerable number were women, who either took their own lives or died at the hands of male family members in mercy killings. This phenomenon had a lot to do with the Chinese tradition that pitted women's lives against the social norm requiring them to make sacrifices, even with their lives, to uphold their family dignity. Although mass suicides among women in the face of foreign invaders did occur from time to time in different parts of the world, the combination of factors that drove women in Zhenjiang to suicide and their male family members to commit mercy killings was by all accounts sui generis in this locale. Throughout the event, the Chinese suspicion of the British was in no way lessened, and neither was the British misunderstanding of Chinese people and their culture.

PART TWO

COMMERCIAL NETWORKS AND TRANSREGIONAL TRADE

IN THE SECOND HALF of the nineteenth century, after the British invasion, Zhenjiang not only recovered but also experienced an economic resurgence, with commercial activity rivaling Suzhou's toward the latter part of the century. One of the main reasons had to do with Zhenjiang's role as a link for transregional trade between merchants above and below the Yangtze River during the transformation of China's commercial system from one primarily based on transregional trade within China and extended to neighboring countries like Japan, Korea, and Vietnam through the intra-Asia trade network to one directly connected with the rest of the globe through the newly dominant Shanghai.[1]

This transformation occurred against the backdrop of global economic changes that saw a primarily expanding Asian economy between 1800 and 1850. The expansion continued between 1850 and 1880, when Asia's export activities were constrained by use of the silver standard while much of the rest of the world had adopted the gold standard. Despite Asia's lack of exports, however, there was a surge in intra-Asian trade as China, Japan, and India competed fiercely for commodities like cotton and silk, as judged by the sudden increase of payments among those countries during that period.[2]

As more opportunities became available in Asia around 1880, when Asian countries began to adopt the gold standard, not only did trade between Asia and the rest of the globe quickly expand, but Chinese merchants also took advantage of the changes in Asia, especially the "opening" of treaty ports in Japan and Korea that provided access to parts of Asia previously denied. It was the combination of the growing importance of the Asian economy and the exceptional ability of Chinese merchants to take advantage of various changes in Asia and around the globe that laid the foundation for Shanghai's emergence as one of the world's major commercial centers at the beginning of the twentieth century, along with Chicago, Buenos Aires, and Calcutta, all of which grew at a speed equivalent to that of Manchester, England.[3]

In this part, I show how Zhenjiang negotiated global economic changes in the second half of the nineteenth century. I examine two discrete yet closely related developments in Zhenjiang: its evolving role as a brokerage town and the process through which its local business community found a way to connect with Shanghai's financial system. I will demonstrate that the entrepreneurial-spirited townspeople in Zhenjiang were capable of surviving the changes by actively participating in them, turning them into opportunities.

4

The Nineteenth-Century Transformation

◇

ONE OF THE REASONS Zhenjiang became part of global economic changes was the arrival of economic powers from Europe and North America in China in the early nineteenth century—an important factor in the transformation of Chinese commerce that gave rise to the new role of Zhenjiang as a brokerage town in China's transregional trade. To better comprehend Zhenjiang's evolving role, we shall first look at how China became a target of the global economic expansion undertaken by the industrialized countries.

THE YANGTZE RIVER AND THE UNEQUAL TREATIES

One of the results of China's defeat in the First Opium War (1839–1842) was the introduction of foreigners from European and North American countries that had recently gained global dominance through industrialization to compete for access to the Yangtze River, one of the main arteries of China's transregional trade. This competition was substantiated by these industrialized countries' forcing the Qing dynasty to sign a series of treaties that gave them access to cities in territories beyond the east coast, such as Zhenjiang.

The first such treaty was the Treaty of Nanjing. Sealed in 1842 between the Qing dynasty and Britain, it designated Shanghai as one of the five treaty ports, along with Guangdong (Shameen Island), Xiamen, Fuzhou, and Ningbo. A year later, the Treaty of the Bogue (or Treaty of Humen) and the Five Articles of Association in Sino-British Trade (*Zhongying wukou tongshang zhangcheng* 中英五口通商章程) were added to give Britain most-favored-nation status and its citizens the right to live and purchase property in the treaty ports. In 1844, the United States and France followed suit and requested similar treaties from the Qing dynasty, resulting in the Treaty of Wangxia and the Treaty of Huangpu, which offered both countries the same privileges as Britain.

In 1856, Britain and France joined forces to launch the Second Opium War in an attempt to extract more privileges from the Qing dynasty. With their superior military forces, the two countries succeeded in forcing the dynasty to renegotiate a treaty to focus on four issues, one of which was the opening of new ports along the Yangtze River. The Treaties of Tianjin were then signed in June 1858 between China and France, Britain, Russia, and the United States, with similar provisions for each country. By virtue of their favorite-nation status, all the countries signing the treaties could enjoy one another's privileges.[1]

Under the Treaties of Tianjin, the cities of Zhenjiang, Nanjing, Jiujiang, and Hankou were among ten new treaty ports. Except for Nanjing (which would not open until 1898), all the cities were quickly opened to these countries. The rule prohibiting foreigners from staying outside the treaty ports for more than one day was abolished; they could travel freely in any part of the country beyond the limit of one hundred *li* (about thirty-three miles) with valid passports to conduct trade and missionary activities along the Yangtze River.[2]

When the treaty was signed, however, one thing still prevented countries from Europe and North America from fully accessing the Yangtze River: the Taiping Rebellion. Under the treaty, foreigners could not move freely along the Yangtze River as long as there was a military confrontation between Qing dynasty troops and the Taiping rebels. To gain that access, Britain went into another round of negotiations with the Qing dynasty in November 1860. The result was the Interim Charter for Trading at Ports along the Yangtze River (*Changjiang gekou tongshang zanding zhangcheng* 长江各口通商暂订章程) as an addendum to the Treaties of Tianjin. The charter allowed the British to initiate trade along the Yangtze River during the rebellion by temporarily subjecting their activities to dynastic approval. In return, Britain promised not to aid the Taiping rebels. Having considered the possibility of collecting more custom dues once the British resumed trade with China, Prince Gong, the head of the Qing dynasty's negotiation team, signed the interim charter, making Jiujiang, Zhenjiang, and Hankou accessible to all Europeans and Americans.[3]

The Chinese soon discovered a loophole in the interim charter. Because of ambiguous wording, the British could interpret it in a way that allowed them to trade freely in any place between Zhenjiang and Hankou. With the attempt to close the loophole, the Qing dynasty initiated a revision of the charter, and thus created the Provisional Charter for Trading at the Ports along the Yangtze River (*Changjiang gekou tongshang zanxing zhangcheng* 长江各口通商暂行章程). The revision contained twelve items, one of which limited British business activities in cities like Jiujiang and Zhenjiang. In exchange, the Qing dynasty no longer required the British to obtain customs permits before loading goods at the different ports prior to their return to Shanghai. The day after the charter with Britain was signed, the Qing dynasty signed a simplified version, the General Agreement for Trading at Ports (*Tongshang gekou tonggong zhangcheng* 通商各口通共章程), which gave countries without favored-nation status the same privileges as those with the status to access cities along the Yangtze River. It also became a template for later agreements between the Qing dynasty and any foreign country concerning access to any river system in China. By then, the British had opened consulates in Jiujiang, Zhenjiang, and Hankou, and the Qing dynasty had opened customs offices in those cities.[4]

In 1862, both the Chinese and British wanted to change the requirement that foreign traders had to go through the customs office in Shanghai before they could trade in Jiujiang, Zhenjiang, and Hankou. At the time, the provincial governments of those cities were unhappy about losing revenue to Shanghai. After negotiations between China and Britain, a new statute was born: the General Charter on Trading along the Yangtze River (*Changjiang tongshang tonggong zhangcheng* 长江通商统共章程). The new charter allowed foreigners to trade in Jiujiang, Zhenjiang, and Hankou, as well as Shanghai, and gave them privileges that made their trading activities along the Yangtze River much more convenient.

The Qing dynasty decided in 1861 to build a major new office for the customs service at Zhenjiang. The project was delayed for four years, however, because of the activities of the Taiping rebels in the area, which also forced the British to temporarily relocate their office near the Jao Mountain.[5] Construction of the office building for the customs service in Zhenjiang finally commenced in 1865, about a year after the Taiping rebels lost their capital in Nanjing, ending their thirteen-year uprising. The office, located in the British concession, was completed in nine months, and the customs station at Qihaokou was moved to the riverbank nearby.[6]

While this was happening, the Qing dynasty sought to restrict the commercial activities of foreign vessels, such as forbidding them from carrying opium and certain local products. The Chefoo Convention (or the Treaty of Yantai) between China and Britain was signed in 1876 and did away with the internal tariff (*lijin* 厘金) or any form of taxation for trade in treaty ports conducted by these countries. Thus, between 1858 and 1876, industrialized countries gained access to the areas along the Yangtze River through a series of treaties and agreements.[7]

SHANGHAI AS A NEW COMMERCIAL CENTER

Making the Yangtze River more accessible to Euro-American powers helped Shanghai become one of the major commercial centers in all of Asia in the second half of the nineteenth century. Shanghai's rise was due to a confluence of factors internal and external to China, among which were global economic and technological changes, such as the use of mechanized technology in transportation and communication around the globe, that accompanied the expanding intra-Asian economy as a whole. During its transformation, Shanghai became connected internally within the territories of the Qing dynasty and externally to the rest of the world. Within East Asia, it became the axis of a commercial network linking treaty ports in China and Japan, of which Zhenjiang was a part.[8]

The city's development during this period was based on its unique geographical location in the middle of several major trade routes inside and outside China. Shanghai was located in one of the most populated areas in China, the lower Yangtze delta, which was the hub of the country's long-distance commerce. Unlike Nanjing, Hangzhou, and Suzhou, Shanghai had a harbor that accommodated large ships. In addition, it also was less than a hundred miles west of the great circle route extending from the west coast of North America to Japan and Southeast Asia, and was at the crossroads of all the major commerce routes in the western Pacific. This geographical advantage was an important reason, among others, that Pacific Rim countries like the United States chose Shanghai as their center for redistributing goods to the rest of China. Within roughly fifteen years, between 1846 and 1861, for instance, trade passing through the city rose from 16 percent of China's total exports and imports to 50 percent, eclipsing Guangdong.[9]

The opening of the Suez Canal in November 1868 put Shanghai in an even more favorable position for trade between Europe and Asia. The canal linked the Red Sea and the Gulf of Suez with the Mediterranean Sea, shortening the distance between Europe and Asia and thus greatly decreasing the cost of transporting goods to China. The canal's impact on Shanghai became evident when European countries like Britain designated Shanghai the first destination of the goods they shipped as they increased their exports to China.[10]

Coincidentally, Shanghai's rapid emergence as an economic powerhouse aligned with changes in the routes for transregional trade. Shortly after the Opium War, the Yellow River changed course, making a stretch of the Grand Canal in Shandong unnavigable and leading to the frequent use of a trade route between Jiangsu and the Gulf of Zhili that had already existed after the Qing dynasty ended the ban on sea traffic in 1683. By then, more and more traders began to rely on a new route from Shanghai to Tianjin by going around the Shandong Peninsula to reach Yingkou (in Liaoning).[11]

These changes accommodated the growing use of steamships in the mid-nineteenth century that made traveling along the Yangtze River, as well as along the east coast, much more efficient than going through the

Grand Canal. Thus, a new structure of trade routes emerged in which Shanghai became the axis along the Yangtze River and the east coast. With the convenience of steamships, merchants shipped goods from central China to other locations through the coast rather than through the canal or overland routes.[12]

Along the Yangtze River, Shanghai, Chongqing, and Hankou emerged as a new economic triad, followed by growth in second-tier cities like Yangzhou, Zhenjiang, and Nantong. More and more merchants along the Yangtze River shipped products to the rest of the country via Shanghai rather than through Zhenjiang to the south of the Yangtze River or Yangzhou to the north.[13]

Meanwhile, Shanghai's ascent signaled the decline of the Guangdong system of trade. After Shanghai's rise, the entire urban network in China and its connections with the rest of the globe were dominated by two major commercial centers, Shanghai and Hong Kong, toward the late nineteenth century; all import and export trade activities between China and the rest of the world went through these two cities. While Hong Kong became the main connection between southern China and the outside world, Shanghai was the primary linkage for northern and central China. Although almost all of the regional ports in China had trade relationships with both cities, their main relationships were among themselves. Transregional trade was forced to reorient to this new arrangement in Chinese commerce.[14]

TRANSFORMING THE SYSTEM OF TRANSREGIONAL TRADE

As Sherman Cochran has suggested, three scholars have made profound contributions to our conception of the system of transregional trade before the mid-nineteenth century and the changes it faced thereafter. G. William Skinner offers us a way to perceive it through a macroregional model within the territories of Chinese dynasties. Using the same model, William Rowe shows us the supraregional trade links by highlighting the power of social networks among long-distance traders that made possible a nationwide market before the arrival of advanced transportation and communication technology in the mid-nineteenth century. Takeshi Hamashita helps us realize the existence of intra-Asia trade networks beyond the territories of the Chinese dynasties via imperial China's tributary system that operated through the common currency of silver beginning in the sixteenth century.[15]

Because of their different focuses, these scholars present different pictures of transregional trade. These differences are reflected in how they conceive of the main characteristics of trade activities among Chinese long-distance traders. Whereas Skinner and Rowe see the division between the trade activities in the core and periphery, as well as on both sides of the boundary between macroregions, Hamashita observes linkages among the merchant groups between open ports and coastal regions, and between those areas and their hinterlands.

Each scholar thus offers a distinctive view of the transformation of transregional trade in the late nineteenth century. Skinner suggests that there was only a limited amount of transregional trade before the end of the nineteenth century, albeit a great deal occurred along the Yangtze River. A national level of market integration was possible only after the signing of the Treaty of Shimonoseki in 1895, as modern technology became available. Rowe sees the significant lack of connection between the central and regional metropolises and the hinterlands within each macroregion rather than between macroregions. He believes that this was the situation until 1889, when "the industrial era in local history" started, despite the fact that it could have begun earlier, when the steamship was brought to China.[16]

Like Rowe, some scholars emphasize the disconnect within China's trade system. For example, Rhoads Murphy sees a wide gap between commercial activities in treaty ports and interior China in the nineteenth century. Wu Chengming perceives the disjuncture between the already well-developed grain trade at the regional level operated by active trade networks and most villages at the bottom of the marketing structure that were still underdeveloped before the nineteenth century.[17]

But Takeshi Hamashita refuses to accept these views because he does not limit his study of the long-distance trade system to the interior of the main territory of Chinese dynasties. He points out that researchers who confine their research within the boundary of a particular state, empire, or nation are still looking through a nation-state pair of glasses. Instead, he asks us to pay close attention to the historical formation of "areas" and "regions" that transcend national boundaries. Based on this approach, he ascertains the existence of the system as an intra-Asia trade network that covered a much wider area, from East Asia to Southeast Asia and, later, to all of Asia.[18]

As Hamashita explains, this Asian network was developed through a maritime system of tribute-trade relations in East Asia, which began to take shape in the Tang dynasty. The linkage among cities and open ports within the network grew throughout the centuries, later producing satellite trade networks and smaller network centers in Vietnam; Choson, Korea; and Tokugawa, Japan. During the eighteenth and nineteenth centuries, more and more port cities became connected. For instance, among them were networks between Fuzhou and Keelung (in Taiwan) that linked Southeast China and Taiwan; and one between Aceh (in modern Indonesia), Malacca (in modern Malaysia), and Guangzhou that linked the Dutch East Indies, Malaya, and Southeast China. As port cities like Naha (Okinawa), Guangzhou, Macao, and Hong Kong flourished in the nineteenth century, the linkage between regions was also extended, as we saw between Fuzhou and Naha and among Guangzhou, Nagasaki (Japan), and Southeast Asia.[19]

As Hamashita elaborates, there were three main components of the maritime system upon which the entire network depended. The first was the coastal regions that intersected the sea and land; the second, the sea-rim zone that comprised coastal areas in which the cities and trading ports were the "key nodes" for the maritime area; and the third, the port cities that linked maritime regions. Long-distance trade provided the connection between port cities and tied the maritime regions together.[20]

Hamashita attributes the vital role of long-distance trade to the "exceptional" capability of Chinese merchants to "turn the system into one that extended the reach of their trade activities" to East Asia and beyond. He gives the examples of merchants from Ningbo, suggesting that they played such an active role in the trade in Nagasaki that the coastal and maritime trade outside China was far more profitable than transregional trade within the main territory of Chinese dynasties.[21]

Hamashita's assessment of Chinese merchants has a lot of support from scholars like Gary Hamilton, who also shows that merchant networks in China grew increasingly stronger from the mid-Ming to late Qing and expanded into Southeast Asia, where they "dominate[d] the domestic economies" in the late nineteenth century. Similarly, Ishikawa Ryota shows that after the Japanese forced Korea to "open" a series of treaty ports in 1876, Chinese merchants moved into places like Seoul to set up business. In addition to Hamilton and Ryota, a group of Japanese scholars has also demonstrated that Chinese merchants were capable of reaching the rest of Asia through their powerful networks.[22]

According to Kazuko Furuta, for example, Chinese merchants relied on their networks to gain an edge against Japanese merchants in the imported-cotton fabric business in Kobe, Japan. Based on his findings, Furuta suggests that the opening of treaty ports around the mid-nineteenth century "stimulated" the rise in significance of Chinese merchants in all of Asian commerce.[23]

Hamashita's conceptualization of the Chinese commercial system informs his view of its transformation during the nineteenth century. Hamashita first considers the 1830s to 1890s a period of "multilateral and multifaceted negotiations" for East Asia as it faced all kinds of challenges from global changes, including those brought by the rapid expansion of the industrialized economy and the worldwide adoption of mechanized technology in transportation and communication. In the midst of these "negotiations," especially during the second half of the nineteenth century, China's long-distance trade extended directly not only into Europe and North America but also among open ports, between ports and their hinterlands, and among different coastal regions all over the world. Because of these changes, Chinese merchants engaging in trade activities were able to operate throughout East Asia between open ports and their hinterlands and coastal regions, as well as with Europe and the United States. Incidentally, this augmentation of trade activity coincided with the end of the triangular trade centering on opium and the Chinese economy recovering from the damages of the Taiping Rebellion, both of which gave Chinese merchants lots of opportunities to move into areas formerly controlled by foreign traders.[24]

How does Hamashita's idea apply to Zhenjiang? Let's first examine the changes that surfaced in the city around the mid-nineteenth century.

FROM RIVER PORT TO BROKERAGE TOWN

The roots of Zhenjiang's becoming a brokerage town can be traced back to the introduction of its river port, originally in a place named Catfish Sheath (Nianyutao 鲇鱼套). It was one of four ports at the conjunction of Zhenjiang, Yangzhou, and Guazhou; the other three were Sixth Trench Entrance (Liuhaokou 六濠口), Seventh Trench Entrance (Qihaokou 七濠口) in Guazhou, and Fairy Temple (Xiannumiao 仙女庙) in Yangzhou.

Catfish Sheath became a river port largely because of timber. Around the turn of the nineteenth century, someone recognized the growing demand for wood in Jiangnan and brought timber to Catfish Sheath to be sold to the merchants who came to Zhenjiang for goods. These lumber traders usually operated in small groups and called themselves "uninvited visitors" (*zilai zike* 自徕自客) to Zhenjiang. They obtained timber in places like Hunan, Hubei, Jiangxi, and Anhui, then tied the wood into bundles of one hundred to two hundred pieces and took them via the Yangtze River to Zhenjiang. They landed at the west corner of the city, which they named Catfish Sheath, after the old port disappeared because of topographical changes. Because Catfish Sheath was created by the timber traders, it was called the "port of timber boards" (*paiwan* 牌湾).[25]

The port soon expanded into a market, where various goods were sold to merchants from across the country. For instance, the salt merchants traveling among Hunan, Hubei, Jiangxi, and Anhui stopped over in Zhenjiang to trade beans, rice, and other grain crops. Those from southern China purchased beans and grains other than rice and wheat to deliver to Southeast Asia. The influx of merchants led to hotels, restaurants, and brothels in Catfish Sheath.[26]

As Catfish Sheath grew and changed, so did three ports nearby: Fairy Temple was the main port for the grains brought from northern Jiangsu, and Sixth Trench Entrance and Seventh Trench Entrance were destinations for salt from Anhui. Merchants from every part of China, north and south of the Yangtze River, traded there. For instance, merchants from Shandong, Zhejiang, and Fujian came to sell grains, and those from Ningbo who brought timber from Fujian also sold seafood from Zhejiang and Fujian. Similar to what occurred at Catfish Sheath, merchants at Fairy Temple, Sixth Trench Entrance, and Seventh Trench Entrance constructed large residential buildings, assembly halls for native associations, and brothels, one of which was the well-known "heavenly palace of imperial concubines" (*tianfei gong* 天妃宫). The Ningbo merchants purchased land for their market street.[27]

Together, the four ports became locations where large quantities of goods, especially grain, changed hands. Their growth and development were commemorated in a popular piece of doggerel that had rhymes like "Catfish Sheath was the market for Zhenjiang," "Sixth Trench Entrance and Seventh Trench Entrance were the markets for Guazhou," and "Fairy Temple was the market for Yangzhou."[28] Most of the rice traded was not locally produced. In fact, local yields, even after a bumper harvest, barely fed the city for three months. Most rice bought elsewhere changed hands in Zhenjiang, attracting a large number of rice traders.[29]

Among the large commodities not affected by the changes in Zhenjiang were the so-called northern commodities (*beihuo* 北货), an assortment of native products from the north of the Yangtze River. The reason was that these products were available only from native producers—unlike sugar, for example, which was dominated by imports toward the end of the nineteenth century. Many of the northern commodities eventually ended up in Taiwan, Hong Kong, Japan, and Southeastern Asian countries, taken there by merchants from the south who bought them in Zhenjiang from sellers from the north. Most of the northern commodities that stayed in China went to Shanghai, Suzhou, Fujian, Chaozhou, and Guangdong. Sales of northern commodities by merchants from the north continued to rise and peaked at the end of the nineteenth century, when products such as jujube, chestnut, lotus, and pepper were added to the list. Because of the nature of trade for these commodities, Zhenjiang continued to attract merchants from elsewhere.[30]

The brokerage business in Zhenjiang began with the so-called business of sugar and northern commodities, which consisted of those two

FIG. 4.1 Junks and hulks in Zhenjiang, 1906–1907. Photograph by G. Warren Swire. Archives and Special Collections, SOAS Library, University of London.

distinct yet closely related businesses. In the beginning, in the early nineteenth century, the business sold mostly one product—sugar—from places like Sichuan, Guangdong, Guangxi, Fujian, and Taiwan. Brown sugar, produced in Guangdong and Taiwan, was the favorite in the local market.[31]

Soon, "Luzon brown sugar" from Luzon Island slipped into the Zhenjiang market. Then, sugar from Indonesia and Cuba arrived, but only for a brief period before the influx of the machine-processed sugar known as white sugar or crystal sugar made by British-owned companies in Hong Kong and brought in by the Jardine Matheson & Co. and Butterfield & Swire Co., Ltd. Local residents were not particularly fond of machine-processed sugar but could not resist the price, and sales of domestically produced sugar started to plummet long before the end of the nineteenth century.[32]

Whereas the sugar business traded just one commodity, the business of northern commodities dealt with roughly twenty agricultural products: bean cakes, daylilies, sesame, peanuts, and various fruits only avail-

able in those areas and highly prized in Guangdong, Fujian, and Taiwan; sesame, peanuts, locust flowers, walnuts, melon seeds, animal skins, and silkworms sold to countries like England, Germany, America, and France; and peanuts, sesame oil, bean cakes (for fertilizer), daylilies, and dried vegetables popular in Southeast Asia and Japan.[33]

There also were stores that sold grains and beans to merchants who came from many parts of the country through the waterways of the Huai River, the Grand Canal, and the Yangtze River. Some were from northern China and places like northern Jiangsu, southwestern Shandong, and northern Anhui. A good portion also came from Wuhu, Hunan, Hubei, and Jiangxi. Most grain traders came from Yantai, Chaozhou, Guangzhou, and Ningbo, followed by Fujian. Some dealers, such as those from Yantai (including Qingdao and Weihaiwei), regularly purchased mung beans from the merchants who came from the south and shipped them north to be turned into dried bean vermicelli that was sold back to merchants from the south. Other merchants, like those from Guangzhou, Chaozhou, and Fujian, specialized in buying rice, wheat, coarse grains, and bean cakes, which they sold along the southeast coast and as far away as Japan and Southeast Asia. Coarse grains and bean cakes were popular with customers in Japan and Southeastern Asia.[34]

The first sign of change appeared after the mid-nineteenth century, when some merchants from Suzhou, Guangdong, Fujian, Chaozhou, and Ningbo stopped showing up. Previously, they had usually bought northern commodities from places in northern Jiangsu, northern Anhui, Shanxi, Shaanxi, Henan, Hebei, and Shandong at Zhenjiang. But then, some northern commodities dealers from Shanxi, Shaanxi, Hebei, western Henan, and northern Shandong began to go through Shanghai instead, in order to trade directly with Hankou, Tianjin, and Zhifu (or Dengzhou port), three places in the Shanghai commercial network (discussed in Chapter 6). The northern commodities at Zhenjiang from this point on were from parts of Jiangsu, like Yangzhou, Huaian, Xuzhou, and Haizhou; northern Anhui and southwestern Shandong, like Jining; and northeastern Henan, like Kaifeng.[35]

Trade in Zhenjiang increased despite the loss of these merchants. That was due in large part to the use of steamships, which made shipping goods to Zhenjiang easier than ever and increased the total amount of commodities being brought into the city. Some merchants started to rely on river steamers (when available) to transport goods, while others resorted to the boats common on the east coast, including sand junks, toe-rope boats, regular fishing boats, and wooden junks.[36]

Zhenjiang experienced another shift in transregional trade around the time when goods from Shanghai started pouring into the city. Some were brought by merchants that had recently set up businesses in Shanghai. For example, after the kerosene lamp was invented around 1853 in the United States (and at the same time by a Polish inventor in today's Ukraine), it was brought to Zhenjiang from Shanghai. This new lamp was much more convenient than those that used animal, vegetable, or tung oil, and people both in the city and in the surrounding areas gradually abandoned their old lamps. Stores, restaurants, and street vendors also made the switch, which meant the markets could be well lit at night. Foreign-built, massive storage tanks for kerosene soon appeared on the Yangtze riverbanks and not only exposed people to products from Europe and North America but also made them realize for the first time that Shanghai, not Guangdong, was the foremost distribution center for these highly prized foreign goods. One of the consequences of this change was that Zhenjiang became one of Shanghai's subdistribution centers for kerosene.[37]

Eventually, about 60 percent of Zhenjiang's commercial activities involved foreign goods, mostly from Europe and North America. This continued to increase in the early twentieth century, when Zhenjiang became the hub for foreign products redistributed north of the Yangtze River, through those who still traded there. By that time, for example, the total value of foreign products passing through Zhenjiang to places like Jiangsu, northeastern Henan, southwestern Shandong, and northern Anhui was 15,250,000 customs taels, whereas agricultural commodities that passed through the city on their way to other countries were valued at only 4,250,000 customs taels.[38]

Meanwhile, demand for rice from Zhenjiang for export to Japan through Shanghai increased, giving the city the opportunity to become a major rice market in the lower Yangtze region between 1866 and 1897. Traders from Shanghai bought rice in Zhenjiang and shipped it to Shanghai's Wusongkou port, then to Japan. It was estimated that the annual amount of rice (including some beans) passing through Zhenjiang in a twenty-year period during this era amounted to around three million bags, with each bag weighing about two hundred *jin* (with a *jin* equal to 1.102 pounds).[39]

Thus, as we have seen, Zhenjiang became a brokerage town shortly after the mid-nineteenth century as the system for transregional trade began its transformation. Zhenjiang gradually became a second-tier city in the economic sphere surrounding Shanghai, which allowed merchants from the north and the south of the Yangtze to trade there while continuing to use the existing water system for transporting goods. This made Zhenjiang an ideal meeting ground for merchants from both north and south.

5
Brokering Multiple Commercial Networks

◇

WHAT KIND OF MERCHANTS went to Zhenjiang to trade, and how were their commercial activities tied into the transregional trade system? For answers, we may look to sociologist Mark Granovetter's theory on social networks. He suggests that economic actions in commercial activities are neither "carried out by atomized actors" nor based on individual motives. If we closely examine the merchants who went to Zhenjiang, we will find that most were not "atomized actors" but rather agents for the large merchant groups in the places they came from, some of which were below provincial level. These merchant groups formed the basis of the major commercial networks in the country and their extensions in other parts of Asia. Thus, to better understand the significance of Zhenjiang's role as a crucial link for multiple commercial networks, we need to take a closer look at these groups.[1]

THE MERCHANT GROUPS

Chinese merchants formed networks with groups (*shangbang* 商帮) mostly based on their places of origin. The word *shang* took on the meaning of "merchant" in the early Zhou dynasty after the people of the Shang and Zhou dynasties began actively engaging in trade. The word *bang* first surfaced in the Tang dynasty and was used for the business associations that organized with one trade represented per street. *Bang* has a broad range of meanings and is used for any formal or informal organization.[2]

There are several ways to categorize the merchants of late imperial China. Peng Chang divides them into three types: rural, urban, and long-distance. Wellington Chan classifies them as licensed versus unlicensed and through geographical location, specific trade, or a special role they played. Because the merchants were very diverse groups of individuals, I have decided to provide a general view based on geographic location.[3]

I need to remind readers here that the decision to categorize merchants by their native places is arbitrary, useful only for the convenience of discussion. Not only were the merchants not always unified or organized along the lines of their native places, but there were also a variety of ways to define what constituted a native place. In some cases, internal divisions resulted in subgroups of larger groups. As William Skinner proposes, this flexibility in group boundaries among merchants indicates that commercial conditions, rather than "local system loyalties," played an essential role.[4]

Among the country's major merchant groups, ten were the most prominent during the late imperial period, especially toward the second half of the nineteenth century. These were Shanxi merchants (Jinshang 晋商), Shaanxi merchants (Shaanbang 陕帮), Huizhou merchants (Huishang 徽商), Zhejiang merchants (Longyou Shangbang 龙游商帮), Suzhou merchants (Dongting Bang 洞庭帮), Ningbo merchants (Ningbo Shangbang 宁波商帮), Jiangxi merchants (Jiangyou Shangbang 江右商帮), Shandong merchants (Lushang 鲁商), Guangdong merchants (Yueshang 粤商), and Fujian merchants (Minshang 闽商).[5]

Shanxi merchants were known for building a powerful financial network centered on remittance banks (*piaohao* 票号) after they had accumulated great wealth from the salt trade. Their quick rise to prominence, as the later discussion will show, had a lot to do with a set of dynastic policies from the Tang to the Qing. They leveraged their wealth to run the largest banking enterprise in the country.[6] Similarly, Shaanxi merchants actively traded salt in Sichuan and Guizhou. Aside from that, however, they were also involved in various business undertakings such as shipping cloth and silk from Suzhou, selling tobacco in Jiangsu and Zhejiang, and selling grain to the army on the west, northwestern, and northern borders, where they also bartered tea, salt, textiles, and ironware.[7] Compared with these two groups, Huizhou merchants were known for their cultural pursuits, which earned them the nickname of "Confucian merchants" (*Rushang* 儒商). They specialized in trading salt and running pawn shops, aside from dealing with a variety of basic commodities like grain, silk, tea, timber, paper, and ink sticks.[8]

Following the Huizhou merchants, the Zhejiang and Suzhou merchants were the most active merchants in the mid-Ming dynasty period. While Zhejiang merchants excelled in jewelry and antiques, Suzhou merchants focused on rice and silk. After the rise of Shanghai in the nineteenth century, however, Suzhou merchants quickly expanded into banking and the brokerage business while maintaining their trade in silk and cotton fabric.[9]

Jiangxi merchants were once very active, zealously trading products such as grain, pottery and porcelain, cloth, tobacco, indigo, medicine, and timber between northern and southern China in the Ming dynasty. By taking advantage of their convenient access to the Grand Canal, the Yangtze River, and Zhu rivers (through the Gan River), they supplied huge quantities of goods to many parts of the country. They were widely perceived as lacking ambition in the late Qing, however. William Rowe's recent research has provided some evidence that contradicted this perception.[10]

On the east coast, there were the Ningbo merchants. Their main commodities were medicine and clothes, and they specialized in trading with Japan, Korea, and countries in Southeast Asia. Their business success relied heavily on native ties that enabled them as a whole to cooperate efficiently with one another in business. After the treaty ports opened, the Ningbo merchants specialized in brokering deals for Chinese and foreigners from industrialized countries. Many were members of the first generation of industrialists during the emergence of modern Chinese industry.[11]

Like their Ningbo counterparts, Shandong merchants enthusiastically traded with other Asian countries. We often associate Shandong merchants with "daring the journey to the Northeast" (*chuang Guandong* 闯关东) starting around the beginning of the nineteenth century, when the Qing dynasty allowed peasants from the interior of the Eastern Pass of the Great Wall to migrate to Manchuria. Part of the group settled in Southeast Asian countries such as Indonesia and became successful entrepreneurs. Also like the Ningbo merchants, they had a significant presence in Beijing, where they controlled the textile, food, and restaurant businesses. Their activities spread well into northern China and along the east coast. By the second half of the nineteenth century, Shandong merchants were also running oil mills and grain stores, specializing in goods like silk, pharmaceutical products, animal hides, and cookware. They also got into the money lending business.[12]

Although Fujian merchants were known for having extensive business relationships with Taiwan, their success relied equally on their ability to trade elsewhere in the country. The Fujian merchants were the most diverse of all, with subdivisions usually formed along the boundary line of a particular area within present-day Fujian province, which often encompassed only a few districts or several counties. The decision depended on how the people in the area identified themselves within specific locales. The most notable subgroups, for instance, were from southern Fujian, Fuzhou, and Xinghu. Not only did each consider itself distinct from those elsewhere in the province, but each also specialized in a particular trade. For example, Minnan merchants predominantly traded with Taiwan, while Xinghua merchants were active players in the Zhenjiang market, where they were heavily involved in trading sugar and northern commodities.[13]

Among all the merchant groups in the country, those from Guangdong had the most diverse organizations and traded the widest range of commodities, even more so than the Fujian merchants. Guangdong merchants were in two large groups, one from Guangdong and the other from Chaozhou (in eastern Guangdong). Like the Fujian merchants, their organization was very flexible, consisting of subgroups formed based on localities that often involved only several districts within the province. Because of this, the group was much less consolidated than others. Overall, along with merchants in Shandong and Fujian, Guangdong merchants were best known for doing business in Southeast Asia, especially in countries like present-day Malaysia and Indonesia.[14]

Although many of these groups emerged before the mid-Ming dynasty, almost all became highly visible in the second half of the dynasty as they grew, accumulated wealth, and expanded their ventures in the midst of commercialization. But commercialization was not the only reason for their ascent; there were various other contributing factors, some of which were measures adopted by different dynasties, from the Tang to the Qing. Despite the fact that most of these measures were intended to promote only the interests of the dynasties, once promulgated, they created opportunities that merchants capitalized on, making them beneficiaries as well.

A good example is the maritime ban intended to prevent piracy at sea. The ban resulted in changes in the major trade routes, making the Grand Canal, the Yangtze River, the Gan River, and the Zhu River the main arteries of the entire transregional trade system. A quick list of similar measures would include Opening Tea-Horse Exchange Market (*chama hushi* 茶马互市), Exchange Cloth for Horse (*buma jiaoyi* 布马交易) or Exchange Silk for Horse (*juanma jiaoyi* 绢马交易), Supplying Grain for Salt Permit (*shiyan kaizhong* 食盐开中), Trading alongside the Army (*sunjun maoyi* 随军贸易), and Paying Levies in Real Cotton (*mianbu zhengshi* 棉布征实).

The Opening Tea-Horse Exchange Market set up bartering posts on the western, northwestern, and northern borders, including Guizhou, Sichuan, Tibet, and Mongolia, to allow merchants to exchange tea from the interior for horses from regions closer to the border. It commenced during the Tang and was discontinued during the Yuan dynasty, then started again in the Ming, until it finally ended in the mid-Qing dynasty. Because of this, some merchant groups, the one from Shaanxi in particular, became enthusiastically involved in growing tea in Hunan and bringing it to the northwestern border.

Likewise, Exchange Cloth for Horse traded silk and cloth for horses on the northern border, mostly in Xinjiang and Mongolia. The policy had the same effect on various merchant groups. The main difference, however, was the trade being directly controlled by the Ming and the Qing dynasties. It ended in 1840, after Russia profoundly penetrated the trading areas.

The policy known as the Supplying Grain for Salt Permit was adopted by the Ming after 1370 but continued into the Qing, although it also existed in its original form in the Song and Yuan dynasties. It allowed the merchants to supply grain to the army in border regions in exchange for salt permits. This particular dynastic measure benefited merchant groups from Shaanxi, Anhui, Shanxi, and Zhejiang. For instance, merchants from Shanxi grew wealthy by selling salt to other parts of the country through permits obtained under the policy. Given the abundance of salt in Shanxi, this happened very quickly.

Similarly, the Qing policy of Trading alongside the Army allowed merchants to transport food and other provisions to the army in the northwest during the dynasty's suppression of the Galdan rebellion. While doing this, merchants also traded with Mongolians. The policy was in place only between 1690 and 1757, starting under the Qing Kangxi emperor, but trade continued once the merchants became familiar with the routes and received the customary protection from the army. Because of this policy, in the ensuing ninety years starting in 1757, some merchant groups successfully established connections between the markets in the Jiangnan region and towns on the northwestern border.

The dynastic measures regarding border areas created opportunities for large merchant groups to extend their reach to the border, but they were not the only ones who benefited. Sometimes a tax policy, such as the Paying Levies in Real Cotton policy, begun by the Ming and ended in the Qing, which required the collection of levies in the form of raw cotton, also provided business opportunities for merchants transporting cotton to the dynasty's capital. The key to their success seems to lie in their ability to discover and capitalize on such opportunities.

Furthermore, all the merchant groups discussed above were sojourners. To borrow William Rowe's description, they were the "wholesale jobbers who carried merchandise to or from the other main urban centers or rural markets." In other words, they were "itinerant," based in urban centers of various sizes to trade all kinds of commodities.[15]

As such, each merchant group had a specialty. The long-distance trade system worked much like an ecosystem in which each group dominated one or several aspects of local commerce while connecting with trade in the rest of the country. Meanwhile, as "outsiders" to those urban centers, they had to rely on bureaucratic largesse to survive. In exchange, they had to constantly make "contributions" to local projects or directly to the officials themselves.[16]

To make a profit, merchant groups had to travel for miles, and thus their footprint covered a vast territory. That kind of mobility, as well as their far-reaching capability, can be seen among merchants from all parts of China. Here is a quick peek at how several merchant groups came to dominate the entire tobacco trade. During the late Ming and early Qing dynasties, for instance, merchants from Shanxi, Shaanxi, Huizhou, Fujian, and Jiangxi were very actively involved in trading tobacco. Merchants from Fujian controlled tobacco in western Fujian and the southern Gan highlands. Sojourning merchants from Huizhou, southern Fujian, and Jiangxi transported Pucheng tobacco (one of the name-brand tobaccos from Fujian, present-day Pucheng County). They also controlled the tobacco cultivated in the lower Yangtze highlands and sold tobacco processed in Anqing throughout Jiangnan. Merchant groups from Shanxi and Shaanxi handled tobacco grown in the Xiang-Gan area. Their business covered the territory from the lower Yangtze region to the Pearl River delta, and from northern cities like Beijing and Tianjin to southern cities like Guangdong. They were eager to enter the markets in Xinjiang, Mongolia, and southern Siberia.[17]

Merchant groups seem to have been concentrated in two areas, although in general those from the coastal provinces were more likely to focus on coastal areas while those from the interior were widely scattered across central and western China. In one pattern, quite a few merchant groups were active exclusively outside their home provinces. For instance, merchants from Zhejiang predominated in Shanghai, Hankou, and Xian but not in their home province because their overseas trade had to go through Ningbo, where Shandong and Fujian merchant groups also were present. The merchant group from Jiangsu was concentrated mostly in the Yangtze basin but left the trade in their native province to the merchant groups from other provinces. Similarly, merchants from Jiangxi let the merchant group from Shandong dominate in their native province.[18]

In another pattern, the merchant groups in Guangdong and Fujian were able to not only exercise a firm hold on their home turf but also

extend their activities to nearby Taiwan and Southeast Asia. Merchants from Fujian dominated trade in Taiwan as early as the tenth century. The province started to depend on rice from Vietnam to feed its population, due to the lack of arable land and a large population, and gradually imported rice from Guangdong toward the sixteenth century. By the second half of the sixteenth century, however, Guangdong had trouble keeping adequate rice supplies and had to import rice from Guangxi. At that point, Fujian was forced to look elsewhere for rice, turning mainly to Taiwan and Thailand. Changes in the sourcing of rice in the sixteenth century made merchants from both Guangdong and Fujian the most active traders in Southeast Asia, much more active than the Portuguese rice traders there.[19]

However, these were by no means the only patterns discernable among merchant groups. As Ng Chin-keong suggests, for example, quite a number of Fujian merchants became active traders in Guangzhou port, while many others were settling in Southeast Asia, when the junk trade was in the decline in the early nineteenth century. Meanwhile, Steven B. Miles reveals that a large number of merchants from Guangdong were operating their business in Guangxi and Yunnan through diaspora networks created by fellow natives who migrated to these provinces through the Pearl River system. This shows the activities of the merchant groups were much more diverse than we previously thought.[20]

Merchants, most of whom represented the merchant groups they belonged to, operated in Zhenjiang through brokers, and the merger of the trade of sugar and northern commodities acted as the crucial juncture. We will now focus on the new generation of brokers that appeared after the mid-nineteenth century.

THE BROKERS

As transregional trade gradually moved away from routes that relied mostly on China's main waterways to those centering on Shanghai, as well as the entire east coast and treaty ports, local commerce in Zhenjiang likewise changed. That was most evident in the trade of sugar and

northern commodities, which began to consolidate. During that time, a new generation of brokers appeared.

Initially, sugar and northern commodities had separate guilds, without a clear distinction between the two. The lack of differentiation came from the mixed memberships of each organization. For example, the guild for northern commodities had members who also dealt in sugar, while the guild for sugar had members who also sold tung oil and ramie. It included traders known as "southern and northern grocers," who were mostly itinerant merchants from different parts of the country, both north and south.[21]

Meanwhile, both organizations had to deal with the merchants flooding into Zhenjiang to trade sugar and northern commodities. The ones from Guangdong, for instance, brought sugar to sell to merchants from the north, and the ones from the north, particularly northern Jiangsu, brought northern commodities to sell to merchants from the south. None of the groups from north of the Yangtze River traded directly with groups from the other side, and they all relied on the sugar and northern commodities guilds as their brokers. Because of the similarities in activities and the overlapping terms of membership, the two guilds gradually merged, hence the emergence of the so-called business of sugar and northern commodities.[22]

The appearance of many new, small brokers in Zhenjiang in the second half of the nineteenth century was launched by the growth of the business of sugar and northern commodities. An important component was the local stores, especially the two largest, from which the first group of small brokers all originated. In the mid-nineteenth century, these stores engaged in all kinds of commerce, ranging from selling seafood from Shanghai to the locals, trading various commodities in Hankou that were brought in from Shangjiang (the area of present-day Jinhua) and Quzhou (in Zhejiang), and brokering deals for petty merchants who came to Zhenjiang to obtain cooking oil (vegetable, soybean, and sesame oil). But after the mid-nineteenth century, increasing numbers of dealers of northern commodities came to the city.[23]

Increased demand for northern commodities led store owners to focus on brokering these goods. Their fellow natives provided funding to build several loading docks on the Yangtze for merchant ships from elsewhere.

Witnessing the quick profits these stores generated, other locals jumped into the business, though many had very little or no capital. One such individual was Wu Zemin.[24]

Wu had previously been a clerk in one of the largest grocery stores. He left to open his own store but quickly closed it, realizing that a brokerage business for northern commodities would be much more profitable and easier to run. He took out a loan from his previous employer and opened one, and, within a short period, he was able to not only repay his debt but also become one of the most active brokers in town.[25]

Although many attributed Wu's success to his honesty and trustworthiness, the real reason was his personal relationships with local officials, through which he received the privilege of assisting the local government in collecting contributions from the city's entire business community. He was given an official title for his service, and he was soon elected chairman of the board of directors of the city's Chambers of Commerce, as recognition from the business community naturally followed.[26]

Unlike Wu, another man, with the surname Zhu, left his store after serving as a manager and thus was able to bring a large number of clients with him. Facing the possibility of losing the majority of his customers, the store owner offered Zhu 50 percent ownership in the store plus a 10 percent dividend on annual sales. Zhu accepted the offer and became wealthy. He later succeeded Wu as the chairman of the board of directors of the city's Chambers of Commerce.[27]

After these two men succeeded in the brokerage business, there emerged a great number of small—mostly one-man—brokerage companies whose operators called themselves brokers (*yahang* 牙行). Because some traded fruit along with northern commodities, they sometimes called themselves "fresh fruit and northern commodities brokers."[28] For us to better understand these brokers, it is necessary to take a brief look at the history of the particular institution of the brokerage, one of the oldest business institutions in China. As a brief survey of its history shows, it existed as early as the Han dynasty, when a practitioner was called a "powerful broker" (*zhanghuei* 驵会) or "broker" (*kuai* 侩). Beginning in the Song dynasty, brokers were divided into two categories: private and government authorized. There were variations in their names in later periods. Regardless of the name difference, all had to pay a brokerage tax, which they simply added to the taxes they charged clients.[29]

The broker's main function was to negotiate deals between buyers and sellers, from whom they extracted a fee. But they also were often responsible for overseeing sales, determining the quality and price of goods, and keeping the market in order. As transregional trade expanded during the Ming-Qing period, so did the role of brokers.[30] Seeing this as a threat to the dynasty, Ming emperor Zhu Yuanzhang attempted to control these middlemen. Then, in 1709, Qing emperor Kangxi shut down all private brokers. No broker could operate without a government license, an offense punishable by jail. Despite this, the number of brokers and their influence on the market increased.[31]

By the second half of the nineteenth century, the services that brokers in Zhenjiang provided were little changed. Besides being middlemen between traders from the north and south, they were responsible for securing loans, collecting debts, and transporting goods for merchants. Although some large groups of merchants had trading firms as well as guilds, none of them traded directly with one another, as dictated by tradition. They all went through brokers. This tradition made brokerage one of the largest businesses in town.[32]

At that time, there were two kinds of brokers in Zhenjiang: small and large. The majority were small, with minimal capital and operating under short-term business licenses from Dantu County (where Zhenjiang was located) after paying business taxes. Because of their lack of funds, they were unable to hold commodities for merchants, even those sent by powerful merchant groups, so they were mainly considered "selling agents," meaning they had to sell their commodities.[33]

Some small brokers focused on luring the merchants entering the city through the Grand Canal. Boats shipping tribute grains through Zhenjiang often carried northern commodities on their way back south, so small brokers would send representatives to meet them on the canal and offer them tobacco, liquor, and prostitutes, or entertain them in gambling houses, to gain their business. The headmen of these boats were the targets of intense solicitation, prompting the saying among city dwellers that "once the flagpole on the boat nodded its head, the [boat headmen] would indulge themselves in three houses: the opium house, the brothel, and the restaurant" (*erquegan diantou, yiri sanlou* 二雀杆点头，一日三楼).[34]

Although many small brokers had regular customers, they still sent clerks, apprentices, or hired hands called agents (*qianke* 掮客) in small junks to solicit business from rice dealers along the banks of the river and canal. These agents were also known as pullers (*lazi* 拉子), because their main job was to pull merchants arriving along the riverbank into their companies. The agents were paid on commission and, to compete, they often brought in the regular customers of their competitors, creating disputes.[35]

For traders from the north, brokers resorted to tactics such as cheating on the price of commodities, asking for commissions, or "eating the food plate" (*chi panzi* 吃盘子). In this last method, brokers would sell goods for much more than standard market prices before the traders had time to learn about local market conditions. After being paid, brokers would attempt to deliver a smaller quantity of goods than the traders had paid for, a scam known as "lacking weight" (*qian fenliang* 欠分量). To accomplish this deception, brokers used scales meant for weighing heavy goods to weigh light goods. Then, they would offer their customers only a rough estimate of the weight during the weighing process. When these methods failed, they resorted to procuring prostitutes or offering sessions of opium smoking in an attempt to renegotiate the payment, or simply refused to pay until the traders yielded to their demands.[36]

This is how grain brokers operated with rice dealers. Four types of businesses handled rice: stores (*dian* 店), firms (*hao* 号), mills (*chang* 厂), and brokerage houses (*hang* 行). These were retailers of rice and other grains (although many also held wholesale licenses) and were mostly located on the south side of the city. Firms were similar to stores but had more capital. Unlike stores, however, they provided the service of transporting rice to various locations across the country. Like firms, mills also had significant capital, but their primary business also included milling rice that they purchased from farmers. Before milling machines were available, all the mills used humans and sometimes animals to husk the rice using a tool that is similar to a burrstone mill but is made of bamboo, thus giving these mills the moniker "husker mills." The last of these four businesses was the brokerage house, consisting of small brokers

FIG. 5.1 Trading goods behind the British consulate building, 1906–1907. Photograph by G. Warren Swire. Archives and Special Collections, SOAS Library, University of London.

specializing in rice. At the peak in the second half of the nineteenth century, there were about a hundred such brokerage houses throughout Zhenjiang and concentrated along the Yangtze and the Grand Canal, where tea booths were set up for business negotiations.[37]

One type of small broker in the rice market was responsible for weighing grain for grain dealers. They were known as "measuring-vessel firms" (*huhang* 斛行) and had to be licensed by the government to operate, so local people usually called them "government measuring-vessel firms." All the rice brought by different merchants was weighed before being transferred to wholesale dealers. Clerks routinely inflated the actual weight of the rice they handled in order to be paid more and also had secret arrangements with the previous kind of small brokers in order to sell the rice for a higher price. In return, brokers gave the firms part of their profits. Knowing this, merchants gave these firms advance payments in exchange for giving an accurate weight. These firms favored small brokers because of their close personal relationships. Most firms, regardless of size, played the same tricks on their customers.[38]

When a food shortage arose, the government sought to control the price of grain. In response, traders usually shipped their grain elsewhere, such as to Chongming (near Shanghai), Haimen (in southeastern Jiangsu), and northern Jiangsu, or as far as the seaports along the east coast. Many waited until the government lifted its price restrictions to return their grain to the Zhenjiang market.[39]

These tactics often led to disputes between brokers and merchants. The result was not always in favor of the brokers, although they often had various local officials on their side. For instance, the Shaanxi merchants once accused a broker speculating in cotton of depressing prices, overcharging for packaging, and stealing cotton from them. The merchants successfully bribed the provincial chief of Jiangsu to obtain favorable injunctions from the provincial government against the broker and to overrule the previous judgment by the county government. To celebrate the victory and further humiliate the broker, the merchants engraved the injunction on a stone tablet that was erected in front of the county government building for a short time.[40]

In many cases, however, small brokers were hired to solicit business for larger ones and were thus called "commission agents" (*jingshou* 经手). These independent businessmen earned fees for bringing buyers and sellers together because of the lack of capital.[41] In Zhenjiang, there was a separate group of big brokers who called themselves "big brokerage houses" (*da hangzhan* 大行栈) or "business agencies" (*daiban zhuang* 代办庄). Although they were labeled "big," this did not necessarily mean they had large operating capital of their own. Instead, they often relied on the backing of locally powerful families, on personal ties to wealthy friends, or on their clout in the local community. Any of these conditions, or a combination, enabled them to secure loans for clients from wealthy investors and later extract their commission from the transactions.[42]

One example comes from a member of the Yan family, one of the largest in Zhenjiang. This individual opened an agency with capital of only about ten thousand taels but could operate a large business because of backing by his locally powerful family, two family friends, and other wealthy people in town.

In another case, Wu Zemin simply relied on his standing in the business community to convince a large, traditional bank in Suzhou to make sizable loans to his clients through his big brokerage house. Wu later persuaded the same bank to make loans to the clients of two brokerage companies owned by his relatives. Interestingly, Wu's action in getting the loan from a traditional bank outside the city did not seem to bother the local banks, since they still profited from the transaction because the clients had to issue credit (*huipiao* 汇票) and receive payment through the local money stores owned by these banks.[43]

There were quite a few local money stores in Zhenjiang. They were very popular because their clients, mostly merchants from the north and south, considered them reliable—so much so that their credit was treated as cash in the local market and was redeemable after an extended period.[44] In some cases, big brokers needed loans themselves because they were directly involved in purchasing, storing, and selling large quantities of goods. Some sent clerks to the areas where northern commodities were produced to purchase the goods at the lowest prices and then ship them back to Zhenjiang to sell at a much higher price. That is why local people often called these big brokers "buying agents" (*maihang* 买行).[45]

During the purchasing and selling processes, however, almost all big brokers took advantage of the northern commodities producers' lack of knowledge about the exchange rates for different currencies in Zhenjiang. Specifically, the price of goods in Zhenjiang's market was determined by the value of silver, but traditionally the payment to producers in the north was in the form of copper coins. Because the circulation of silver became rare in transactions, the value of silver appreciated as quickly as the value of copper coins depreciated. Big brokers knew that the northern commodities producers were not always up to date on exchange rate fluctuations and continued to pay for sugar in copper coins but asked for silver in return. This kind of behavior was one reason that some merchants eventually set up trading posts to bypass brokers.[46]

These trading posts generally were of two kinds—one belonged to those from the north, and the other, to those from the south. The ones for northerners had trademarks, some of which were backed by the traditional bank in the north to indicate their specialty in dealing with northern commodities. They also formed guilds. For some reason, there was confusion in the way local people identified the native origins of these trading posts. For example, local people considered the trading post founded by the Shanxi merchants to be owned by Henan natives, because the same Shanxi merchants also owned several remittance banks and traditional banks in northeastern Henan.

Likewise, the trading posts run by Nanjing natives were considered to be owned by Beijing natives, because the Nanjing merchants were called the Jing Group (*jingbang* 京帮) and the "jing" in "Nanjing" was the same as in "Beijing," which was in the north. Besides this confusion, infighting among trading posts over trivial matters was constant. Trading posts owned by merchants from Shandong and Shanxi were known for skirmishes and created quite an uproar in the local market.[47] Southern merchants also had trading posts and guilds, which were equally infested, if not more so, with the same problems as the northern ones. For example, several trading posts—around twenty, at one point—were created by Guangdong merchants alone and formed two separate guilds based on the two major subgroups.[48]

The southerners' trading posts, aside from buying northern commodities from the north and selling them in the south, all acted as agents for companies overseas, some of which belonged to the overseas Chinese. In the sugar business alone, for example, they represented companies in Luzon (Philippines), Indonesia, Cuba, and Hong Kong (specifically, the Jardine Matheson & Co. and the Butterfield & Swire Co., Ltd.). At the same time, they acquired northern commodities not only for Chinese communities in Hong Kong and Southeast Asia, but also for merchants from countries like Japan and Korea and across Europe. Generally, the larger trading posts were more likely to be involved in this, whereas the smaller ones were more active in selling sugar from Southeast Asia because of the overall decline in the sugar trade.[49]

In accordance with the local business custom, however, neither foreign agencies nor their subsidiaries traded directly with merchants from the north. Instead, they went through the big brokers—not the small brokers—because only these were deemed qualified (*you zige* 有资格) to deal with foreign businesses. Somehow, this custom prevailed for some time, and no one seemed to question it.[50]

Another unspoken rule was the so-called tacit mutual understanding (*xinzhao buxuan* 心照不宣) between the big brokers and representatives of the Guangchao merchants. Guangchao merchants would not purchase northern commodities directly from local stores. The big brokers would send clerks to either Guangdong or Hong Kong to lay in a stock of sugar.[51]

This understanding later proved to be a double-edged sword, however. For instance, although it allowed big brokers to dominate the sugar business, it also prevented them from finding new sources of sugar outside Guangdong and Hong Kong. Because of this, the big brokers were unable to prevent Guangchao merchants from stealing customers by offering low-priced, inferior sugar from Hong Kong. Because the big brokers depended on brokerage fees that came as a fixed percentage of each deal, they preferred to deal only in higher-priced sugar. Still, they tolerated this intrusion because they believed the benefits outweighed their losses.[52] Having seen the dominance of big brokers in trading with foreigners, most traditional local banks offered them favorable conditions such as delayed payments. The big brokers profited by deliberately delaying payments and using the money in the meantime to purchase goods for quick sale, a tactic that was very profitable.[53]

Meanwhile, when foreign companies laid in stocks of northern commodities in Zhenjiang, they would be issued an empty transit pass, which the Chinese called a "foreigner's pass" (*yangdan* 洋单), through which companies declared the value of their goods at the maritime customs service in Zhenjiang. The benefit of such forms was that officials at the Chinese native customs stations would show utmost courtesy to those holding them, letting their boats go ahead of Chinese boats. This allowed shippers not only to save time going through customs but also to avoid paying the *lijin* tax at the Chinese native customs station.[54]

Many merchants from Guangdong were able to bypass different channels for their benefit. For example, when locally grown daylilies were in high demand in Hong Kong, Guangdong merchants employed boatmen to transport them. Whenever a boat was stopped by native customs, the shippers would show their transit pass, and the officials would treat the boat as foreign owned. Even when these boats arrived at a native customs station after the stations were closed in the evening, the boatmen would beat a gong to alert the customs officials, who would immediately inspect their permit and let them pass.[55]

Very soon, this pass became a valuable commodity that foreign companies and merchants from the Guangchao merchant group sold to merchants from elsewhere. It was particularly useful for those who had large quantities of northern commodities and sugar awaiting shipment to different parts of the country through the Grand Canal.[56] This practice aroused resentment and jealousy among all brokers. In 1902, Wei Xiaopu organized a group of more than twenty of his cohorts to form a large business corporation. They requested from the authorities a transit pass that would treat them the same way as foreigners, even after the native customs were abolished in 1901. Although the government granted permission, it also issued a new "transport permit for Chinese merchants" only to those participating in Wei's new business corporation. After this, every participating broker was given a newly registered trademark and was granted a status similar to foreign trading companies. These brokers thus began to call themselves "foreign firms."[57] Afterward, Wei created an organization for the purpose of acquiring the same transport permit from the maritime customs in Zhenjiang for brokers who were not in his organization. While president of the organization, Wei created an office specializing in helping those who were granted transport permits to go through customs.[58]

So far, we have learned about the different kinds of brokers and their activities that enabled them to play a major role in linking diverse groups of merchants from various parts of the country during the transformation of China's transregional trade. In the late nineteenth century, however, as Zhenjiang gradually became a second-tier distribution center for goods from Shanghai, it faced the opportunity to merge its commercial network into Shanghai's.

6
The Shanghai Commercial Network

ONE OF THE MAIN OBSTACLES the local business community in Zhenjiang encountered in the late nineteenth century was the difficulty connecting to the Shanghai commercial network that emerged after the opening of treaty ports in Japan (beginning in 1854) and Korea (beginning in 1876). As Shanghai gradually became one of Asia's key commercial centers, Zhenjiang needed to connect to the network to reach the much bigger markets in East Asia and around the world. One of the main problems was how to gain recognition from Shanghai's financial sector, given the need to overcome hurdles such as the exchange of currencies and honoring of business credit.

As Takeshi Hamashita indicates, the multilateral financial arrangement is one of the vital aspects of Asia's commercial networks, providing the mechanism upon which commercial interactions among different networks operate. To find out how members of the local business community in Zhenjiang overcame these difficulties, we will consider their efforts to establish financial arrangements with their counterparts in Shanghai, paying close attention to the details of those arrangements to understand the extent of the difficulties faced and efforts to overcome them.[1]

EMERGENCE OF THE SHANGHAI COMMERCIAL NETWORK

One of the most significant changes after the rise of Shanghai during the opening of treaty ports in China and in Japan and Korea was the emergence of the Shanghai commercial network. Maria Fusaro defines a commercial network as a creation by "a group of people who are in contact consistently over a sustained period through commercial interests and actions."[2] But what kind of network was this and how did it possibly differ from others around the country? To answer these questions, we need to first look at how the network emerged.

The Shanghai commercial network was the result of the intensive commercial activities of Chinese merchants who took advantage of global changes in the nineteenth century—including the new treaty ports in China, Japan, and Korea, and new technology in transportation and communication—to expand into a new set of urban centers in East Asia in the second half of the nineteenth century.

These merchants belonged mostly to the existing commercial networks in China, the merchant groups. Unlike the commercial networks in premodern southwestern Europe, these merchant groups were structured based on native place origin. But similar to those in Europe, they did more than connect with each other in those cities: each merchant group created a separate merchant community in every major urban center. They used the markets as "interfaces" to conduct business with one another.[3]

By joining the Shanghai commercial network, Chinese merchants were able to operate in a transnational setting, a much larger, urban setting that linked cities in the Chinese interior with the rest of Asia, as well as with the rest of the globe through open ports, coastal regions, and their hinterlands. In many ways, the Shanghai commercial network was not the only commercial network of Chinese merchants in China or Asia, but it was the fastest growing, largest in scale, and the best globally connected network of Chinese merchants in the second half of the nineteenth century.

According to Japanese economist Kazuko Furuta, the opening of treaty ports in China and other parts of Asia connected Shanghai with trade routes in several directions. One led to North China and the Yangtze delta region, and another also led to Kobe. Through these linkages, there emerged a commercial network centered around Shanghai, of which Zhenjiang and Wuhu were parts. This network, termed by Furuta "the Shanghai network," consisted of treaty ports in China and Japan. In China, this included Fuzhou, Wenzhou, Ningbo, Zhifu, Tianjin, and Niuzhuang on the east coast; Zhenjiang, Wuhu, Jiujiang, and Hankou along the Yangtze River; and in Japan, Nagasaki and Kobe.[4]

Within this network, Shanghai became the import center for Hankou, Tianjin, and Kobe, rather than for Zhenjiang and Ningbo, as one may assume (due to Zhenjiang's and Ningbo's proximity to Shanghai). In 1875–1877, for instance, Hankou and Tianjin received the largest volume of imports. Hankou's share was about 25 percent of the total, while Tianjin was next at around 20 percent. Furuta believes these figures indicate the role of Hankou and Tianjin as redistribution centers for the greater Yangtze region and North China. Although Zhenjiang and Ningbo were treaty ports near Shanghai, their volume received dropped significantly. Kobe was next in its share of received re-exports, for instance, at 7.16 percent in 1875, 5.09 percent in 1876, and 5.33 percent in 1877. That could only mean, as Furuta points out, that Kobe was an important destination for the re-export of goods, such as gray shirting from Shanghai, for example.[5]

Furuta attributes the emergence of the Shanghai commercial network partially to the exceptional networking ability of Chinese merchants in Japan. Since the opening of Kobe as a treaty port, those merchants had been very successful in outcompeting their Western counterparts and transported a large volume of goods from Shanghai to other ports both safely and cheaply through steamship routes created for this purpose.

Furuta cites the research of another Japanese scholar, Shin ya Sugiyama, to show that the Chinese could not have taken advantage of Western steamship technology so effectively without the cheap services and the body of knowledge that they inherited from their predecessors, the "itinerant trade groups" (*kebang* 客帮) who excelled in transregional trade within China before the mid-nineteenth century. Furuta paints a vivid picture of how the commercial network around Shanghai worked in the cotton textiles business: "during this period cotton fabric was steadily imported into Kobe, and almost all of it was handled by Chinese merchants in the form of re-exports from Shanghai. The origin of most of the cotton manufactures was Britain, and Shanghai must thus be evaluated as a link between Britain, the place of production, and Japan, the place of consumption."[6]

Similarly, Takeshi Hamashita stresses that the opening of treaty ports in East Asia helped form a trade triangle of Inchon-Shanghai-Osaka, which created linkages stretching to Tianjin, Yingkou (in Liaonin), and Vladivostok to the north, and Nagasaki, Hong Kong, and Singapore to the south. In Hamashita's words, "this trilateral group, plus Nagasaki, was an integral part of the larger network of trade and payment settlements."[7]

By the end of the nineteenth century, Shanghai already had become the crucial link between all of East Asia and Europe. As Hamashita shows, for instance, China officially allowed rice to be sold overseas after 1895. From that point on, there emerged a trade pattern among three countries in which the Japanese concentrated on rice and soybeans, while the Chinese monopolized the trade of English cotton fabric and other products that required substantial capital. Almost all the cloth manufactured in Manchester and sold in East Asia was first shipped to Shanghai, then to other destinations. For the Korean market, Japanese traders had to purchase textiles and other products in Shanghai and ship them to Korea.[8]

We shall now find out how the local business community in Zhenjiang connected to the network. We start with the beginning of commercial ties between Zhenjiang and Shanghai.

THE OPIUM STORE

The first commercial tie between Zhenjiang's business community and the city of Shanghai grew out of the opium business. After Shanghai gradually replaced Guangdong as the largest commercial center in the country, around the mid-nineteenth century, many wealthy opium dealers from southern China moved to Shanghai to set up distribution businesses. Concurrently, in Zhenjiang, there emerged a group of local opium store owners who, unlike their predecessors, depended on supplies and financial support from opium sellers in Shanghai. Incidentally, this started Zhenjiang on the journey of gradually merging into Shanghai's business circle and becoming part of the newly formed Shanghai commercial network.

Among the largest businesses in Zhenjiang shortly before the Opium War were "opium stores" (*tuzhan* 土栈) that sold opium as a foreign product. Opium slipped into the city with the first batch of foreign goods and was considered foreign medicine. It was shipped to the city by the Guangdong merchants, some of whom were sent directly by the Guangdong Thirteen Trades Monopoly (*Guangdong shisan hang* 广东十三行).

The Chinese considered opium to be medicinal as early as the Tang dynasty, long before the British brought it to China. In the Ming dynasty, Chinese medicine men already knew how to produce a powerful drug from the opium poppy plant by extracting sap from the head. The dynasty allowed opium to be imported from India and taxed it like any other imported good.[9]

Incidentally, almost all foreign products appearing in Zhenjiang in the early nineteenth century were shipped there by merchants from other parts of the country; the local people who bought and used them had no idea that they came from foreign countries. For instance, some stores owned by merchants from Beijing sold foreign products along with women's makeup and embroidery supplies, calling the products "miscellaneous goods from Beijing and Guangdong" (*jingguang zahuo* 京广杂货). Grocery stores that sold sugar and rosin produced in foreign countries and in Guangdong called them "sugar and rosin from Guangdong and Fujian" (*minguang tangxiang* 闽广糖香). Some merchants obtained various foreign products from Suzhou and sold them as native products from Suzhou in stores nicknamed "native Suzhou." Similarly, merchants from Guangdong and Fujian brought opium, which made people believe that it had been cultivated in Guangdong and Fujian.[10]

At one point, as many as twenty to thirty opium stores sold opium in the city, most of which were owned by merchants from Guangdong and Chaozhou. Despite the fact that almost all opium store owners were sojourners, they were quite familiar with local customs; some had close personal relationships with local officials, who helped them obtain the local government licenses required by the dynasty.[11]

There was no clear distinction between "government-approved" and "privately owned" opium stores, except through public perception. Because all opium products brought to China by the British were taxed by the government, local people usually called the stores selling them "government-approved opium stores," the opium they sold "government-approved opium," and the opium paste "government-approved opium paste." But these stores also sold opium produced within the country, called "privately sold opium," without paying the sales tax required of foreign imports. To restrict the selling of untaxed opium, the Qing dynasty issued tax stamps to be placed on each package being taxed and required that all opium sold on the market carry the stamp. For convenience, the government issued special tax stamps for small packages.[12]

Later, after Zhenjiang became a treaty port, the government set up a trading company, nicknamed "the British brokerage house" because it was located in the British Concession, to manage the taxed opium from Britain. Every opium shipment arriving in Zhenjiang had to be taxed and stamped before it was distributed to sellers. Realizing that this cut into their profits, many opium store owners decided to sell opium in smaller quantities to attract more buyers and set up little shops called "penny opium stores" to regain their profits. As a result, opium stores proliferated in the city near the mid-nineteenth century.[13]

One visible change in Zhenjiang after Shanghai began to rise as the economic center of Asia in the second half of the nineteenth century was the emergence of a new group of opium store owners. Unlike those originally from Guangdong, Chaozhou, or Huzhou, whose opium businesses were directly linked to their home provinces, these new owners were Zhenjiang natives whose business depended on their extensive relationships with suppliers in Shanghai, who provided opium and, sometimes, financial investments. Many of these suppliers were natives of Guangdong, Chaozhou, and Huzhou who relocated to Shanghai.

One example of this new breed of opium store owners was Yu Baichuan. He started out in Guazhou, going door to door selling wares he kept bundled on a pole that he perched over his shoulder. He often took breaks in a small, penny opium store whose owner was from Chaozhou, and befriended the owner after helping him out in exchange for letting him rest there. When the owner decided to return to his native home, he gave the store to Yu. Before leaving, the store owner helped Yu establish personal relationships with his opium suppliers in Shanghai, where most opium by then originated from. These connections soon proved very valuable to Yu, an unknown in the Shanghai business community, which essentially operated on credit, and allowed Yu to obtain the first shipment of opium on credit.[14]

Yu's business took off, and he soon opened a grocery store on Zhenjiang's busiest street. He then formed a partnership with an opium store in Shanghai owned by a Chaozhou native named Guo Demao, and they opened a large opium store in Zhenjiang. Through the store, Yu sold opium on the north bank of the Yangtze River. With the money earned, Yu purchased shares of company stock in Guo's opium store in Shanghai. After Guo opened a commercial bank in Shanghai, these shares made Yu a wealthy man. One sign of Yu's success was that many small opium stores pretended to be affiliated with him.[15]

Yu was not the only local opium store owner in the city whose success had a lot to do with his relationship with wealthy business owners in Shanghai. There is a long list of people who benefited, and like Yu, they all moved into other businesses after the opium trade in the city and across the country sharply declined in the late nineteenth century due to the Qing dynasty's effort to restrict opium consumption.[16]

The rise of businesspeople like Yu is a clear indication of the significance of local connections with Shanghai. But how were local businesses in Zhenjiang, and not only those selling opium, tied into Shanghai's financial system to become part of the Shanghai commercial network? The answer lies in the efforts of the local bankers' association that emerged near the end of the nineteenth century. But before we examine those endeavors, let us take a brief look at what kind of local banks existed in Zhenjiang and how Shanghai played a part in the growth of local banking services that led to the rise of the bankers' association.

THE CHINESE TRADITIONAL BANK

When Zhenjiang became a treaty port, it was home to a dozen money lenders. Among them were traditional banks (*qianzhuang* 钱庄), remittance banks (*piaohao* 票号), jewelers (*yinlou* 银楼), and pawn shops (*dangpu* 当铺), with the last two engaged only occasionally in money lending. One of the city's biggest remittance banks was the branch office of Rishengchang (日升昌), the largest of its kind in the country and based in Shanxi. After the death of its owner in 1849, its business declined. This provided the opportunity for traditional banks to become the primary banking institutions in town before European-style banks appeared around 1910 (although European-style banks emerged elsewhere in China right after 1897).[17]

Most traditional banks originated as money stores, whose owners usually had large enterprises for goods such as clothing and rice. Local people thus called them "money and clothing stores" or "money and rice stores." Because some also sold opium, they were also called "money and opium stores."[18] Initially, their main services were exchanging currency and making small loans, but that changed when Shanghai gradually became the hub for supplying and selling goods for local businesses. Increasing commercial activities between Zhenjiang and Shanghai prompted the need for banking services such as money transfers and business credit. Some money stores expanded their services beyond accepting deposits, making commercial loans, and issuing private bank notes and called themselves "banks" (*qianzhuang* 钱庄) instead of "money stores" (*qiandian* 钱店).[19]

The growth in banking services was soon matched by an increase in the number of traditional banks. For example, Zhenjiang had about ten traditional banks in the 1860s and 1870s, but by the end of the 1890s, there were thirty-two, although some were subsidiaries of larger, special-purpose banks. For instance, the two largest traditional banks had separate branches for customs services.[20]

The funds moving through traditional banks grew threefold in the second half of the century. In the 1860s and 1870s, the annual amount was around one hundred thousand taels. By the 1890s, the amount had increased to around three hundred thousand taels yearly, bringing sizable profits.[21] Growth in traditional banking attracted new, outside investors, most of whom owned real estate or other businesses elsewhere, to open banks in the city. These included Zhou Fujiu, originally a salt merchant from Anhui who had various stores in Yangzhou; Wang Jialu and Liu Guanjun, merchants from Suzhou who became major landlords in Zhejiang; and Liu Guanjun, who had land and other real estate in

Hangzhou, Shanghai, and Qingdao (in Shandong), some of which he operated under the fake identity of a British trading company.[22]

Some investors owned different types of stores in the city; others had several traditional banks. For example, Wang owned a large silk fabric store, and the large traditional bank he owned in Zhenjiang was one of several in different cities owned by relatives of the governor of Zhili, Li Hongzhang. Similar to what happened in Hankou, these individuals not only developed personal bonds, but also refrained from competing with businessmen from their home provinces. It did not take long for them to merge into the local business community by, for instance, accepting the paper currency they issued.[23]

Because traditional bank owners brought sizable capital to Zhenjiang, locals described their practices as "using another's water to fill one's own bottle" (*yibizhuzi* 挹彼注兹), meaning using outside capital to enhance business within the city. Local businesses were not the only benefactors of these loans; anyone engaged in regular trading in Zhenjiang was able to obtain loans from traditional banks, including traders from northern Anhui, northeastern Henan, southwestern Shandong, Wuhu, and Jiujiang.[24]

The plethora of traditional banks soon led to the formation of a bankers' association, the "money trade guild" (*qianye gongsuo* 钱业公所). In 1891, the bankers' association established a meeting hall, where members gathered to set prices for the market, trade with each other, and discuss matters related to their common economic interests.[25]

Both the "guild" (*gongsuo* 公所) and "association" (*huiguan* 会馆) appeared in China roughly in the sixteenth century—although associations were formed a little earlier—when commercial activities increased and merchants began to settle down near their markets and formed trade organizations. The number of organizations held steady until roughly 1860, after the second group of treaty ports was created following the Arrow War (also known as the Second Opium War), and the country saw another proliferation between 1900 and 1909, before they started to phase out toward the very end of the Qing dynasty.[26]

The word *gongsuo,* which usually translates as "public hall," is often used for an association of people in the same occupation, and *huiguan,* which means "assembly houses," for organizations of people with a common place of origin. It may be true in most cases that associations were more interested in promoting native-place sentiment, whereas guilds were more concerned about trade issues, although the names were often used interchangeably.[27]

Several studies of Beijing have indicated that there were considerable differences in the two organizations, often determined by their location. Those inside the city were mostly for scholars and officials having the same native origin. According to a rough estimate, 86 percent of associations inside Beijing were established to host scholar-officials, whereas only 10 percent to 20 percent were commercial and handicraft associations. Of those outside the city, however, almost all, including guilds, were gathering places for merchants and craftsmen, mainly focusing on business interests.[28]

Associations and guilds typically had the same organizational structure. Of the two shared by all types of business organizations—the simplex and multiplex—associations and guilds both had the simplex structure and were large, formal organizations based on trade. Because they both functioned as trade organizations, it is difficult to distinguish them, although guilds were supposedly "organized along the lines of trade rather than local origin" and associations "were not . . . trade organizations."[29]

The main reason for associations to operate like trade organizations was that their main goal was to promote commerce, just like the guilds. On the one hand, associations were essentially formed by the "merchants traveling to a city in search of new markets [who] set up organizations there to represent the interests of their home area." On the other hand, the difference has to do with the way membership was constituted: the business firm, not the individual, became a member. And contrary to what many assumed, native ties played a small role in forming this type of business institution.[30]

In Shanghai, however, associations and guilds were mostly formed by merchants of the same trade but also along native-place connections. They were not only similar in nature, but also in function, all categorized as a "trade organization *cum* native tie." In other words, they were "organizations of fellow-provincials which expressed trade interest."[31]

This framework does not fit some of the associations that emerged in Chengdu, however. To take the one formed by Zhejiang natives as an example, despite the fact that all of its members belonged to the merchant group from the province, none of its bylaws pertained to anything other than its members' economic concerns. Similarly, its regulations stated nothing about promoting native-place sentiment, charitable activities, or ceremonies related to native-place identity, all of which were assumed to be the usual functions of an association.[32]

Nevertheless, not only was there a great deal of overlap between the two organizations, but their roles—including those of associations, guilds, and merchant groups—were much more complex than previously realized. In other words, one should not be surprised to see that while some associations were involved only in matters related to the native-place origin of their members, others functioned only as trade associations. Meanwhile, some guilds engaged in trade activities, while others served as native-place associations.[33]

We shall now take a close look at how one particular organization facilitated Zhenjiang's commercial connection with Shanghai, in a series of measures the association took to grant local businesses recognition by private financial institutions in Shanghai and to receive permission to operate in Shanghai's market, both crucial to Zhenjiang's entrée into the Shanghai commercial network.

CONNECTING TO THE SHANGHAI COMMERCIAL NETWORK

Once the bankers' association was formed, its organizers devised a set of business rules and a requirement for members to behave honorably. The owner of a medium-sized, traditional bank later introduced a new accounting system modeled after the one just adopted by modern-style banks in Shanghai in 1897, a system that had been promoted by the noted Qing official Sheng Xuanhui (盛宣怀). Both measures elevated business standards and increased efficiency in banking, setting the stage for expansion into Shanghai.[34]

The bankers' association next set up an agency in Shanghai, one of the first such agencies established there by traditional-style banks from the lower Yangtze region in the last decade of the nineteenth century. Like others of its kind, the agency offered a storage service and lodging to regular clients traveling from Zhenjiang to Shanghai. It also actively solicited business, arranging payment for business transactions and gathering business intelligence. More importantly, however, it guaranteed the authenticity of letters of credit issued by local traditional banks that opened branches in Shanghai.[35] After the practice of using letters of credit was introduced in 1822, it was adopted across China, especially in large cities like Shanghai, but bankers there were reluctant to accept such letters from relatively unknown people in Zhenjiang. The bankers' association relied on its name and presumed reputation to solve this dilemma.[36]

Businesspeople in Zhenjiang called the guarantee "seeing the ticket, then setting the date" (*jiangpiaopiqi* 见票批期), meaning issuing a date for the delivery of payment once the letter's authenticity was confirmed. After a traditional bank from Zhenjiang issued such a letter of credit, the receiving bank in Shanghai would take it to the bankers' association for authentication; afterward, a date would be set for delivering the actual payment. By providing this service, the bankers' association gradually won acceptance by traditional banks elsewhere.[37]

Meanwhile, the bankers' association also created a rule calling for every traditional bank to honor the letter of credit issued by any other member of the association and to advance payment expeditiously. This single rule allowed both the traditional banks and traders from Zhenjiang to shorten the delay in obtaining goods from Shanghai and resulted in significant increases in profits for Zhenjiang organizations conducting business in Shanghai.[38]

But this was only one of the bankers' association's accomplishments; another was in assessing the value of local currencies against those accepted in Shanghai. This task was by no means small. The many different kinds of currencies used, and the fact that each was made differently, led to profound confusion and turmoil in the currency system across the country.

In the first half of the nineteenth century, for example, China's common currencies were silver ingots and silver dollars. Copper coins were fractional currency to be used as small change, with common denominations in *wen* (文, equal to one cent), *guan* (贯), or *chuan* (串)—both of the latter equal to one thousandth of a cent. In addition, traditional banks printed their own paper currencies. While most traditional banks used silver and the Qing dynasty accepted only silver for tax payments, local people still used copper coins in their daily transactions.[39]

During the same period, the most widely used currencies in Zhenjiang were silver ingots: the one known as the "two-four ingot" (*ersi baoyin* 二四宝银) was used within the city, and another, the "Zhenjiang two-seven ingot" (Zhenjiang *erqibao* 镇江二七宝), was used in trade that Zhenjiang conducted with parties elsewhere. "Two-four" and "two-seven" reflected the purity of the silver.[40]

In Shanghai, silver dollars were favored in the late nineteenth century because they were convenient to carry and easy to calculate, whereas copper coins were popular in rural areas. Spanish silver dollars minted in Spanish Mexico were widely used in the lower Yangtze region, and Eagle silver dollars, minted in Mexico after the country gained independence in 1812 and no longer produced Spanish silver dollars for Spain, were also popular.[41]

By the time most of the large, traditional banks in Zhenjiang had set up branches in Shanghai near the very end of the century, the Spanish silver dollar had become scarce, largely replaced by two new kinds of silver dollars. One was the Dragon dollar (*longyang* 龙洋), produced in 1889 in Guangdong, and the other, the British dollar (*zhanrenyang* 站人洋), issued by British banks after first minting the currency in Mumbai and Kolkata, India, in 1895.[42]

Although the Zhenjiang two-seven ingot was among the first currencies from the lower Yangtze region to be accepted in Shanghai, it still had to be converted to Spanish silver dollars, for years the unofficial silver standard in Shanghai markets. But because there was a lack of Spanish silver dollars in circulation, their conversion was against the value of the Spanish silver dollar—called "virtual silver" (*xuyin* 虚银)—instead of the actual coin itself.[43] The conversion method was known as the "Shanghai nine-eight rule for the dollar" (Shanghai *jiuba guiyuan* 上海九八规元), which originated in the bean cake market in the old town of Shanghai before the city became a treaty port. "Nine-eight" indicated that the Zhenjiang two-seven ingot had 98 percent of the value of the Spanish silver dollar.[44]

Aside from the calculation itself, conversion brought other difficulties. The scales used to weigh ingots during the minting process were made differently from place to place. Because of this, for instance, cities such as Nanjing and Yangzhou had ingots made at a slightly reduced weight compared to those minted in Zhenjiang. The silver ingot used in Wuhu had a higher level of purity: the fifty taels of silver ingot contained silver worth fifty-three taels of fine silver (*wenyin* 纹银), the Qing dynasty standard. In Anqing, two kinds of silver ingots were used, one with fifty-four taels, worth fifty taels of fine silver, and the other worth much less. Then, the conversion process had to account for the "value assessment in Hankou" (*hangu* 汉估), or the conversion rate there. It also needed to reflect the bank-to-bank exchange rate, or "inter-bank offered rate" (*chexi* 拆息).[45]

The responsibility of sorting out the currency confusion had previously rested on the shoulders of the "public assessment bureau" (*gongguju* 公估局) established in the mid-Qing to assess the values of the currencies used in different areas against the value of fine silver. Among the earliest public assessment bureaus, the one in Beijing was run by the dynasty, whereas all others, including those in Hankou and Tianjin, were privately owned, usually by merchants, although they had to be recognized by the local government and bankers' associations. The first public assessment bureau in Shanghai was founded in 1850 by an Anhui native. Before that, when the city was still on the rise, the task of evaluating currencies was left to each traditional bank in Shanghai.[46]

In Zhenjiang, there had been a privately owned public assessment bureau. For ingots from Zhenjiang to be accepted in Shanghai, Zhenjiang's public assessment bureau had to assess their value initially before turning them over to their counterparts in Shanghai for verification of the assessment. After the bankers' association in Zhenjiang was accepted by Shanghai's financial institutions, it decided to take over the task. At home, it also had twice-daily announcements of the market value of the main currencies in Shanghai and Hankou. Efforts such as these made by the bankers' association helped Zhenjiang overcome a major hurdle in currency transfer, which was essential for the business community in Zhenjiang to successfully join the Shanghai commercial network.[47]

The result of Zhenjiang's connecting to Shanghai was twofold. On the one hand, it allowed Zhenjiang's financial institutions to become part of the Shanghai commercial network and thus act as the intermediary between Shanghai's financial market and the traditional banks in some areas of the lower Yangtze, as well as north of the Yangtze River. For instance, the emerging status of the bankers' association among Shanghai's private financial institutions soon came to the attention of traditional banks from the lower Yangtze region and northern China, all of which were looking for the opportunity to extend into Shanghai. The bankers' association in Zhenjiang thus received a lot of business inquiries from these traditional banks. Through its arrangement, traditional banks in Zhenjiang formed partnerships with their counterparts from other parts of the country, which allowed merchants from areas such as along the Huai River and Grand Canal to reach Shanghai's market.[48]

Later, traditional banks from places like Yangzhou, Hankou, Nanjing, and Jiujiang began to use the traditional banks in Zhenjiang to transfer funds with Shanghai. As a result, the daily price of the silver dollar set by the bankers' association in Zhenjiang became one of the important references for the exchange rate in those regions, which earned Zhenjiang the nickname of "silver wharf" (*yin matou* 银码头), meaning the center of funding transfers among the merchants from those areas.[49]

THE END OF THE BROKERAGE ERA

Commercial activities in Zhenjiang plummeted in the first decade of the twentieth century, after reaching their zenith around the turn of the century. One superficial cause was the flood in northern Jiangsu province in 1906, which made it impossible for brokers in Zhenjiang to collect payments from the area and caused them to lose a lot of southern clients who traded through them. The real cause, however, was a combination of factors that altered trade routes and thus changed the way transregional trade was conducted.[50]

One factor was the introduction of railroads on both sides of the Yangtze River, which gave merchants direct access to cities like Shanghai, Tianjin, and Beijing. In 1906, the Beijing-Hankou railroad (originally named the Luhan railroad 卢汉铁路 or Pinghan railroad 平汉铁路) was completed, which made it possible to transport goods from north of the

Yangtze River between Chongqing and Beijing. In 1908, the Shanghai-Nanjing line was finished, directly linking Shanghai and Nanjing and encompassing Zhenjiang on the south side of the Yangtze River. Then, the railroad between Tianjin and Pukou (in Nanjing) became operational in 1911, connecting Hebei, Shandong, northern Anhui, and Jiangsu to Tianjin and Nanjing. Trains thus became a good option for passenger travel and shipping. The Tianjin-Pukou railroad caused Xuzhou (in Jiangsu) to replace Zhenjiang as the hub for the transshipment of goods from both north and south. In addition, boats from Huojiaqiao (in the eastern part of Yangzhou) shipped goods brought by train on the Tianjin-Pukou line directly to Yangzhou and Shanghai, further making Zhenjiang irrelevant.[51]

The high cost of shipping by rail led a good number of merchants from the north to continue to rely on boats. By the early twentieth century, however, the section of the Yangtze River along Zhenjiang was silted up by sand to the extent that it was impossible for ships, including the relatively small river steamers favored by shipping companies, to dock, which made doing business in Zhenjiang through its river port very difficult and expensive.[52]

At the same time, the condition of the Grand Canal also deteriorated, so it was not an alternative. After the Yellow River changed course around 1855, the number of traders from the north going through the canal was in steady decline. Though a small number came from southern Shandong and northern Jiangsu through the sections of the canal that were still navigable, they eventually stopped, as the lack of maintenance made conditions even worse. When merchants from the north no longer showed up in Zhenjiang, the city's role as the connection between north and south ended entirely.[53]

Like the trade in sugar and northern commodities, trade in grain and beans also went downhill in 1897, after Li Hongzhang, the viceroy of Zhili and minister of Beiyang, suggested moving the grain market from Zhenjiang to Wuhu. After that, most grain from the upper Yangtze River and Anhui province—two of the main sources of grain—bypassed Zhenjiang. As a result, merchant groups from Guangdong, Chaozhou, Ningbo, and Fujian relocated to Wuhu, further signaling the decline of the grain business in Zhenjiang.[54]

The slide continued as every foreign company using river transportation closed its office in the city by 1908. The only companies remaining were owned by Zhenjiang natives, all operating under the identity of foreign companies to avoid being bullied by Qing officials demanding handsome bribes. This took away every bit of residual business the brokers might still have had with foreign companies. Zhenjiang's legacy as a brokerage town for transregional trade ended roughly in the first decade of the twentieth century.[55]

◆

Chinese local society negotiated global economic changes intensely in the second half of the nineteenth century, when Shanghai became a leading economic center of Asia. While the changes subjected Zhenjiang to the inpouring of machine-made products from industrialized countries, they also accelerated China's commercial transformation in transregional trade that had been, for the most part, operated among China's macroregions through the country's primary river system. As the result of the transformation, China further extended its global reach through its open ports and coastal areas, as well as between those areas and their hinterlands, in Asia and the rest of the world.

This transformation changed the lives of the people of Zhenjiang. Once the number of agents representing major merchant groups dwindled in the local market, the city saw a large number of new brokers. By using various methods and relying on local tradition, these individuals reoriented the city into a brokerage town. To take advantage of the commercial opportunities afforded by the changes, the local business community made every endeavor to connect to the Shanghai commercial network, a transnational network of Chinese merchants whose enterprises spanned Asia and Europe. By maneuvering around the obstacles generated by the confusion over common currencies and the lack of credit recognition, it also succeeded in merging local commerce with commerce in Shanghai.

PART THREE

NEGOTIATING TECHNOLOGY

SOCIOLOGIST CLAUDE FISCHER USES a billiard-ball analogy to criticize the main approach of technological determinism that sees technology only as external to society and deprived of human agency. He suggests, instead, that one should focus on the people who use technology rather than the impact of technology on the larger society. Following Fischer's suggestion, in this part, I show how steamboat business owners as well as ordinary people in Zhenjiang negotiated the "new and alien technology" as Chinese local society became part of the global technological transformation of the nineteenth and early twentieth centuries.[1]

I use Zhenjiang as a case study to demonstrate how the negotiation took place, the nature of the negotiations, and their outcomes. I illustrate the Chinese experience with mechanized technology from the perspective of how people not from technology's origins struggled through the adoption process as technology spread. I assume that the process of negotiating technology is global, applicable not only to those living where the technology originated.[2]

To better understand how Chinese urban local society experienced steamship technology, I focus on what I call "the age of the steamboat," a period when the smaller steamboat was widely adopted in China, especially in the inner waterways (*neihe* 内河) of tributary rivers and lakes connected to major rivers like the

Yangtze. The age of the steamboat started roughly by the end of the nineteenth century, coinciding with Japan's entrance into Chinese inner waterways after 1895. It progressed into the era that saw the appearance of the Beijing-Hankou railroad (1906), which heralded the decline of steamship-based, long-distance shipping. And it gradually ended in the early 1930s with the Nationalist government's aggressive agenda in public road expansion and incorporation of the steamship into a rail-road-water system of transportation.

Although we usually associate steamships with "big technology," steamboats were widely used by common people as an affordable alternative to the wooden boats they had relied on for centuries. As Zhenjiang's experience will show, commoners widely embraced the technology because it enabled them to travel via small streams into the regions where most people lived.

7

Steam Navigation as a Means of Dominance

STEAM NAVIGATION TECHNOLOGY was brought to China in the nineteenth century as a byproduct of Euro-American military and economic endeavors. As a result, China entered the global scale of technological change characterized by mechanization. Before we investigate how Chinese local society participated, we shall first examine how the steamship served as a means of dominance, first for Euro-Americans and then the Japanese, and the Qing dynasty's reaction to this foreign technology.

THE STEAMSHIP AND EURO-AMERICANS

Shortly after the mid-nineteenth century, some business corporations from industrialized countries in Europe and North America set their eyes on China's vast market. Their main goal was to use the steamship that was newly available in their countries to take over China's freight shipping business and export all sorts of machine-made goods to China, and, vice versa, to ship native Chinese products, most of which were raw materials, back to their countries. For this purpose, they entered the Yangtze River.

The Yangtze River was their prime target because it was accessible to steamships and allowed penetration into China's vast interior. One six-hundred-mile stretch of the river between present-day Shanghai and Hankou could accommodate five-thousand-ton ships. During the high-water summer season, the same channel could accommodate ten-thousand-ton ships. Furthermore, from the main river, a steamship could access the river's major tributaries.[1]

The earliest steamship companies in the region were Russell & Co. and Augustine Heard & Co., two American trading houses deeply immersed in trading in Asia. It was no accident that the Americans were the first to dip their toes into the Yangtze River, for American-made steamships with low-draft side-wheelers (or propellers) were more suitable for the river than those made in England, another country that excelled in steamship manufacturing.[2]

Samuel Russell established Russell & Co. in Guangdong in 1824. After making a considerable profit, the company created the Shanghai Steam Navigation Co. (SSNC hereafter) in 1862 as a public, joint-stock company based in Shanghai. Its shareholders included some Chinese natives as well as British merchants. Augustine Heard & Co. was founded by brothers John and Albert Heard in 1840, and at one time had a division in Hong Kong. After Shanghai became a treaty port, the company opened an office there, with its main business in freight shipping between the treaty ports along the east coast of China.[3]

The Americans were not the only ones interested in using steamships in China; so were the British, although they initially were somewhat reluctant to engage fully in the business due to their early conviction that the steamship was unsafe and its use in shipping unprofitable. Over time, they abandoned that idea and aggressively pursued this interest. Meanwhile, in 1861, the steamship *Governor* sailed between Hankou and Shanghai, carrying five hundred to six hundred tons of goods in each direction. The ship was owned by Dent & Co., a British company founded at the beginning of the nineteenth century by British merchant Thomas Dent.[4]

At that time, the Taiping Rebellion was still underway. Most parts of the lower Yangtze were still in the hands of the rebels who controlled Nanjing. Shortly after the rebels took control of the lower Yangtze region, between 1853 and 1854, the Americans, British, and French sent delegates to meet with the rebel leaders to discuss continuing access to the region. Since the rebels held the view that all races and nationalities were part of a brotherhood, they permitted foreign vessels to enter their territory, as long as they did not aid the Qing dynasty.[5]

More foreign steam shipping enterprises appeared along the Yangtze River in the early 1860s. Some had a long history of involvement with China. For example, Jardine Matheson & Co. (JMC hereafter), founded by the Scotsmen William Jardine and James Matheson, opened in Guangdong shortly after 1832 to engage in the opium trade. Others were already well established in Europe. For instance, the Ocean Steamship Company was a subsidiary of Alfred Holt & Co., one of the best-known shipping concerns in England. There were also companies like Melchers & Co., whose main business was to manage fleets for European shipping corporations that did not have offices in China. Melchers & Co., opened in 1806, was one of the oldest shipping concerns in Germany and had European shipping giants as clients, including Germany-based Norddeutsen Lloyd. These enterprises linked the lower Yangtze River with major seaports in the North Atlantic. For example, in 1865, Alfred Holt & Co. employed three large steamships to travel between Liverpool and Hankou, thus linking Shanghai and Hankou with Liverpool.[6]

The period between 1862 and 1867 was marked by fierce competition among the foreign steamship companies. By 1867, SSNC had gained the upper hand by acquiring the entire fleet of Dent & Co., as well as all JMC properties. During the unfolding crisis in Shanghai's financial market, a result of the financial crisis in London that affected the entire shipping business, SSNC seized the moment to force JMC, Dent & Co., and Augustine Heard & Co. into signing an agreement that prevented them from reentering the market for the next ten years.[7]

Despite SSNC's increasing dominance on the Yangtze River, however, the shipping business for foreign companies continued to grow after the opening of the Suez Canal on November 17, 1869, which cut in half the distance from America and Europe to Asia. The canal sparked additional interest among the countries doing business in China. The early 1870s were thus marked by renewed competition among steamship companies, during which SSNC faced a new competitor, the China Navigation Company Ltd. (CNC hereafter) owned by John Swire & Sons Co. and Morris Lewis & Co. By then, some Qing officials also expressed interest in the steamship.[8]

THE QING DYNASTY AND STEAM NAVIGATION

The Qing dynasty's experimentation with steamship technology began in the early 1860s, about two decades after steamships were brought to the country. As foreign steam shipping companies expanded on the Yangtze River, some Qing officials, as well as wealthy merchants, considered building or purchasing steamships. One of the officials was the governor-general of Liangjiang, Zeng Guofan. In 1861, while in Anqing to fight the Taiping rebels, Zeng founded the Anqing Arsenal with the initial purpose of manufacturing guns and cannons. He had already sent his assistant to the United States to purchase the necessary machinery. At the arsenal, Zeng gathered six people, including a self-taught chemist and a self-educated mathematician, and issued the directive to build a steamboat.[9]

With almost no knowledge of steam engines, the group turned to a translated article published in an English science journal. Three months later, they had a prototype steam engine. They then proceeded to build a steamboat with a wooden body the length of three *zhang* (each *zhang* equals 10.93 feet). As soon as they finished it two years later, they realized that the steamboat could only travel about one *li* (about 0.311 miles) per hour because of insufficient steam pressure from the engine.[10]

A year later, the Qing army led by Zeng defeated the Taiping rebels, clearing the way for Zeng to move to Nanjing with his arsenal. At the new facility, the same group built a new steamboat based largely on the design of their first one. Zeng was so pleased that he named the steamboat *Yellow Crane* (Huanggu 黄鹄) in homage to the mythical crane that flew thousands of miles with ease. Ironically, other than pleasure outings for Zeng's family, the steamboat was never used to transport goods or passengers. After three years, the craft fell apart due to lack of maintenance.[11]

In 1872, the Qing dynasty initiated its effort to create a steamship company. The person put in charge was Li Hongzhang, then governor-general of Zhili, after the Tongzhi emperor accepted his detailed plan for a dynasty-sponsored steamship company. Li's core strategy was embodied in his "nine methods," which included incentives for merchants to use steamships to transport tribute grain. Li accepted the recommendation from one of his assistants to form business partnerships with merchants within a partnership known as "government-merchant joint management" (*guanshang heban* 官商合办) after he realized that the dynasty did not have sufficient funds to run the entire operation. Li's main concern was not to hand the entire matter to the merchants. Because of that, he later refined the formula into "government supervision and merchant management" (*guandu shangban* 官督商办), which strengthened the dynasty's control. Afterward, he suggested that the dynasty adopt the concept as the principle.[12]

Li distributed a proposal for a Chinese shipping company to various merchant groups, especially among those in Guangdong and Fujian. When Zeng Guofan died on March 12, 1872, Li became the sole authority over matters related to the shipping company. In October 1872, he ordered the setting up of headquarters for a company in Shanghai that he named the China Merchants Steam Navigation Co. (CMSNC hereafter). Afterward, Li appointed Tang Tingshu (唐廷枢), an expert on maritime transportation, its chief executive. The company also elected Sheng Xuanhuai (盛宣怀), a well-known figure in the Self-Strengthening Movement, as chairman of the board of directors.[13]

As initially planned, the company would rent steamships from the Jiangnan Arsenal and Fuzhou Shipyard, two dynasty enterprises that built steamships. The officials managing the shipyards were reluctant to follow the plan, however, because they saw no personal gain in doing so. They informed CMSNC that there were no ships to rent and the shipyard would not produce any in the foreseeable future due to a lack of funds. CMSNC then purchased four steamships from foreign countries and transferred another from Zhejiang to the Yangtze River.[14]

On the surface, the founding of the China Merchants Group reflects the Qing dynasty's willingness to accept steam navigation. In reality, it was largely due to the dynasty's growing need to transport tribute grain.

As the Grand Canal continued to deteriorate, the dynasty used the sea route for transporting tribute grain, determining that restoring the Grand Canal was too costly to be worthwhile. In addition, because of a shortage of wood, fewer large ships were available. The dynasty, therefore, considered steamships an attractive alternative.[15]

THE JAPANESE IN INNER WATERWAYS

The signing of the Treaty of Shimonoseki was in many ways a turning point in China's steam navigation history. Not only did it allow Japan to become the main player in the steam shipping business, but it also ushered in a new era of Japanese dominance in China's inner waterways through its use of small steamships.

Japan was technologically advanced by the end of the nineteenth century. As latecomers to China, Japanese companies had to compete with conglomerates from other industrialized nations. To gain the upper hand, the Japanese looked for new opportunities and discovered that most of the Chinese interior was connected to the country's main river system through vast inner waterways. They decided to focus on these waterways to access the heartland.

When the treaty was signed, however, China's inner-river ports and lakes were off-limits to foreigners; over the years the Qing dynasty had gradually allowed some foreign vessels to dock at specially designated "non-treaty ports" (*fei tiaoyue kouan* 非条约口岸), although not the inner waterways. The Japanese companies, therefore, urged their government to pressure the Qing dynasty to make available some inner waterways, especially tributaries of the Yangtze River. As a result, the Qing dynasty in 1898 issued its "Regulation for Navigating in Inner Waterways" (*neigang xingchuan zhangcheng* 内港行船章程), which listed locations accessible to foreign vessels. Because these locations were all on tributary rivers and lakes, the new regulation extended the reach of foreigners to the inner waterways.[16]

The first Japanese company to capitalize on this opportunity was the Osaka Mercantile Steamship Co., Ltd. (Osaka Shōsen Kabushiki-gaisha, OMSC hereafter). Right after arriving in China in 1897, the company placed two steamships into service between Shanghai and Hankou, as well as between Hankou and Yichang (Hubei), to compete with JMC, CNC, and CMSNC. A year later, it moved into inner-river ports such as those in Jiangyin (in Jiangsu) and Huangshigang (in Hubei). Subsidized by the Japanese government, the company became a formidable contender in the steam shipping business.[17]

The Treaty of Shimonoseki also provided Japan access to the newly added treaty ports of Shashi, Chongqing, Suzhou, and Hangzhou. Because most inner waterways were far away from customs stations, some Japanese companies focused on passenger transportation rather than freight shipping in the triangle area of Shanghai, Suzhou, and Hangzhou.[18]

The first Japanese company to step into this business was the Daito Steamship Co., Ltd. (Daito Kisen Kaisha, DSC hereafter) founded by Daito Hiroyuki & Co. In 1901, the company established service between Suzhou and Shanghai, then between Suzhou and Hangzhou. A year later, it extended its business reach to locations such as Zhenjiang.[19] Seeing DSC's move, a smaller Japanese company, Konan Steamship Co. (Konan Kisen Kaisha), joined the venture. Formed in 1901 by a group of Japanese businessmen who shared a common interest in exploring Hunan province after reading an investigative report on the region's economic potential, the company found its niche in freight shipping in the inner waterways between Hankou and Xiangtan (Hunan).[20]

The Qing dynasty signed two more treaties, in 1902 and 1903, to give foreign companies full access to China's entire network of inner waterways: the Sino-British Treaty on Commercial Navigation (*Zhong Ying xuyi tongshang xingchuan tiaoyue* 中英续议通商行船条约) and the Sino-Japanese Renewed Treaty on Commercial Navigation (*Zhong Ri tongshang xingchuan xuyue* 中日通商行船续约). The former offered British companies the same treatment as Chinese ones; the latter allowed Japanese companies to use the inner waterways for business as long as they obtained licenses from the Chinese authority.[21]

Two years after the signing of these treaties, the consulate general of Japan at Zhenjiang sent an official correspondence notifying the highest-ranking authority in Zhenjiang that the Japanese company DSC would open steam freight and passenger transportation businesses in Zhenjiang on May 4, 1905, mostly through the inner waterways between Zhenjiang and Qingjiangpu (in Jiangsu). It also planned to set up offices on the Zhenjiang-Qingjiangpu route as well as branch offices in other locations. The consulate indicated that this was in accordance with the recently signed Sino-Japanese treaty of commercial navigation. Immediately after getting permission, DSC brought ten steamboats to Zhenjiang.[22]

These efforts were part of a broader strategy for creating a network of shipping routes in East Asia by linking river ports on the Yangtze River and in the inner waterways to major trading ports in Japan. For instance, as soon as the Japanese companies moved into the Shanghai-Suzhou-Hangzhou triangle, they linked with Osaka, one of Japan's largest trading ports. By the mid-1900s, companies like the Japan Mail Shipping Line (Nippon Yusen Kabushiki Kaisha) had thirteen steamships in regular service between Hankou and several large Japanese ports, in addition to its inner shipping route between Shanghai and Wuhu.[23]

A major development occurred in 1907: DSC, OMSC, the Japan Mail Shipping Line, and the Konan Kisen Steamship Co. were merged into one large steam shipping corporation with a new name, the Japan-China Steamship Co. (Nisshin Kisen Kaisha, JCSC hereafter). Right after the merger, JCSC mapped out a presence on the Yangtze River, in every major river port as well as tributaries. With a subsidy from the Japanese government and its combined capital, the new corporation was poised to outcompete all other steam shipping enterprises, and, in particular, CNC, JMC, and CMSNC.[24]

JCSC made it very difficult for other companies to survive. The first to feel the pressure were German companies such as North German Lloyd (Norddeutscher Lloyd), which had just begun showing an interest in shipping on the Yangtze River by forming a joint venture with Melchers & Co. and extending the shipping routes after relying on Melchers & Co. for this for years. The Hamburg American Line (Hamburg-Amerika Linie) and Arnhold & Karberg & Co., which formed a joint venture at the turn of the century, were caught in a similar situation. Soon, North German Lloyd had to remove its ships from the Hankou-Yichang line. The Hamburg American Line also sold its two ships and withdrew one of its powerful diesel-powered ships from the Yangtze River. Like the Germans, some French companies pulled out of the business. For instance, by 1911, the Pacific Steam Navigation Co. (Compagnie Asiatique de Navigation) had to sell its ships to CNC and JMC after contracting its business to another French company.[25]

Similarly, some large British, Australian, and American companies failed to catch up with the Japanese in their attempts to get into China's inner waterways. Most confined their business to the triangle area of Shanghai, Suzhou, and Hangzhou. Thus, by the first decade of the twentieth century, Japanese steamboat transportation companies dominated China's inner waterways in the Yangtze River's tributaries—and then China launched its own, private steamboat operation.[26]

THE ISSUE OF PRIVATE OWNERSHIP

Private individuals in China owned steamboats beginning with Zeng Guofan's experimentation with steam navigation technology and as some wealthy investors acquired several steamboats from foreign countries to start a shipping business on the Yangtze River and the inner waterways. This created a situation for which the Qing dynasty was utterly unprepared. In the ensuing confusion over how to deal with private ownership, Qing officials discussed whether steamboats should be allowed for freight and passenger transportation, especially in the inner waterways.

In December 1864, the commissioner of customs and Shanghai Taotai issued eighteen regulations to allow steamboats privately owned by Chinese the same privileges as foreign vessels at treaty ports, which continued to be operated solely by the Chinese. A few months later, however, Li Hongzhang, acting governor-general of Liangjiang, issued an order denying access to river ports in Liangjiang (modern-day Jiangsu, Jiangxi, and Anhui), particularly ones in the inner waterways. To get around this, some Chinese steamboat owners hired foreign ship crews, while others, who were yet to start their businesses, decided to invest in foreign companies. Realizing the situation, Ying Shibao (应时宝), the chief commissioner of customs, issued a set of new rules to replace the ones offered by Li, and these allowed Chinese steamboats to use inner-river ports. However, soon after, Li Hongzhang, joined by Zeng Guofan, reinstated the restrictions.[27]

In 1882, several local notables in Jiangsu filed a petition with Zuo Zongtang (左宗棠), governor-general of Liangjiang, for permission to own steamboats for freight shipping between cities such as Suzhou, Hangzhou, and Yangzhou, some of which were accessible only through the inner waterways. While granting permission, Zuo prohibited the use of steamboats for transporting passengers.[28]

Shortly after that, in 1884, the Qing dynasty issued the decree "General Principles on Chinese Merchants Purchasing and Building Steamships" (*Huashang gouzao lunchuan zhangcheng* 华商购造轮船章程), granting permission to travel with privately owned steamboats in the inner waterways, especially for Qing officials. The decree, however, also imposed a great number of restrictions against private ownership of steamboats in general. For example, it required private owners to register with the dynasty; steamboats were only allowed to transport officials or operate in some other official capacity, but not for commercial freight shipping or passenger transportation; and the boats had to be easily identifiable by their appearance. Regardless, the decree set off a frenzy of ownership of private steamboat transportation companies. Most operated only in the triangle area and their main customers were Qing officials.[29]

It was not until 1890 that the Qing court finally realized the potential benefit of having private Chinese companies compete with foreign companies. Over the next five years, the dynasty issued a series of decrees to clear the way for the commercial use of privately owned steamboats. Despite that, however, many Qing officials continued to resist. For instance, two years after the dynasty changed its mind, Liu Kunyi (刘坤一), governor-general of Liangjiang, stated in memorials to the emperor that he intended to restrict private ownership of steamboats to prohibit them from carrying passengers or freight anywhere except the treaty ports and inner waterways between Suzhou and Hangzhou.[30]

The situation was similar among local officials, many of whom imposed restrictions and showed no mercy to those who failed to uphold them. For instance, one notable local had his boats confiscated shortly after he started a private steamboat transportation company. In Suzhou and Shanghai, local officials forbade a wealthy individual to open a business after he spent several thousand taels building a steamboat to commercially transport cargo and passengers between Suzhou and Shanghai. Despite these difficulties, private steamboat transportation companies continued to appear.[31]

As we can see, steamship technology was brought to China by industrialized countries as a byproduct of economic activities pursued for global dominance. These activities led to the Japanese taking over the inner waterways of the Yangtze River's tributaries, especially in the lower Yangtze region. After the Qing dynasty decided to adopt steamboat technology for its own use, many Qing officials continued to resist private ownership of steamboats for passenger transportation. This resistance became part of the backdrop against which the Chinese urban local society negotiated with foreign technology, and to see how it did so, we now turn to a group of private steamboat owners and ordinary people in these local communities.

8
The Role of the Steamboat

DAVID ARNOLD, THE AUTHOR OF *Everyday Technology*, says, "While it cannot be denied that many of the machines that most immediately capture our idea of technological modernity—the railroad, automobile, cinema, computer—originated in the West and were first developed there to meet Western needs and Western tastes, this does not mean that their histories, once they were transferred to other societies, to other cultures and places, were merely the extension and fulfillment of their Western forms." Here I will examine how once steam navigation technology arrived in China, people adapted it to serve their purposes, despite facing numerous obstacles. My focus will first be on a group of private steamboat transportation business owners and the organizers of a local charity group. That is because, as historian of Indian technology Smritikumar Sarkar rightfully describes, any technology only becomes useful to society when entrepreneurs become interested in using it. Individuals like these business owners and like-minded community leaders played a key role in adopting the new technology, for they had the entrepreneurial drive to first take advantage of the opportunities it brought.[1]

NEGOTIATING CHINESE IDENTITY WITH STEAMBOATS

One of the main changes in the inner waterways shortly after the turn of the century was the appearance of several steamboat transportation companies. Not only were those companies owned by Chinese private individuals, but their purpose was to challenge Japanese dominance over the inner waterways. Working to fulfill their ambition, these company owners faced difficulties from both the foreign companies and Chinese officials. Their very survival was often an uphill battle that sometimes cost them their Chinese identity.

The first private company that appeared in the inner waterway's triangle area was the Daishengchang Steamship Co. (戴生昌轮船局, Daishengchang hereafter). Founded in 1891 in Shanghai, the company initially called itself a bureau whose main business was to transport officials in the area. Between 1899 and 1901, Daishengchang extended its business to Zhenjiang and other locations, not all of which were reached through the inner waterways. By then, the company had twenty steamboats, and it built landing docks and storage facilities in all of these locations.[2]

The owner of the company was Dai Siyuan (戴嗣源), a Zhejiang native who came from a family deeply involved in the activities of his native merchant group, one of which was sea shipping. Because of his family background, some Qing officials asked Dai to transport army supplies from the mainland to Taiwan for the dynasty during the Sino-Franco War (1883–1885), for which he earned an official designation. Dai later decided to stay in Taiwan and become a Japanese citizen when Taiwan came under Japanese rule after 1895. In 1897, Dai contracted his entire business to JMC and a British shipyard, Boyd & Co. When Dai's son became a Japanese citizen in 1905, he declared his company a Japanese enterprise.[3]

Dai's action was not unusual among Chinese owners of private steamboat transportation companies. Between 1898 and 1901, it was common for Chinese private companies to operate under foreign holdings. Some registered with foreign consulates, which in return offered their countries' flags, business permits, and license plates for use on the boats. To better understand this phenomenon, we will now take a closer look at the methods companies used to obtain foreign identities.[4] The first

FIG. 8.1 Steamboat in Zhenjiang in 1906–1907. Photograph by G. Warren Swire. Archives and Special Collections, SOAS Library, University of London.

example is from a company founded in 1901 in Shanghai by a Zhejiang native who was also an agent of a British company at that time. Because the owner claimed his business under his British employer, the company applied for a British business license. After that, all of its steamboats and tugboats carried British flags on their shipping routes.[5]

In the second example, a company owned by a merchant in Shanghai opened several branch offices along the Yangtze River, including one in Zhenjiang, for which freight and passenger transportation in the inner waterways was its main enterprise. To obtain a foreign identity, it offered 30 percent of its stock to a British company that had no actual involvement in its business operations.[6] The third example is a company founded by a local official and several wealthy individuals in Zhenjiang. The company specialized in transporting both passengers and freight along the inner waterways. To appear foreign, the company took an office inside a building operated by a British firm.[7] These are only a few of a great many examples. The phenomenon was so widespread in the lower Yangtze region that at one point more than two thousand vessels flew foreign flags, according to witnesses in Zhenjiang. Most of these vessels were ordinary wooden sailing boats.[8]

One explanation for this phenomenon may come from a document that points to government corruption as the main cause. In 1917, the Jiangsu governor's office under Governor Qi Yaolin (齐耀琳) issued an order to stop local officials like river bailiffs (*hekuai* 河快) from extorting extra fees and contributions. The order concluded by saying that, because of these officials, Chinese businesses were flying foreign flags and joining Western churches.[9]

Nevertheless, despite the reasons for hiding their Chinese identity, these private companies generated considerable pressure on the larger companies on the inner waterways owned not only by foreign corporations like JCSC but also by the Qing dynasty and CMSNC in particular. At the turn of the century, CMSNC's fate was uncertain. At first, during the Boxer Rebellion (1900), the Qing dynasty reverted the transporting of tribute grain back to China's main river system, since the invasion of the Eight-Power Allied Forces made the sea route almost impossible, and this brought a temporary boom to CMSNC's business. Right after the rebellion ended, however, the dynasty converted all taxes in the country from grain to silver, to meet the increasing demand for silver from the industrialized countries and to pay off indemnities. That decision in many ways signaled the end of tribute grain transport because there was no longer a need for it. The grain transportation system was officially terminated a few years later.[10]

In 1902, CMSNC realized the consequence of these changes: the loss of its largest source of income and main mission. It then reinvented itself by creating its largest subsidiary, the China Merchants Inner-Waterway Steam Navigation Co. (招商内河轮船公司, CMIWSNC hereafter), with headquarters in Shanghai. It also set up dozens of branch offices in various cities along the Yangtze River, including one in Zhenjiang. CMIWSNC first operated in the triangle area.[11]

As soon as CMIWSNC got into shipping in the inner waterways, it faced competition from Daishengchang and the Japanese company DSC, already established on these rivers. To fend them off, CMIWSNC negotiated an agreement with both of them in 1903 to form a joint venture. Together, the three companies dominated the waterways for a while.[12]

Through the joint venture, CMIWSNC grew into a large-scale operation on the inner waterways. The company expanded its shipping route into places like Zhenjiang, thus creating a network that covered the lower Yangtze region. Therefore, CMIWSNC was not much affected by the Qing dynasty's decision to abolish tribute grain transport in 1904.[13]

Meanwhile, the combined strength of the three companies forced other private companies into smaller tributaries of the Yangtze. Their smaller steamboats were able to access rivers that most larger steamboats could not reach, enabling them to thrive.[14]

Just as the market for steamboat transportation on the inner waterways was getting crowded, there appeared the Dasheng Steamship Co. (大生轮船公司, Dasheng hereafter), founded by Zhang Jian (张謇) in Nantong. Zhang started his venture in steam shipping shortly before 1900 by renting a small steamboat to transport products from his enterprise to Shanghai, as well as passengers between Nantong and Shanghai.[15]

In 1903, Zhang and several others from Nantong formed a company specializing in inner waterway transportation around Nantong, which led to the establishment of the Dada Inner Waterway Steamship Co. (大达内河轮船公司, DIWSC hereafter), which carried both goods and passengers between Nantong and Lusi (in Jiangsu).[16] In 1904, Zhang teamed up with two wealthy and powerful Zhejiang natives to create a new steamboat corporation comprising three separate entities. All three transported freight as well as passengers using the inner waterways. They quickly extended their service to sixteen locations between Shanghai and Yangzhou and increased their shipping routes between Nantong and some cities in the lower Yangtze region, including Zhenjiang.[17]

In every place where his steamboats docked, Zhang built wharves. For locations that were unsuitable for this, small wooden boats ferried passengers to the steamboats. By 1912, Zhang had a large fleet of steamboats, including a steamship, most of which were built by Zhang's shipyard to travel on the Yangtze River and its tributaries.[18] While this was under way, two developments emerged in China and Europe that deeply affected steam navigation in China: the appearance of the railroad and the outbreak of World War I.

GLOBAL CHANGES AND LOCAL REALITY

The building of railroads after 1906 and the outbreak of World War I in 1914 created the biggest change in Chinese steam navigation. The two worked in consort to trigger the decline of steamship-based, long-distance shipping on the Yangtze River, but in the meantime boosted steamboat-based freight and passenger transportation on the inner waterways. These changes produced new winners and losers and unexpectedly benefited the private shipping company owners.

The railroad played a significant role in revamping the major routes of transregional trade. For example, after the completion of the Beijing-Hankou railroad in 1906, the Shanghai-Nanjing railroad in 1908, and the Tianjin-Pukou railroad in 1911, goods from Anhui and northern Jiangsu were taken to Xuzhou (in Jiangsu) and Bengbu (in Anhui), rather than to Zhenjiang for shipment by train to Shanghai. This greatly reduced the amount of goods going through Zhenjiang by steamship to other parts of the country or overseas.

The same happened with imports from overseas. Goods such as refined sugar, textiles, and tobacco were shipped by rail to Zhenjiang from Shanghai. The remaining goods that Zhenjiang continued to handle were mostly for local consumption or for customers in surrounding areas and were transported by steamboats or wooden boats through the inner waterways.[19]

Shortly after the railroads appeared, World War I broke out. The perils of war caused a sudden plunge in the supply of European goods on the world market as well as a shortage of companies transporting Chinese raw materials to Europe due to the dangers in the sea. As a consequence, transcontinental shipping between Asia and Europe by steamship was greatly reduced. For instance, when the war started, China saw a 20 percent drop in the number of European ships on the Yangtze River, a trend that continued until three months before the war ended near the end of 1918.[20]

Under the impact of the railroad and the war, most foreign companies, except those from Japan, began to withdraw from the Yangtze River, sensing the end of the steamship era in China. Right after the Tianjin-Pukou Railroad was finished, for example, most of those companies closed their branch offices in Zhenjiang, leaving JCSC the only foreign company with a branch office in the city.[21]

At the same time, there was a steady increase in some goods being transported through the Yangtze River's tributaries even during the war. The reason is that neither the railroad nor World War I had affected steamboat-based, short-distance transportation on the inner waterways as much as long-distance steamship shipping on the main body of the Yangtze River. That is because the steamboat had advantages over the train when it came to connecting many points along the Yangtze River. On the other hand, many people, especially farmers, still preferred steamboats to trains for transporting small quantities of goods or for personal travel because it was cheaper, more flexible, and more convenient.[22]

For example, farmers from the regions of the Huai (淮河), Xia (下河), and Chuanchang (串场河) rivers carried a large number of agricultural products like chickens, fish, and eggs daily on the two most popular steamboat routes in the lower Yangtze region—Shanghai to Yangzhou and Shanghai to Qidong—to Shanghai. This earned those steamboats the nickname "chicken-and-duck boats" (鸡鸭船). The farmers sometimes could negotiate a discounted price if the boat failed to stay on schedule. In addition, a large number of people traveled by steamboat from Jiangsu to Shanghai to look for work.[23]

Steamboats were often the alternative when trains were overcrowded or unavailable. In July 1920, for example, a few trading companies in Zhenjiang had just received a large shipment of talcum powder, wheat, and other miscellaneous grains from the upper Yangtze River but were unable to transport them out of Zhenjiang to separate destinations because there was no train available. The companies had to ship the goods by steamboat.[24]

In large part because of the rising need for inner-waterway transportation, there also was a rise in the number of privately owned companies specializing in this service through the 1910s. We can observe this by looking at Zhenjiang. In the 1910s, there were more than two dozen private steamboat transportation companies, including those with foreign identities. Some were newly formed; others were recently revived following bankruptcy. There were also some branch offices opened by large Chinese companies from elsewhere, a few of which provided freight and passenger transportation through the inner waterways, especially in the triangle area.[25]

The immediate fallout of this development was fierce competition. *Shanghai News* had a vivid report in 1913 on the situation in Zhenjiang, stating that at one time the three largest steamship companies on the Yangtze River were CMIWSNC, DSC, and Daishengchang. After CMIWSNC was confiscated by the Beiyang warlords (*beiyang junfa* 北洋军阀), new ones emerged. At that time, the cost of steam transportation was still quite competitive, and every company charged the same amount, leaving a thin profit margin. After a new company appeared that year and charged much lower rates on its main route between Zhenjiang and Yangzhou, a price war started. When another company appeared with a much lower price, competition became even more widespread. This continued into the mid-1910s and was so tense that the local government in Zhenjiang decided to intervene. In 1917, local officials mediated an agreement that allowed companies to have different shipping schedules. The agreement failed to remedy the situation, however.[26]

Incidentally, as private companies crowded the steamboat transportation market, the Japanese company JCSC ended its principal operation on the inner waterways. In 1915, it withdrew from the triangle area, and in 1920 it downgraded all of its branch offices, including Zhenjiang's.[27] The reason was rising anti-Japanese sentiment that began in January 1915 after Japan presented twenty-one demands to China. Major cities and small towns experienced boycotts and protests that eventually permeated the countryside and caused most people to shun Japanese businesses. Aside from that, however, was the growing pressure of Chinese competitors, especially private companies on the inner waterways. In concert, these two changes dealt a blow to the Japanese shipping business, causing it to withdraw from China.[28]

Right after the Japanese companies left the inner waterways, there was a sudden increase in Chinese private steamboat transportation companies. In fact, about ten new companies appeared at the same time in 1921 in the upper Yangtze River area, and they all extended their reach to the lower Yangtze. In the summer of 1922, coal prices surged worldwide, making many companies in the lower Yangtze unable to maintain their profit margins. Competition from the new companies and the rising cost of coal forced some out of business, while others reduced the frequency of travel along minor shipping routes.[29]

Nevertheless, continuous demand for steamboat transportation on the inner waterways brought in even more private companies. In Zhenjiang, for example, most companies remained in business between 1923 and 1924. When some cut their service between Zhenjiang and Qingjiang, others immediately filled the gap.[30]

Several companies hastily resumed operations by doubling their shifts on some minor routes, allowing them to quickly become part of the emerging inner-waterway shipping network. By the mid-1920s, several such networks had taken shape around Zhenjiang, Suzhou, Wuxi, Changzhou, and Nanjing. Thus, by the time the Nationalist government took control of the country, Chinese private steamboat transportation companies had taken control of the inner waterways. Part of the success of steamboat transportation companies could be attributed to the guilds these companies formed under the Qing dynasty to support their interests and provide protection from predatory warlord governments after the dynasty ended.[31]

BUSINESS ASSOCIATIONS AND STATE AUTHORITIES

One thing we need to explore is the role of guilds in the day-to-day struggles of the steamboat transportation business owners who survived the pressure from state authorities under the Qing dynasty and different warlord governments that all sought control of the steamboat transportation business and imposed heavy taxes. The steamboat transportation companies formed guilds in response to this pressure.

The first guild for the steamboat transportation business appeared in Zhenjiang in 1907 and was headed by Hu Xuesi (胡学思), a wealthy individual. That year, the prefectural government received an application from Hu and his cohort to form such an organization that would include members in the upper reaches of the Yangtze River, the location that fell under the same prefecture's jurisdiction, as well as an affiliated group in the salt shipping business. A similar organization had already been formed unofficially, but it was only for companies located in the lower reaches of the Yangtze River.

After the petition was filed, an order from the prefectural government arrived at the county government office, indicating that the government would place a magistrate in the position of the chairman of the organization's board of directors. The order also directed the magistrate to "follow the bylaws to exercise his power to reorganize the association." It seems this practice of having local officials serving as the heads of the local trade unions was the norm in Zhenjiang in the late Qing.[32]

Right after the Qing dynasty ended, there was a slight augmentation of organizational activities among the private steamboat transportation companies, most of which sensed the new freedom from government control. The steamboat companies specializing in commercial shipping met in Zhenjiang in September 1912 and came up with a new organizational structure. This time, the meeting elected an honorary president from among the members themselves. The bylaws of the association showed that the companies joining this organization were aware of the dominance of foreign companies in the steamship shipping business, which indicates that some organizations like this had already become keen to preserve the national interest against foreign economic powers.[33]

One of the main issues these associations had to deal with was being squeezed by various state authorities seeking financial gain. A common tactic was to levy high taxes, which the companies took countermeasures to evade. Therefore, tax fraud was rampant over the years, particularly once the competition became brutal. For example, a steamboat transportation company in Zhenjiang avoided the tax by taking boats for transporting government tax silver and using them instead to ship local products to Shanghai, Wuxi, and Changzhou. Activities such as this were so common that the local government in Zhenjiang ordered all the companies to show their receipts and accounting ledgers.[34] On another occasion, a local official discovered that a great many private steamboat transportation companies in Zhenjiang were not registered with the authorities or had several boats sharing a single registration. These companies apparently did this to evade boat taxes.[35]

More often than not, provincial authorities under the various warlord governments intervened in tax fraud cases for their own benefit. In January 1912, for example, local officials in Zhenjiang received an order from the provincial government under Governor Wang Hu (王瑚) to investigate a subsidiary of CMIWSNC that was previously run by Sheng Xuanhuai (盛宣怀), one of the prominent "official-industrialist entrepreneurs" in China, after Sheng was deprived of all his official titles and positions following his defection to the American embassy. The government suspected that the company had engaged in tax evasion by producing fake receipts and falsified accounting records on the number of shareholders and number of shares owned. Right after the investigation, the government confiscated the company's assets and sold them, using the income to purchase army supplies for the provincial garrison army.[36]

In another case, in 1914, the provincial government in Jiangsu under Governor Han Guojun (韩国钧) ordered the custom house of Jiangsu to supervise the boats of a private steamboat transportation company as they traveled through the inner waterways, to see if they were loading and unloading goods for foreigners and attempting to evade paying taxes. A few days later, there was a similar order for another company that was also suspected of tax evasion.[37]

In all those cases, the business associations were caught in the middle between state authorities and their own members. Since most steamboat transportation business owners considered the authorities' efforts to eliminate tax evasion to be nothing but robbery, they relied on the association to take a firm stand against the authorities. The following incident from 1923 is a case in point illustrating how business owners were suspicious of the authorities' intentions and also shows us the important role of guilds in representing their members against the authorities.

In 1923, the Jiangsu provincial government under the governorship of Han Guojun decided to establish a local office, the Maritime Administration Bureau, in Zhenjiang to supervise the steamboat transportation business to prevent tax evasion. When the news arrived in Zhenjiang, the plan met with strong opposition. Representatives from several business associations visited the Chambers of Commerce in Zhenjiang, asking it to present a petition to the provincial government against such a plan. The chamber decided to act on behalf of the associations by making a public announcement, stating that "the Maritime Administration Bureau in Zhenjiang looks like something that will protect the interest of the shipping business, but it is one that robs the businesspeople . . . How can anyone with a heart tolerate this!"[38]

Under pressure, the provincial government eventually closed the bureau, but the bureau chief disregarded this and continued demanding payment of miscellaneous fees, which created even more of an uproar. Another petition followed and was joined by the Chambers of Commerce of the lower Yangtze region, whose headquarters were in Shanghai, as well as other steamboat business associations from along the Yangtze River. The bureau chief finally decided to give up his office and shut down the bureau.

In many ways, this was a victory for the guilds under their concerted efforts and strong support from organizations in neighboring areas. This would not have happened without the increase in organizational activities among private businesses in the 1920s, however, which was made possible by the growing number of steamboat transportation companies. Because of this, more business associations were launched in Zhenjiang.[39]

While the guilds protected their members from predatory state authorities, they also assumed responsibility for thwarting the collective power of boatmen and other workers. For example, in June 1921, boatmen and tugboat workers in CMIWSNC decided to form unions and sent an application to the provincial government of Jiangsu. The application was blocked by the company, with the assistance of a business association.[40]

Steamboat transportation companies occasionally used guilds to settle business disputes with other industries. In April of 1923, for example, a group of steamboat business associations jointly filed a complaint with the Jiangsu provincial government under Governor Chen Taoyi (陈陶遗) against a mining company they accused of disrupting their business. The government referred the case to the provincial government in Hubei (where the mining company was located) and urged the office there to settle the dispute. In this way, guilds contributed to the success of the private steamboat transportation companies in taking over the inner waterways of the Yangtze River by the mid-1920s.[41]

There was another kind of steamboat-related organization, a local charity group called Puji (普济). Unlike the private steamboat business association, it had to rely on donations to operate. Quite a few steamboat transportation business owners were patrons. Puji went through long periods of struggle because of its constant lack of funding and at times ineffective leadership, which made survival difficult. Beyond that, the organization received no support, either financial or administrative, from local authorities, even though it performed many public functions that were the local government's responsibility. The next section discusses the charity's experiences with the steamboat.

THE STEAMBOAT AND LOCAL CHARITY

Ever since the steamboat appeared in Zhenjiang, leaders of a local charitable group set their eyes on it with the intent to use it as a free ferry service at Zhenjiang and Guazhou. Ferry service had existed in Zhenjiang as early as the Tang dynasty (618–907) and was run by the local government, and thus was known as the "government ferry service." Junks or rafts were used before the steamboat came along, and the service was always free. By the late nineteenth century, Zhenjiang offered two ferry services, both providing passenger transportation between Xijingdu (in Zhenjiang) and Guazhou (in Yangzhou). One was a charity called Puji, and the other, a commercial service called Tongji (通济), although it charged a very low fee.[42]

Puji was founded by three wealthy individuals in 1872 and used large wooden boats. Local officials supported the operation and required local businesses, especially money stores, to make regular contributions toward its upkeep. The three founders formed the Zhenjiang Riverboat Charitable Ferry Bureau (镇江江船义渡局, ZRCFB hereafter) and elected Yu Baichuan (于百川), a well-respected community leader, as chairman of the board of directors. Working with another local charitable organization that was formed earlier for a similar purpose by a different group of community leaders, ZRCFB assumed the responsibility of rescuing people involved in boating accidents and providing a ferry service after the Yangtze River swallowed the entire ancient city of Guazhou in 1895, causing it to be completely submerged.[43]

Until the Tang dynasty, Guazhou had been connected to the north side of the Yangtze River, but the continued accumulation of silt shifted the river stream upward toward Yangzhou, eating out Guazhou inch by inch and creating a piece of land on the Zhenjiang side. Over an extended period in 1895, waves pounded the riverbanks at Guazhou until the entire city collapsed. The thriving Qihaokou market disappeared along with it.

This greatly affected Zhenjiang because many businesses used the market in Guazhou to connect with dealers from north of the Yangtze River. Despite Guazhou's disappearance, the need for ferry service between Zhenjiang and Guazhou remained. Soon, as a plan for building a new market town in Guazhou got underway, the need increased.[44]

The organizers of Puji knew that the steamboat was one way of meeting this need, but their decision was delayed by a series of internal events, beginning with leader Yu Baichuan's death in 1902. ZRCFB elected his nephew as chairman of the board of directors, but he became ill and resigned in 1907, after which ZRCFB replaced him with Yu Baichuan's son. Thus, Puji's goal of acquiring a steamboat was delayed for almost twenty years since its founding, because of poor leadership and insufficient funding.[45]

That changed in 1921, when Puji elected an influential community leader, Lu Xiaobo (陆小波), chairman of the board of directors. At the time, Lu was a major investor who owned or co-owned around two dozen local enterprises ranging from the water company to a modern hospital. He was widely considered a successful entrepreneur, similar to Zhang Jian in Nantong. Lu was able to bring in the funding needed to acquire a steamboat.[46] Puji expanded its ferry service to include the nearby island of Xiannumiao. With many business leaders from around Zhenjiang providing financial support, Puji was finally able to purchase its first steamboat in 1923, making Puji much more popular than Tongji.[47]

Tongji noticed the difference right after Puji's steamboat went into service, which was during a major holiday, when so many people crossed between Zhenjiang and Guazhou that Puji could hardly keep up with demand. On the other hand, Tongji had very few passengers despite its low fare, so it eventually shut down the business and used one of the wooden boats to provide a free ferry service to the poor.

Meanwhile, Tongji's owners also planned to purchase a steamboat. With the hope of obtaining financial support from the local authorities, they filed a petition to the provincial government of Jiangsu under the governorship of Han Guojun, imploring it to order the local authorities to provide funds. The provincial government responded by first explaining that it did not have funds for Tongji, then ordering the magistrates of Dantu and Jiangdu counties to help raise funds. None of them complied, because they did not see that as their responsibility.[48]

After two years, Puji's popularity dwindled because of the changes occurring across the country, as well as a major land use dispute involving some local steamboat transportation companies. First, the war between the various warlords intensified near Zhenjiang, disrupting steamboat transportation in general, including Puji. In 1925, for example, war broke out in Danyang County in Zhenjiang province between the warlord army of the Zhili clique led by Sun Chuanfang (孙传芳) and the military of the Fengtain clique headed by Zhang Zuolin (张作霖). When Sun's army moved into Zhenjiang, Puji had to suspend its service, and when Sun's army expressed a desire to use Puji's boats for a military campaign, the leaders of the Puji organization had to hide their steamboat.[49]

Shortly after the army moved out of Zhenjiang in 1926, the idea of abolishing the charitable ferry service surfaced among a group of small steamboat transportation company owners who wanted to use a piece of land occupied by Puji. They argued that Puji had no right to deny them access to this public land, since Puji used it to load and unload heavy goods, and that heavy customer demand and the threat from flooding and erosion meant they deserved the same access for their own businesses. The dispute grew into a local campaign against Puji, forcing it to close. But Puji regained its footing toward the end of 1926, after the Red Cross in Zhenjiang asked it to transport some goods. The Red Cross paid for the service, and Puji was able to resume its charitable activities. In addition, by flying the Red Cross flag, Puji avoided harassment from the warlord army. Other steamboat transportation companies soon followed suit, and with this competitive advantage lost, Puji gradually cut back on its ferry service.[50]

Local entrepreneurs and the organizers of the charity group Puji negotiated steam navigation technology in the context of a multitude of challenges, including those caused by global and local changes. These individuals succeeded in taking control of steamboat transportation on the inner waterways and maintained the local charity service only by circumventing obstacles in their social milieu. Nevertheless, through negotiations, they were mostly capable of accomplishing what Ralph Schroeder, a British scholar of science and technology, sees in the relationship between technology and its users in general: actively transforming technology for one's needs.[51]

9
Foreign Technology and Local Society

◇

WE WILL NOW LOOK INSIDE the "black box" (to use Langdon Winner's phrase) to discover how local communities as a whole negotiated the new and alien technology of steam navigation by handling various issues themselves, and how the state's growing presence under the Nationalist government transformed the way local communities experienced this technology. I will pay specific attention to ordinary people who interacted with the technology in everyday life. The technology brought the people of Zhenjiang a mix of issues that varied from locale to locale. As the steamboat age mostly coincided with the ending of the Qing dynasty and the lapse in national authority during the warlord period, the local communities of Zhenjiang were left to themselves to deal with many unprecedented challenges introduced by technology. We begin by looking at a situation that arose after the steamship became available in China: the inundation of foreigners and foreign government representatives on the local scene.[1]

THE FOREIGNER AS A LOCAL ISSUE

Ever since steam navigation made travel from the North Atlantic to China's interior much easier, foreigners from the region appeared on the local scene much more frequently. Interactions between them and the locals occurred under a variety of circumstances, which often generated different outcomes. In some cases, as we will see, these exchanges subjected the local communities of Zhenjiang to direct intervention by foreign governments.

The first example is an encounter that took place in June 1890, when a major fire engulfed a store-filled commercial area in Zhenjiang. The damage was estimated at about three hundred thousand taels of silver, a staggering sum at that time. Coincidentally, an American gunboat was docked nearby, and the marines aboard immediately left the boat to help extinguish the fire. They also stopped some looters from entering the properties. Through their bravery and skill, they managed to isolate the fire to keep it from spreading. The property owners were deeply moved by the marines' deeds and thanked them profusely.[2]

While this event involving American soldiers created positive feelings, the next example of foreign involvement had the opposite result. The incident took place in May 1911, when a foreigner working for a Swiss petroleum warehouse boarded a small sampan and headed toward a passing steamship with the intent of having a conversation with the ship's owner, most likely an old acquaintance. En route, however, the ship bumped the sampan. The sampan overturned, throwing the passenger and the two Chinese boatmen into the river. The steamship came right away and rescued the foreigner but left the two Chinese behind to drown. Although the response from the local communities was not recorded, it can be assumed that this would have generated resentment toward foreigners.[3]

Occasionally, local people had the opportunity to watch the skirmishes that erupted between Chinese soldiers and the crew members of foreign ships, such as the one that occurred in September 1916, involving a steamboat owned by the German Litong Steamship Co. It started when the boat was fired upon while passing by Zhenjiang. The crew members identified the aggressors as Chinese soldiers, presumably from a warlord army nearby, because their hair was styled in pigtails. The only motive the German crew could figure out was resentment because the boat blocked their access to the river. The crew members immediately returned fire, and although no one was hurt during the incident, the steamboat suffered minor damage. When the shooting ended, the soldiers held the boat until its Chinese crew members persuaded the soldiers to let it leave. Given the fact that the damage was minor, the boat captain decided not to file a complaint with the Chinese authorities. Still, the incident was a major topic of conversation in Zhenjiang, since many local residents watched from the hills as the amusing spectacle unfolded.[4] Despite the fact that these events involved foreigners, and even though local people were left behind to perish in some cases, local authorities showed no interest in the incidents. Their general attitude was to avoid any dealings with foreigners. That changed, however, when foreign embassies got involved.

One example took place in 1916, when heavy rains that lasted for several days caused the Yangtze River to rise. Massive waves pounded the river dike at its busiest point, close to where some people lived. Meanwhile, passenger steamboats owned by Daishengchang and Yonghe docked there, making the waves larger and potentially pushing the dike to collapse. Many of the local people approached the companies to persuade them to dock elsewhere until the storm passed. Daishengchang agreed to the request, but the Yonghe company refused. This enraged the people, who proceeded to douse one of the boats with kerosene and set it on fire. However, they mistakenly burned a boat owned by Daishengchang rather than Yonghe. No one was injured, because the passengers had already left and the crew ran away when the fire was set.[5]

Both the Japanese and British embassies got involved in the case, alarming local townspeople. First, the Japanese embassy in Nanjing felt that it had the right to intervene because not only was Daishengchang initially registered with the Japanese embassy as a Japanese business, but it was also a joint venture with the Japanese steamship company DSC. The embassy sent a member of its military staff to Zhenjiang to solicit the local officials' punishment of the guilty parties. As soon as the representative learned that those people lived in Jiangdu County, he asked city officials to notify the Jiangdu magistrate, who sent the county police to investigate and to suppress the still-angry crowd, who now sported guns.

To please the Japanese official, the magistrate accompanied him to the incident scene.[6]

Negotiations to settle the damage soon ensued in Zhenjiang. They did not take place between the Japanese and Chinese only, however, but between the Japanese and the British, on one side, and the Chinese, including officials from the Zhenjiang Prefecture and several community leaders, on the other. The British were involved because Yonghe was previously registered as a British company with the British embassy. Negotiations proceeded for days and then stalled, mainly over Chinese objections to the request that those involved in the incident pay three to four thousand taels to compensate for the damages. Eventually, the community leaders decided that it was best for the communities to reach a settlement. They paid one of the officials a personal visit to persuade him to accept their terms, which included collecting payment for the local authorities themselves, and the official agreed. The case was finally settled.[7]

A year later, a similar incident occurred between two steamboat transportation companies that were both registered with the British government. It started with a Yonghe steamboat carrying about eighty passengers between Nanjing and Yangzhou at dusk, when visibility was low. One of the steamboats from Hongan was traveling the same course. By the time it saw the other boat, it was too late to avoid a collision. The Yonghe boat sank almost immediately, and the boats that came to the scene were able to rescue only around twenty passengers. Interestingly, in this case, the British embassy for whatever reason decided not to get involved in the settlement. Nevertheless, remembering previous incidents with steamboat transportation companies operating under foreign identities, officials in Zhenjiang Prefecture investigated the incident and helped arrange the settlement between the two companies.[8]

As these examples show, the appearance of the steamship created unprecedented situations for the local communities of Zhenjiang, some of which involved foreign embassies. All of this put significant pressure on residents and local officials, who were mostly inexperienced in dealing with foreigners, let alone with powerful foreign government agencies. For most, steam navigation technology and foreign embassies' interference with local affairs were seen as equally treacherous.

ACCIDENTS AS LOCAL MATTERS

Many local residents considered the steamship to be dangerous and problematic. One source of this perception was their unfamiliarity with steam navigation technology and the lack of safety in the technology itself. Frequent accidents involving steamships shaped the opinions of residents, including local officials, regarding this foreign technology.

Accidents were part of steam navigation in China since the technology's inception. For example, the *Shanghai News* reported on January 8, 1873, that a powerful thunderstorm had blown a steamship owned by SSNC to shore near Zhenjiang. Quite a few people drowned as a result. A separate report in a December 1907 issue of the *Pictorial News,* another Shanghai-based newspaper, cites a much more serious accident on a steamship owned by the JCSC that was involved in an accident near Jiaoshan Island, resulting in the drowning of about two hundred passengers. In addition to these accidents, there were also collisions between steamships, such as the one reported in February 1910, which involved a landing-stage boat owned by the Melchers & Co. and a craft owned by another steamship company.[9]

Although these accidents happened around Zhenjiang, local officials paid them no attention because they did not occur within their jurisdiction. When that was not the case, however, officials were forced to respond. After one accident in 1917, for example, local authorities ordered all steamboats to have a sufficient number of life preservers in the event of future accidents that might involve a large number of people. The order specified that ticket prices would be increased to cover the expense.[10]

Local officials were alarmed when an accident involving a high-ranking official traveling through the town occurred in March 1900. The situation put them in a very awkward position. The incident involved one of the landing-stage boats, and the ships always had problems connecting with them. There were quite a few incidents in which passengers, as well as dock workers, fell to their deaths while crossing them. Realizing the danger, the CMIWSNC warehouse manager placed a large net underneath its landing-stage boat every time a ship arrived. Other companies followed suit. This time, however, the net was worn out and failed to catch the passenger, who just happened to be a high-ranking Qing official, a commissioner from Anhui. His assistant and onlookers tried to find his body but were not successful.

This accident disturbed the local officials responsible for the safety of high-ranking officials passing through the jurisdiction. They ordered the CMIWSNC warehouse manager to repair the net and ordered the companies whose landing-stage boats did not have nets to install them. These orders were not strictly followed, however, because these officials did not have direct authority over the shipping companies. The Qing dynasty delegated authority over anything related to steam navigation to the Subprefectural Office for Vessel Management of Zhenjiang Maritime Customs (Zhenjiangguan lichuan ting 镇江关理船厅) agency. In other words, local officials in Zhenjiang had to go through the agency to reach the steamboat transportation companies.[11]

Cases in which bureaucracy prevented local officials from exerting their authority occurred quite often. Once, for example, when the Yangtze River rose significantly after days of heavy rainfall, officials deemed steamboat travel on the inner waterways between Zhenjiang and Qingjiang (in Jiangsu), one of the two main routes, unsafe. Instead of issuing an order to the steamboat transportation companies directly, however, they had to first ask permission from the administrative office of Zhenjiang Maritime Customs.[12]

So far, what we have seen is the variety of changes that the arrival of the steamship brought to Zhenjiang. These changes often added to the administrative burden of local officials and created difficulties in the daily lives of ordinary residents. The new technology brought not just problems, however; as a matter of fact, in some cases, it provided opportunities for local communities to better themselves. How these opportunities were realized is the question we shall now explore.

STEAMBOATS AS SOLUTIONS

The first attempt to use steamboats to solve local problems was made by the governor of Zhenjiang Prefecture in 1900 as he pondered how to make the small wooden boats then in use safer during thunderstorms. They were usually covered under a water transport bridge, also known as a canal lock, used for regulating the water levels of a large stream and a small stream in the Grand Canal. For years, the bridge provided an ideal hiding spot. Over time, as the number of wooden boats increased, however, it became overcrowded, and the governor decided to look for an alternative.

He narrowed down the options to two. The first was to use the small lake, known as Lotus Lake, on the east side of the small stream. The governor thought that if he enlarged the lake to a few dozen *mu* (each *mu* equals 0.165 acres) and connected it to the canal, the boats could weather storms there. On the other hand, he also knew that the lake was dry before winter, when no water entered from the canal, which was at a lower altitude. Furthermore, the water would be too shallow during the spring, and the lake was in danger of disappearing altogether as silt continued to accumulate. Dredging the lake would cost ten thousand taels of silver, a large sum at that time, and then an additional one thousand taels every year to maintain the depth.

The second option was to purchase a three-story landing-stage boat with a metal exterior, like a floating building. The CMIWSNC warehouse manager told the governor about his company's use of a landing-stage boat with the company's wooden boats. Every time there was a storm, the company parked its boats behind its landing-stage boat, which served as a wall to block the wind. The governor calculated that the same amount needed to dredge the lake could purchase ten landing-stage boats that could form a protective barrier during storms, with several dozen *zhang* (each *zhang* equals 3.65 yards) between them—enough to protect a lot of wooden boats. Although the fixed cost of maintaining landing-stage boats every ten years remained, their purchase price could be justified by using them as landing stations for commercial boats. The governor ultimately filled Lotus Pond and turned it into dry land for rent to local businesses, and used the rent collected to purchase landing-stage boats. He also built a wall to protect small boats during storms.[13]

The governor of Zhenjiang Prefecture was sufficiently open-minded to use the introduction of the steamboat to address the safety problems of wooden boats. Local authorities in Zhenjiang, however, were not in favor of adopting foreign technology, even for the benefit of a large segment of the population. This lack of support was only one of the hurdles that local communities had to overcome in adopting a new technology to improve their lives. Because of various changes in local society during this period—including changes in the local power structure and in state authorities during the warlord period—it was rather difficult for local communities to access new technology even after it had been introduced. This changed when the Nationalist government came into power.[14]

TECHNOLOGY AND THE EVERYDAY STATE

Before the Nationalists took over the country, two major changes had already impacted personal travel via steamboat: the appearance of buses and the construction of intercity roads. The latter accommodated the former by providing the necessary conditions for acceptance in places like medium-sized and smaller cities.

Zhang Jian's success in Nantong brought a wave of enthusiasm for building new types of roads in Jiangsu. In 1921, under the initiative of a recently formed voluntary organization, the Chinese National Road Building Association (中华全国道路建设协会), many socially active and locally influential individuals in medium-sized and smaller cities along the lower Yangtze River started to build intercity roads to connect with Shanghai and one another. In Zhenjiang, this organization was called the Bureau of Northern Jiangsu Road Management (江北路政总局), and its mission was to create the city's main road, the Zhenjiang Intercity Road. Efforts like this led to the completion of several intercity roads in Jiangsu in 1927. The appearance of new roads set the stage for the popularity of buses for personal travel.[15]

Bus companies mushroomed in Jiangsu in the 1920s. The first in Zhenjiang was founded in 1927 (shortly after the Nationalist government took over the country) by a business owner right after the Zhenjiang-Yangzhou intercity road was finished. At first, the local government permitted only tourist buses but the company soon was allowed to add regular bus service between Zhenjiang and Yangzhou.[16] Initially, traveling by bus was more expensive than by steamboat; for this reason, it was not well received. It gained some public acceptance only after the bus companies deliberately coordinated their schedules with those of trains, making the bus more convenient than the steamboat. More bus companies were formed after that. Even the local government wanted to join the action by running its own buses. Although the appearance of intercity road and bus had mounted a serious challenge to steamboat transportation, the steamboat's role was truly transformed after 1928 under the Nationalist government's effort to create a public road system.[17]

Shortly after the Nationalist government founded its capital in Nanjing, it began to design a "Linked Public Road" (联络公路) system, centered in Nanjing, with the clear goal of building a national network of roads. To create such a system, the Nationalist government issued "four longitude and three latitude plans" (四经三纬方案) in 1928.[18]

In May 1928, the Jiangsu provincial government released its Guidelines for Public Road Construction in Jiangsu Province (江苏省修筑公路条例) to implement the central government's initiative. The provincial government would build three kinds of roads: provincial, county, and village. There would be nine provincial roads to connect Jiangsu with neighboring provinces. In 1929, the provincial government relocated its capital to Zhenjiang, making Zhenjiang the nucleus of the planned network of roads for Jiangsu province.[19]

The Nationalist government's effort intensified with the founding of the National Economic Committee (全国经济委员会) in 1931. The committee determined that public roads would not only connect major cities but also link these cities with medium and smaller-sized cities, some of which at the time could be reached only through the inner waterways. A year later, the committee revised its plan, after the Military Commission (军事委员会) proposed to connect eleven major, strategically important roads in seven provinces to create a Seven-Province Linked Public Road (七省联络公路). Under the new plan, eight out of the eleven roads would go through Zhenjiang and Yangzhou.[20]

While these changes took place at the national level, the Nationalist government gradually increased its control at the local level, including control of the use of steamboats. The government not only drastically increased the state presence in the local communities of Zhenjiang but also changed ordinary peoples' daily experiences with steam navigation technology. Like the previous period, the Nationalist era had its share of problems and challenges that required the government's attention. For instance, two years after the Nationalist government took charge of the country, three steamboats were robbed, and the perpetrators were none other than members of the Nationalist Army. The incidents occurred on the *Fengheng* (丰恒), *Jigui* (吉桂), and *Fengyu* (丰豫) steamboats owned by Zhenjiang Fuyun Steamboat Co.

The robberies occurred after the *Fengheng* set sail with passengers on board. As it passed Jiangdu County, shots were fired from behind a temple and the shooters ordered the boat to stop. Then, about seventy or eighty robbers boarded the boat to take valuables from passengers and crew members. Meanwhile, the *Jigui* arrived at the same location. The plunderers divided their group into two, with one boarding the *Jigui*. The *Fengyu* arrived a few minutes later, and the same thing happened. The robbers fired on those who refused to give up their belongings and severely wounded one passenger who was pregnant. Even an official from the Shanghai Maritime Customs House was not spared; he began to cry after the robbers took 376 silver dollars from him. After they finished, the plunderers put their booty into three small fishing boats and threw the boiler cover and steering wheel of each of the steamboats into the river to render them inoperable.

The whole incident lasted two to three hours. The total loss was calculated to be tens of thousands of silver dollars. Despite the magnitude of the incident, local officials failed to name any suspect, even though several of the criminals wore military uniforms under their outer garments. Although robberies by the Nationalist Army were not common during the period, incidents of this type did occur from time to time.[21]

In the early days of Nationalist government rule, however, the government did little to respond to or prevent such incidents because it wasn't paying sufficient attention to the local society. Similarly, as we can see in the following cases, the provincial government did not get involved in the organized protests by dock workers and boatmen against local officials not long after the Jiangsu provincial government was established on November 1, 1927.

The first major protest happened on January 27, 1928, after a steamboat owned by a private company collided with the local government's inspection steamboat, knocking everyone on the inspection boat overboard. Although everyone except one boatman was rescued, the officers lost some weapons and decided to arrest several boatmen from the other boat. Afterward, the other boat's company repeatedly tried to negotiate a settlement but failed in every attempt.

Soon after, boatmen in Zhenjiang formed an association to rescue their detained peers. The association demanded that the government office release the boatmen and let the county court decide who was responsible for the collision. After the office dismissed the demand, the association organized about five hundred boatmen for a public protest and filed petitions with the Public Security Bureau in Zhenjiang responsible for making the arrest, with the county government in Dantu, and with the local office of the Nationalist Party. At the same time, the association filed a lawsuit in county court against the bureau's detention of private individuals without a court order. Under this pressure, the bureau released the detained boatmen.[22]

A little later, in March 1928, boatmen in Zhenjiang organized to request a wage increase. Before they approached their companies, they met to discuss strategies and realized that each company paid a different wage that varied day by day. They decided to request a 20 percent wage increase across the board for those earning higher pay and a 50 percent increase for those earning less. Instead of making demands directly with the companies, the boatmen elected representatives to attend the shipping steamboat business association's meeting, where they would present their request and try to gain members' support. They finally got the companies to yield to their demands.[23]

Four months later, a large number of workers went on strike, demanding another pay raise. This time, they added four cents for each heavy item they handled. Several thousand workers on 130 barges participated. They elected four representatives to petition the local government and continued to strike until their demand was finally met.[24]

As we can see in these three cases, the provincial government did nothing to intervene, even though it was well aware of what was happening. As soon as the Nationalist government was fully functional by the end of 1928, however, the provincial government became actively involved in local affairs, in stark contrast to its previous attitude. It tightened its grip on the steamboat business associations, considering them a greater threat to their state-making efforts than those formed by the workers and boatmen. As illustrated in the following example, the government gradually deprived those organizations of all power and control over their businesses.

Shortly after the Nationalist era started, the provincial government of Jiangsu reorganized these associations. Under their guidelines, an umbrella association, the Zhenjiang Shipping Business Association (Zhenjiang hangye gonghui 镇江航业公会, ZHG hereafter) was formed in February 1928 to replace all the existing associations in Zhenjiang, although the new organization was set to be jointly managed by representatives from each steamboat transportation company.[25]

The umbrella organization assumed an unusually close relationship with the government. The first sign of this came in July 1928, as ZHG issued a report that too many steamboats traveled too fast in the middle of the Yangtze River, causing more collisions and showing no regard for loss of life. This case was different because ZHG required its members to observe the speed limit set by a government agency instead of its own.[26]

Following this, in September 1928, the Zhenjiang Chambers of Commerce initiated a project to raise funds for dredging parts of the Yangtze River and the Grand Canal in the city. They invited river engineers and construction experts from government agencies to meet at the chamber office to discuss the matter. As a courtesy, they also invited representatives from ZHG.

During the meeting, it was decided that the cost of the project would be covered by a shipping surcharge of 10 percent of the shipping fee. Forty percent of the funds raised would be used to dredge the Grand Canal, another 40 percent would go to dredging the river, and the remaining 20 percent would be used for running a steam navigation school. The committee would be responsible for issuing a special stamp for the surcharge, as well as for depositing the funds with a local bank, either traditional or modern, once the surcharges were collected. The attendees decided that the Chambers of Commerce and ZHG would form a special subcommittee to manage the funds to prevent embezzlement or waste. With the provincial government's approval, the project went ahead.[27]

Two years later, however, the provincial government formed a regulatory committee to supervise ZHG's management of the surcharge for the river dredging projects. This time, government agencies were added to the special committee and assumed management roles along with ZHG and the Chambers of Commerce. New bylaws were developed that stated the committee would only manage 10 percent of the surcharge levied from the shipping fee. A new office, the Surcharge Collection Office, would be opened to oversee the printing of shipping tickets and enforce the collection of the surcharge, although, in theory, the office would be subject to the authority of the committee.

Along with the committee restructuring came a different arrangement for managing how the surcharges would be levied and authorization of the use of funds, both of which were essential to the interests of the ZHG members. The new bylaws stipulated that every time there was a need to draw funds, the engineering office and construction bureau would first submit their proposals for committee review. Once approved by the committee, the proposal would be forwarded to the Department of Construction of the Jiangsu provincial government for final approval. Only after the provincial government authorized the appropriation of funds would the engineering office and the construction bureau in Zhenjiang be able to draw the funds. Under the new arrangement, neither ZHG nor the Chambers of Commerce had a voice in the decision-making process for any project related to steam navigation.[28]

As this case makes clear, the provincial government gradually deprived the steamboat business associations of all their power by steadily shifting decision-making to government agencies. The result was that the associations had no say in any matter related to steamboat transportation. One example involved a payment scam and occurred on two tugboats in January 1931. Afterward, the chief executive officer of ZHG reported the incident to a government agency rather than conducting an investigation himself. Several months later, a similar incident took place. ZHG was informed that individuals were trying to swindle the local business community by soliciting contributions and pretending to hire boatmen to start a locally based shipping company, and ZHG again let the government handle the case.[29] After these incidents, the steamboat business associations grew increasingly dependent on the government to protect their members' interests. Meanwhile, the government stepped up its oversight role in matters related to steamboat transportation, including the most trivial issues of day-to-day management.

For instance, in April 1931, an official was found on a steamboat without having a ticket. Enraged, he tried to arrest the cashier responsible for checking tickets from passengers. After the incident, ZHG filed a complaint with the provincial government on behalf of the steamboat transportation company, asking for justice in the matter. The provincial government then issued an order to the Nationalist Party's provincial headquarters to investigate and discipline the official.[30]

As these cases indicate, by relying on the government, ZHG altered its previous mission of protecting its members, while the National government gained greater control over local matters related to steamboat transportation. To see in detail how the strong state presence in steam navigation impacted the lives of ordinary people, we shall undertake a microscopic examination of the way steamboat accidents were settled.

Because these incidents often permanently affected people's lives, those in the local communities paid close attention to how they were settled. Meanwhile, because the government usually regarded such settlements as major tests of its ability to govern, it assumed full responsibility for settling them. Thus, each major steamboat incident could easily lead to a clash between the state and local communities.

THE CASE OF THE *BENNIU*

The accident occurred on July 15, 1929. The *Benniu* (奔牛, *Raging Bull*) steamboat from the Lisu (利苏) company had about 270 passengers on board as it traveled downriver near Jiao Island. When it saw another steamboat, from the Datong (大同) company, rushing from a distance, it pulled to a position parallel with it. Suspecting that the other boat intended to engage in a race, the chief engineer of the *Benniu* ordered the boiler operator to raise the water temperature to speed up his boat. The boiler had just been repaired, however, and was unable to sustain the high pressure from the steam. It exploded, spewing hot water and fire throughout the boat.

Many passengers were injured, and some jumped into the river, although most could not swim. About seventy passengers died, and more were badly wounded. After sending all the injured to the hospital, the company reported the incident to the county court and the Public Security Bureau under the local government. Shortly after the incident, some government agencies and local organizations, including the steamboat business association and the workers' union, launched separate investigations. The victims' families also formed their own organization.[31]

On July 20, a meeting was held at the house of the owner of the Lisu company for the purpose of coordinating the investigation and supervising the settlement negotiations. The chairman of the county headquarters of the National Party presided. During the meeting, an ad hoc committee for investigating the incident and managing reparation payments was formed. The attendees included representatives from all the relevant government agencies and nongovernmental organizations including the newly formed association of the victims' families, as well as delegates from the local communities who had no voting rights. The meeting elected some representatives from government agencies and local organizations as committee members.

The committee first decided to seize two steamboats from Lisu and turn them over to the custody of the Zhenjiang Chambers of Commerce for later use as reparations. After the committee learned that Lisu had two other steamboats outside Zhenjiang, one in Nanjing and another in Gaoyou (in Jiangsu), it asked the county government of Dantu to communicate with the county governments of Jiangning (in Nanjing) and Gaoyou to seize the boats and escort them to Zhenjiang, also for use as reparations. The committee offered two thousand silver dollars seized from Lisu to the victims' families to cover the cost of their meals. The families that were willing to take the bodies of their loved ones immediately were given twenty silver dollars each on sight, to later be deducted from the total amount of reparations received.

There were discussions at the meeting about whether Datong was also responsible for the incident. Quite a few attendees suggested that Datong be punished as well, claiming that, immediately after the incident, Datong raised its ticket price for all passengers, including the victims' family members, to take advantage of the fact that it was the only company in service along the route now that Lisu was out of commission. The meeting ended with the victims' families feeling underrepresented. About ten days later, they held a demonstration in front of the provincial government to demand a fair settlement, the immediate payment of reparations by the responsible company, and the punishment of the individuals responsible.[32]

Separate from this ad hoc committee, the Department of Transportation of the Jiangsu provincial government conducted its own investigation and discovered that while the boiler had not been moved, the safety valve had been tampered with before the accident. Investigators were unable to determine whether the safety valve had been stolen or if something else had happened. Meanwhile, the boiler showed no signs of being cracked, which implied that the explosion did not occur because of an existing crack, although the explosion was so powerful that it not only threw metal debris and scalding water at the passengers but also forced some passengers into the river. Oddly, all the crew members ran away before the explosion, except the chief engineer, who was killed in the explosion. The investigator suspected that the boiler operators had deliberately reduced the amount of water in the boiler in an attempt to increase its temperature and speed up the boat in anticipation of a race against the other boat. They also speculated that the crew of the *Benniu* wanted to win the race in order to have bragging rights and because they were told that steamboat transportation companies often rewarded their crews for winning this kind of race. The investigating team recommended that the government arrest the crew members and have them stand trial.[33]

At the same time, the harbormaster of Zhenjiang Maritime Customs, who was on the scene shortly after the incident, conducted an investigation too. He stated in his report that he saw that the back side of the boiler had been completely blown away, causing metal pieces and hot water to be flung at the passengers, instantly killing some of them. He said that he believed the boiler's safety valve had been altered and was nonfunctional. He suggested that the boatmen had altered the safety valve on purpose to enable the boiler to hold more steam pressure, which eventually caused the explosion. The harbormaster reached a conclusion similar to that of the ad hoc committee and recommended the same action by the government.[34]

Meanwhile, the Department of Construction of the Jiangsu provincial government conducted another investigation and reported its findings. Contrary to the previous reports, this one found the foreign inspectors at Zhenjiang Maritime Customs responsible for the incident because they "were really careless" when they inspected the boat before the incident, as well as several other reasons, such as using a boiler that was too old and using the wrong crew members. The report concluded by strongly arguing that the foreign inspectors "could not deny being guilty" and "our government shall stand its ground on the right to thoroughly investigate the matter" to "eliminate the long-term malpractice of the maritime customs."[35]

Finally, the Provincial Office of the Ministry of Civil Affairs filed a report with the administrative office of the Jiangsu provincial government. The report stated that the ministry had already notified Dantu county court, before the court reached its decision on the case, to seize and auction off the property of the Lisu company's owner to obtain funds for compensating the victims' families, who badly needed money and comfort.

After a few days, however, the court informed the ministry that a civil lawsuit had not yet been filed, and the court was unable to proceed with the compensation before reaching a verdict. The court had to follow the proper legal procedures, and there was no wiggle room on the matter. In the same report, the ministry indicated that they had heard that the company's owner, Yu Shicheng, was willing to declare bankruptcy and auction all his property to pay reparations. Because the parties had not reached an agreement, however, the settlement process had stalled. The ministry asked why the court and agencies had not proceeded and urged the county court and other government agencies to do so.[36]

In August 1929, the Jiangsu provincial government discussed the incident during its regular session upon receiving all the reports, including the one from the Provincial Office of the Ministry of Civil Affairs. The provincial government's responses to the Department of Transportation indicated that the meeting resulted in the following decisions: to seize the property of Lisu's owner and liquidate it to fund the reparations; to allow the case to be handled by the court through the newly established legal system; and to have provincial government officials supervise the settlement process.

The office laid out steps for settling the incident. First, the provincial prosecutor would file charges, then the victims' families would file lawsuits following legal procedures. Finally, the ad hoc committee for the incident would manage the reparation payments. The Provincial Office of the Ministry of Civil Affairs and the Department of Transportation were put in charge of supervising the entire process.

After learning that the victims' families objected to the amount of compensation—450 silver dollars per victim—the provincial government notified the Dantu county court that it would increase the amount to one thousand silver dollars per victim, in addition to what was provided by the local government. The funds would be distributed to the families by one of the provincial government offices. The government asked the families to go back home with the money and await further notification regarding reparations.[37]

In Number 1929, during a meeting of the Jiangsu provincial government, the Department of Transportation and the Provincial Office of the Ministry of Civil Affairs both reported on their efforts to settle the *Benniu* incident. The government decided to allow the ad hoc committee for the accident settlement and the association of victims' families to be jointly responsible for supervising the settlement process. The only responsibility the government assigned to the Zhenjiang Chambers of Commerce was to confirm the addresses of the victims' families.[38]

As the aftermath of the *Benniu* case shows, the Nationalist government gradually succeeded in taking over all matters related to steam navigation. It achieved this not only by subjugating all community organizations like the one made up of victims' families and the local steamboat business association under its bureaucratic control, but also by extending its reach within the local communities to all aspects of daily life involving the use of steam navigation technology. The Nationalist government thus turned itself into an "everyday state" that deeply affected the lives of ordinary people.[39]

THE END OF THE STEAMBOAT AGE

The end of the steamboat age was the beginning of a new era in transportation that featured the emergence of a "linked water-rail-road" (*shui tie lu lianyun* 水铁路联运) system of which the steamboat was a part. This transformation resulted from several developments in the country, including the building of intercity roads with new technology, the use of buses for personal travel, and the Nationalist government's effort to create a national public road network that connected roads with railroads and river ports. These developments lured customers away from steamboats and relegated steamboats to a secondary position behind buses and trains. The steamboat thus lost its previous glory, although it continued to play a significant role in river transportation through the period under study.

As some of the plans were implemented, a consensus among the road system planners arose that there was a need to connect the roads with railroads and river ports. Their idea about "intermodal freight transport" (*lianyun* 联运) soon became popular across society at large. In the beginning, there were two separate concepts: "rail-water intermodal freight transport" (*tieshui lianyun* 铁水联运) and "water-road intermodal freight transport" (*shuilu lianyun* 水路联运). These later became a single "water-rail-road intermodal freight transport" (*shuitielu lianyun* 水铁路联运). Under this concept, steamboat stations would be connected with train and bus stations; a person only needed to purchase one ticket for all forms of transportation.[40]

In the midst of the endeavor to create a system of "intermodal freight transport," however, the role of the steamboat shifted from a primary means of shipping freight and passengers through the inner waterways to a connecting tool for buses and trains. Because of the change, most steamboats were limited to the short distances needed for local transportation, although they remained active in areas unreachable by bus or train. This transformation ultimately triggered the end of the steamboat age, just before the outbreak of the Sino-Japanese War.

◆

As Zhenjiang's history reveals, China was drawn into global technological changes after industrialized countries brought steam navigation technology to China in both steam-propelled gunboats and steamships used for economic activities. Once in China, however, the technology became something people had to negotiate before they could fully incorporate it into their lives to serve their specific purposes.

The negotiation took place in a social context distinguishable by the Qing dynasty's suspicion of the misguided use of the technology by common people and the local officials' general lack of enthusiasm for adopting foreign technology. In addition to the official restrictions, ordinary people encountered many unusual circumstances created by the arrival of the new technology. Some gave rise to local issues that strained social relations between officials and local population, between steamboat companies and local communities, and between the Chinese and foreigners.

But even this did not deter steamboat business owners from adapting the technology to their commercial needs. They seized upon every opportunity afforded by the changes in the country and around the world to gain control of China's inner waterways, notably when public anti-Japanese sentiment was heightened and during World War I. Meanwhile, local community leaders persevered in using steamboat services as a local charity. Together, the steamboat business owners and local charity organizers were willing to accept the new technology despite the occasionally deadly consequences deriving from their lack of sufficient knowledge about, and the embedded risk in, such technology. Through sheer relentlessness, they made the steamboat a practical tool for daily travel.

One factor that stands out in this history is the significance of state involvement in the people's negotiation process. As we have observed, in the nineteenth century the Qing dynasty and its state officials played an important role in the way the Chinese people experienced the Opium War and participated in the commercial transformation. Similarly, during the early twentieth century, the state—through the Qing dynasty, the warlords, and the Nationalist government—continued to impact the lives of the people going through global changes, through policies, administrative intervention, and financial support (or the lack thereof, especially during the warlord period). That was obvious especially when China was under the Nationalist government. By tightening its grip on Chinese local society through state making, the Nationalist government alleviated some of the difficulties the people of Zhenjiang encountered. At the same time, however, its state-making measures blurred the boundary between the state and local society, costing local communities their autonomy.

Conclusion

◇

ONE OF THE ESSENTIAL yet most challenging undertakings in studying Chinese history of the nineteenth and early twentieth centuries has been discerning how Chinese local society interacted with global changes, some of which were intertwined with the exertions of industrialized countries. To meet the challenge, I have presented a "thick description" of the life experiences of people in Zhenjiang in negotiating three global changes: the rise of modern imperialism, the intensification of economic integration, and technological transformation. These changes materialized in the lives of the people during the outbreak of the Opium War, China's commercial transition, and the country's adoption of steam navigation. They enable us to see the historical processes in which global changes coalesced with local changes to reshape Chinese society.

The interaction between the global and the local was characterized by local society's negotiation with global changes, as ordinary people struggled to survive amid the devastation brought forth by outside forces, to circumvent hurdles arising from the new reality, and, at the same time, to capitalize on the opportunities afforded by the changes. The result of the negotiation was the combination of global and local changes into a single process that transformed local society. The driving force of negotiation was the desire of people in each local community to survive global changes and improve their lives by taking advantage of those changes. They made efforts to turn difficulties into opportunities on which they could capitalize to support their particular interests and needs. They thus became active participants in global change, not mere recipients, accommodators, or adaptors.

Before the nineteenth century, China had been connected with the rest of the world after a world market (or markets) surfaced. Linkages with different parts of the world were extended after the sixteenth century as the world became increasingly interrelated. Despite the Ming and Qing dynasties' intermittent ban on maritime trade, those linkages were never broken; instead, they persisted through the country's tributary system and the commercial activities of Chinese merchants. Because of this, China became a center of intercontinental trade among Europe, America, and Asia to shape global commerce after the sixteenth century and held a dominant position in the global silver exchange in the seventeenth and eighteenth centuries. Nevertheless, China's connection with Europe during that period remained indirect. Ironically, it was the Opium War, an outgrowth of modern imperialism, that played an inadvertent role in turning that connection from indirect to direct.

The war "facilitated" increasing connectedness as it brought individuals from two continents into face-to-face contact. In Zhenjiang, besides being a "messy business," the war inadvertently served as a negative means of bringing invader and invaded into an "interaction" characterized by a self-destructive reaction from the local population to the invader and by deepening misperceptions regarding the other side by both the British and Chinese. We may attribute this outcome to a sui generis combination of causes produced by the confluence of the global and the local factors. The outcome was tragic for the Chinese people.

From the very beginning, the British undertook the invasion of Zhenjiang for the purpose of cutting off the grain transport route, the bloodline of the Qing dynasty. The British military aimed to teach the Qing dynasty a lesson, which led them to attack Zhenjiang. Their target was not the city's ordinary people, yet the attack resulted in great harm to them. Meanwhile, the Chinese lost in great part due to the lack of military knowledge and expertise by the officials charged with defending against a powerful foreign army equipped with advanced weaponry. Even worse, some of their personal views, moral characteristics, and judgments hindered rather than assisted the local population facing the British invasion. As a case in point, officials like Hailing played a significant role in making residents desperate before the first shot was even fired. The action of state officials was thus often the determining factor in the outcome of local crises.[1]

A number of contributing causes led the people of Zhenjiang to great despair, one of which was the xenophobic suspicion that all foreigners were evil-minded. As Frederic Wakeman once noted, a suspicion such as this could easily become "explosive" enough to compel Chinese people to risk their lives against foreigners and the Qing dynasty, even as the dynasty attempted to prevent them from doing so. In Zhenjiang, this suspicion led to residents' extreme actions to avoid capture, such as jumping off a hill to their deaths and the drowning of women and children by soldiers in response to the approaching British.[2]

Still, xenophobic suspicion alone was not sufficient to drive women to mass suicide and men to mercy killing; another reason was anguish over the possibility that women would shame their families if violated by the invader, and in particular a foreigner invader. This shame was deeply embedded in the Chinese cultural tradition that prizes women's chastity over their very lives.[3] A state-sponsored "chastity cult" that encouraged women to become "chastity martyrs" had existed since the Song dynasty. Self-mutilation and suicide became rather common as a way for Chinese women to preserve their chastity. The Qing dynasty promoted the cult of female chastity, as well as fidelity, in an effort to claim legitimacy as a Chinese dynasty. This cultural tradition certainly influenced women's decision to take their own lives in Zhenjiang.[4]

In this regard, we may interpret the actions of the women in Zhenjiang as what Émile Durkheim has deemed "altruistic suicide," dying to uphold a social norm. He considered this type of self-destruction "obligatory" since it occurred mostly in communities where individuals were highly integrated into society and therefore lost their singular value. Because of this, Durkheim suggests, it was their duty to die as society requires.[5]

But committing suicide in the face of a foreign invader was found not only among the women in traditional China; a similar phenomenon also existed in other countries. A leading scholar of African history, Selwyn Cudjoe, has discovered that a large number of Native Americans and Africans committed suicide when confronted by a powerful European imperialistic army.[6] Other examples were also found among women in the last days of Nazi Germany and imperial Japan at the end of World War II.[7]

Although there is a similarity between the women in Zhenjiang and elsewhere, fearful for their lives and terrorized by the possibility of being violated, there were also differences in the sources of their fear and the ways it was augmented. In both Germany and Japan, for example, government propaganda played a leading role, infusing fear into the hearts of women and leading them to decide they would rather die than face the horrible alternative.[8]

In Zhenjiang, that fear was deeply rooted in the Chinese historical memory of wartime atrocities, such as the Manchu army atrocities against the population at Yangzhou and Jiading at the founding of the Qing dynasty. The Han Chinese literati secretly kept the memory alive with the help of works such as *Diary of Ten Days at Yangzhou* and *Account of the Jiading Massacre,* despite the dynasty's prohibition against such literature. Wartime atrocities continued, as we see later during the Taiping Rebellion, when the rebels took Nanjing and were allowed to ransack and rape. In each case, countless people, especially women, committed suicide by hanging, drowning, and self-immolation. As R. Gary Tiedemann correctly points out, "mass suicides after the fall of a city were . . . a recurrent phenomenon in the history of Chinese warfare."[9]

That memory was awakened in Zhenjiang by the distressful news about the British killing people and raping women in Zhapu and about Shanghai's quick fall to the British. Because of this, the people of Zhenjiang were plunged into helpless terror. Just as Rush W. Dozier, a specialist in the emotion of fear, says, "humans dread helpless terror more than any other kind of fear." This was the driving force for mass suicides and mercy killings.[10]

Regarding mercy killings, it is undeniable that male dominance over women, one of the features of Asian society, played a role in these men's actions and in the women's suicides. As one study shows, during the Ming-Qing period, men and women had a different and distinct moral sensibility that often resulted in women's self-destruction through suicide to meet the moral requirement of their patriarchal families. Chinese soldiers in Zhenjiang might have committed mercy killings as a way of forcing women to fulfill such a requirement, similar to Japanese soldiers who carried out executions of Japanese women during the American invasion.[11]

Can we then consider those mercy killing and suicides a passive form of resistance against a European imperialistic army? According to Cudjoe, a "passive form of resistance" is a "reaction needed to . . . preserve human dignity, and to ennoble the human spirit." If we compare the actions of the people in Zhenjiang to those in America and Africa, we find that the suicides and mercy killings in Zhenjiang were based on a very different combination of factors, albeit in similar form.[12]

Nevertheless, suicides and mercy killings were not all that happened during the battle in Zhenjiang. Indeed, through the battle and its aftermath, soldiers on both sides as well as the people of Zhenjiang had the opportunity to observe the adversary and form impressions. As a result, the British learned to distinguish between two kinds of Chinese soldiers, the Manchu and the Han. They also acknowledged Chinese wisdom and skills and became aware of the inner strength of Chinese soldiers who received medical treatment. But the British continued to attribute the suicides and mercy killings to the barbaric nature of the Chinese, or Asian culture in general, while they labelled Hailing's suicide "heroic" and considered the brave behavior of the Chinese soldiers honorable.

Meanwhile, the people of Zhenjiang observed the British soldiers through their daily contact. That made some women curious about the foreigners, as indicated by their coming out to see the British officer who visited the Qing officials. Interactions between invader and invaded might have produced what globalization specialist Paul James considers the "effect" of most warfare: it "extend[ed] the social relations, even if those relations are combative or divisive."[13]

The changing atmosphere between the British and Chinese notwithstanding, suspicion and distrust against the foreign invader persisted among the Chinese. Not only did the people of Zhenjiang believe that their suspicion about the foreigners' evil intent was confirmed by the deaths of women, children, and the elderly, but also that the British were barbaric, inhuman, and ruthless. Furthermore, fear was ingrained in their minds, as seen in the facial expression of the monk who could not control his awkward laugh when approached by the British soldier.

Thus, evaluating what occurred in Zhenjiang during the Opium War leads us to recognize that Chinese local society's negotiation with modern imperialism was characterized by the war serving as a negative form of liaison for the people of Zhenjiang and the British. Not only did the negotiation produce tragedy, but it also deepened misperceptions between the two sides. In doing so, the war turned local communities within Zhenjiang into places where global changes manifested in modern imperialism and the local changes deeply embedded in Chinese historical roots became irrevocably intertwined.

Turning from the war to China's commercial transformation as it unfolded in the second half of the nineteenth century, we have seen Chinese urban local communities, like the ones in Zhenjiang, exposed to a slew of economic forces from far beyond the territories of the Qing dynasty. The deeper level of change in those communities came from a combination of global and local factors, however, one of which was the rise of Shanghai.

Although the emergence of Shanghai itself embodied a multitude of global economic changes, it also was a direct result of Chinese merchants' ability to seize the opportunities available to them beginning in the mid-nineteenth century to create a transnational commercial network in East Asia: the Shanghai commercial network. This not only allowed the existing Chinese commercial networks formed by merchant groups to collaborate in a transnational setting but it also connected local markets in China with the rest of the globe through open ports and coastal regions, as well as with their hinterlands. One of the major impacts of the Shanghai commercial network on Chinese society was to facilitate the transformation of the Chinese commercial system, and especially transregional trade, its main component within the territory of the Qing dynasty.

Even before Shanghai's rise, there were multiple changes in transregional trade, some of which were due to the decline of the Grand Canal and the shifting of river routes that rendered some sections unusable. More changes began to surface around the mid-nineteenth century, when new trade routes opened along the east coast, aided by the use of steamships. The rise of Shanghai coincided with those changes to hasten the transformation of transregional trade. Many merchants relocated their business operations to urban centers other than Zhenjiang in the Shanghai commercial network—such as Hankou, Tianjin, and Yantai—before Zhenjiang was merged into the network. These merchants' "interest-directed economic actions" (to borrow the phrase of sociologist Ronald Burt) clearly indicated an ongoing realignment process to move transregional trade away from China's internal water system to align with the new Asian commercial center, Shanghai.[14]

Despite its loss of merchants to other urban centers, however, Zhenjiang survived the changes by turning itself into a brokerage town for merchants from both sides of the Yangtze River, who continued to trade there. During the second half of the nineteenth century, Zhenjiang became a hub for the exchange of commodities between merchants from the north and south, who brought various goods from as far as Taiwan, Southeast Asia, and countries on other continents (such as Cuba). At the same time, many shipped native products obtained in Zhenjiang back to their home bases to be sold later in places including Hong Kong and Southeast Asia.

Most merchants who came to Zhenjiang belonged to the country's major merchant groups. The binding factor for each seems to be common native origin, although affinity deriving from family and kinship also played a role. Similar to what sociologist Harrison C. White discovered in Europe, each member of a merchant group carried multiple identities, with separate ties to disparate people, and played many different roles simultaneously within the network. Over the centuries, merchant groups in China, or rather the commercial networks themselves, expanded their sphere of activities and scope of their network throughout Asia and to other parts of the Pacific by taking advantage of various opportunities, especially those afforded by the trade policies of different dynasties.[15]

All the merchants who came to Zhenjiang had to adhere to the local custom of going through brokers in order to trade with merchants from the other side of the Yangtze River. This enabled brokers to control the market through methods such as dictating prices to their advantage. One way of comprehending the source of their power is through the theory of social relations. According to economic historian Karl Polanyi, all economic systems in premodern societies were deeply "embedded" in social relations, dominated by non-economic institutions such as family and kinship. Only after the rise of the "modern exchange economy" were markets institutionalized for contractual exchanges.[16]

If we look closely, we find that all trade activities in Zhenjiang were conducted essentially through personal relations, albeit not always through families and kinship; brokers functioned primarily through manipulating those relations. The group of brokers plying northern commodities and sugar relied very much on their personal connections with local officials and the wealthy to gain acceptance in the local market. They used wining, dining, and procuring prostitutes to build personal relationships. And they continued to resort to personal relations when securing loans, collecting debts, and arranging the transport of goods for merchants.

To understand brokers' power in controlling the market, we may refer to Harrison C. White's model of tripartite relations in social networks. A basic principle in social relations is that "the structure of relations between actors determines the content of those relations." For instance, if two parties in a group have to go through a third party to communicate with each other, then the structure of relations in the group is "asymmetric." And in an "asymmetric" relationship, the third party has the power to control the other two, which gives it the advantage. We can thus discern where brokers got their power: from the local custom that created asymmetry among all involved, itself part of the Chinese brokerage tradition.[17]

Furthermore, this study has allowed us to realize the persistence of brokers in Chinese society well into the late Qing period. From previous work, we have learned that brokers held sway in local markets in the Ming dynasty. With licenses from the government, they acted as a go-between for peasants and long-distance traders. In the early Qing dynasty, however, long-distance traders gained direct access to peasants without having to go through brokers, partially because of the increasing power of merchant groups. Then, by the late Qing dynasty, merchant groups further consolidated their power over the supply chain in local markets, causing the power of brokers to sharply decline even further. The brokerage system simply vanished.[18]

This study has shown that not only did brokers continue to play an important role in local markets in the late Qing, but they also enjoyed a great deal of power in those markets during that period. Observing this reality in Zhenjiang, I share the view of Gary Hamilton, Chang Wei-an, Sherman Cochran, and Loren Brandt that there were very few changes in Chinese local communities regarding private business institutions during the nineteenth century, despite the decline of the Qing state and the arrival of industrialized countries to China.[19]

Becoming a brokerage town was not Zhenjiang's only major transformation in the second half of the nineteenth century. Another was the process that enabled the local business community to join the Shanghai commercial network. Although the process started after the mid-nineteenth century, it was rooted earlier in the century, when a group of local opium sellers began to emerge in the local market. Unlike their predecessors, these local dealers relied mostly on personal ties with wealthy individuals in Shanghai, some of whom were opium suppliers themselves, for financial support. These relations thrived even after the opium trade declined by the late nineteenth century and laid the foundation for Zhenjiang to become part of the Shanghai commercial network.

One issue Zhenjiang's local business community encountered during the process was difficulty in making financial connections due to the confusion in currency values and exchange rates, as well as a lack of recognition and acceptance by their counterparts in Shanghai. We may better understand these challenges by turning to two analyses. According to Peter Spufford's study of credit in premodern Europe, credit and other methods of payment were avenues for the financial connections necessary for market exchanges among merchants; European historian Craig Muldrew and American sociologist Mark Granovetter state that social relationships provided the essential guarantees for credit in premodern societies.[20]

The situation in Zhenjiang aligns with these analyses very well. In the second half of the nineteenth century, credit served as the chief means through which business was conducted between Zhenjiang and Shanghai.

Before the rise of the modern banking system, the only way credit could be guaranteed in Shanghai was through personal relationships. These personal connections fell far short in accomplishing that, however, facilitating the establishment of the bankers' association. Through a series of measures intended to strengthen personal relations, its leaders demonstrated outstanding strategy as well as an intuition for the inner workings of Shanghai's business circles and private financial institutions. The association also promoted business ethics among its members through a set of rules governing business behavior and a new accounting system modeled after the one just adopted by modern banks in Shanghai in 1897. Furthermore, the organization set up an agency in Shanghai to guarantee credit issued by traditional banks in Zhenjiang.

Beyond that, the association took on one of the most difficult yet important tasks of sorting out the differences in currencies and assessing their value for the exchange rate between local businesses and Shanghai. As Robert Gardella and Andrea McElderry discovered, this lack of a "standard measurement system and medium of exchange" was one of the main reasons that foreign merchants were unable to enter China's transregional trade. Based on their findings, we may well assume that the same confusion could have prevented Zhenjiang from entering the Shanghai market. Thus, the bankers' association accomplished nothing short of paving the way for its local business community to connect with Shanghai.[21]

Based on this evidence, I beg to differ from some regarding the role of guilds. Among historians of China, there has been debate regarding the role of guilds in the success of merchants in spurring economic growth. Several studies painted a negative image for the period during which China was subjected to Western economic intrusion. Only in recent years have studies, such as that from Man-hong Lin, contradicted that perception by showing instead that guilds helped merchants in Taiwan prosper in the face of Western competition.[22]

Guilds such as the bankers' association in Zhenjiang contributed greatly to the success of merchants by rising to the challenges of the period and going beyond their main functions locally, such as in setting market prices, regulating trade between businesses, promoting native sentiment, and organizing charitable activities. Furthermore, Chinese merchants in general were capable of taking advantage of all the changes in the country, including those related to the global economic expansion of industrialized countries, to enhance their interests and succeed in their economic endeavors.

Therefore, the second half of the nineteenth century was indeed a period of Chinese local society's intense negotiation with the global changes that saw growing economic connections among different parts of the world and the deep penetration of global economic forces—some of which came from the undertakings of industrialized countries—into Chinese local society. As a result of the change, Shanghai became a hub of the commercial network in Asia, hastening the transition of China's transregional trade into one that extended to the rest of the world. These changes created a distinctive situation for Zhenjiang as the city began to lose its historical dominance in transregional trade. Facing the situation, a new generation of brokers emerged to turn the city into a brokerage town. At the same time, business leaders used their skills in building personal relations and applied innovative measures to traditional commercial institutions to connect the local business community to the Shanghai commercial network. By making these local changes, they positioned Zhenjiang squarely within China's commercial transition.

Examining the technological aspect of China's historical changes, I focused on how the people of Zhenjiang negotiated a new and foreign technology with the same goal that they demonstrated during the city's commercial transformation—not only surviving change but also leveraging change to improve their lives. As we have seen, the people in Zhenjiang (including the steamboat business owners) went through a period of intense negotiation with this new and alien technology not only because of the individual social context within which the negotiation took place, but also because of the distinctive endeavors they had to undertake in order to meet the multifaceted challenges of both global and local changes.

Zhenjiang became part of the global scale of technological transformation for water transportation after industrialized countries brought the steamship to China during and after the First Opium War. The same technology that allowed British gunboats to navigate the Yangtze River was used to flood China with mass-produced products from industrialized countries. Steam navigation was introduced to China as a byproduct of these changes, bringing Chinese local society into the global scale of technological transformation that centered around the inventions of industrialized countries.

What the technology meant for the people in Zhenjiang, however, was more than a new way to travel the waterways, but rather a set of new challenges and opportunities for daily life. While technology enabled travelers to reach Shanghai much more easily than before, it also resulted in a slew of collisions that too often involved the loss of life. In many ways, the use of this novel and foreign technology led to a set of distinctive circumstances that sometimes benefited local communities but other times wreaked havoc on them. For those living in Zhenjiang, therefore, the arrival of the steamship brought continuous negotiation with technology in everyday life, similar to what people in India experienced after the railroad appeared in that country.[23]

The people of Zhenjiang underwent the process of negotiation while their local communities were under the constant influence of world events such as the outbreak of World War I and the fluctuation of coal prices in the world market, all of which had an impact on a global scale. Although the war diverted the attention of European countries away from China, it became one of the main reasons, along with the advent of the railroad, for the decline of long-distance steamship shipping. Just as local companies reaped the benefit of those changes, the sudden rise of coal prices in the world market almost bankrupted them. The direct correlation between global and local changes as seen in Zhenjiang indicates that the Chinese urban local society could no longer remain "local" and had already been deeply penetrated by the global.

Meanwhile, as historian of technology Thomas Hughes points out, "technology is messy and complex" and full of unintended consequences. Because of the messy and complex nature of steamship technology, the people of Zhenjiang sometimes had to face catastrophes such as exploding boilers, mid-river collisions, and drowning passengers. These situations were usually derived from people's unfamiliarity with the new technology, or from the safety hazards embedded in the technology itself. In addition, as another unintended consequence, ordinary people had to face various predicaments caused by the appearance of foreigners or the intrusion of foreign governments in local affairs.[24]

The arrival of technology therefore increased the tension between the families of the victims of steamboat mishaps and the steamship companies, between ordinary people and local authorities, and between the Chinese and foreigners. As historian Edward Beatty suggests, the relationship between technology and social context has an interactive nature such that "adopting new technologies and assimilating new know-how" often brings "friction" to social relations.[25] Furthermore, Donald A. MacKenzie and Judy Wajcman remind us that technology and society are not separate entities. Ritika Prasad, Edward Beatty, and David Arnold have all indicated that social context played a significant role in the spread of Euro-American technology in other parts of the world.[26]

For the people in Zhenjiang, the negotiation with technology bore some individual characteristics because of the social context within which it took place. On the one hand, the Zhenjiang social context shared many variables with the larger Chinese society, such as the Qing dynasty's reluctance to adopt foreign technology and the hesitation among Qing officials to allow private ownership of steamboats, except for use in transporting officials. Like the rest of the country, Zhenjiang was subjected to prolonged warlordism, a period when it was a "stateless state"—to borrow Hussein Adam and Ali Mazrui's term for Somalia when that country lacked a unified central authority.[27]

On the other hand, however, specific local factors influenced the negotiation by those living in Zhenjiang, including the individual makeup of the local polity. Local communities could have adopted steamship technology because there was a group of daring local entrepreneurs willing to embrace new and foreign technology even without support from the local officials or knowledge about the technology. Another reason was the city's geographical location, which made the people of Zhenjiang, with those along the Yangtze River, more likely to be impacted by the arrival of the steamship than those far from the Yangtze River. Local variables made Zhenjiang's negotiation with technology utterly distinctive.

By highlighting the significance of social context in technological change, I by no means intend to imply that I subscribe to a social constructivism that perceives the negotiation process as predetermined only by the variables within the context. Instead, I see people in general as capable of changing their experiences with technology by relying on their efforts, wisdom, and skills in capitalizing on opportunities while circumventing obstacles.[28]

Similar to people in other parts of the world (like India), those living in Zhenjiang encountered many obstacles with steamship technology. In some cases, the steamboat business owners were forced to deal with corrupt local officials by registering with foreign embassies to hide their Chinese identity. Nevertheless, through these rather unconventional methods, they rose above adversity, taking back their inner waterways from the Japanese immediately after the Qing dynasty loosened its grip on private ownership of steamboats. By specifically adopting the steamboat—so-called creole technology and relatively "old" technology in its countries of origin—they not only made it the most practical tool for transporting people via the country's small rivers but also achieved what cultural commentator Raymond Williams has suggested society must accomplish with any technology: to make it the extension of human capacity. Therefore, by depending on their own efforts, wisdom, and skills, these individuals were able to navigate the challenges and turn challenges into opportunities.[29]

It is undeniable that Chinese state authorities—including the Qing dynasty, warlords, and the Nationalist government—played major roles in the local population's negotiation with technology. According to Ritika Prasad, the experience of negotiation is characterized not by the specific changes and challenges people in a particular location face, but by the "combination of resources and constraints through which people could navigate them." If we apply Prasad's method of analysis to Zhenjiang, we find that neither the Qing dynasty nor the warlords were able to provide resources, either administrative or financial, for the local communities during the negotiation, despite the fact that some local officials under these authorities showed interest in using the new technology. In fact, just the opposite occurred. Both the Qing dynasty (which prohibited the use of steamboat for commoners) and the warlords (who maintained a predatory attitude toward tax collection) constrained the adoption of technology by the steamboat business owners. This combination of resources (or the lack thereof) and constraints forced them to struggle with new technology in isolation.[30]

The Nationalist government, however, not only altered the combination of resources and constraints but also extended its bureaucratic control into most aspects of ordinary people's lives, including experiences with new technology. It achieved that through aggressive state-making measures, including financially supporting the charity-based rescue group and directly overseeing the day-to-day steamboat transportation business. While doing so, the government gradually asserted its power over local society by pushing local organizations to the sideline. Because of these efforts, the Nationalist government made local people's negotiations with new technology no longer a "distinctly local matter," as they were before the end of the Qing dynasty. These findings have added more evidence, from the perspective of China's technological changes, to the claim that the Nationalist government became an entity similar to the "everyday state" seen in Japan, India, Egypt, and Pakistan during those countries' development of technology.[31]

Historians C. J. Fuller, Véronique Bénéï, and Salwa Ismail have discovered that for Japan, India, Egypt, and Pakistan, the major impact of the "everyday state" is often found in blurring the boundary between the state and society when people negotiate technologies. From our assessment, we can also see the similarity in that the boundary between the state and society was certainly disappearing in Zhenjiang when the Nationalist government enlarged the state's role in dealing with steamboat accidents and when it micromanaged every aspect of the settlement following a major explosion, including paying additional compensation following a disagreement between the victims' families and the local government. This study thus confirms what scholars like Prasenjit Duara have suggested about the Nationalist government being aggressive in state-making, deeply penetrating Chinese local society before the 1937 Sino-Japanese War.[32]

Therefore, as a part of global technological changes, the people of Zhenjiang negotiated steam navigation technology, a new and foreign technology produced in industrialized countries, in the early twentieth century. The negotiation occurred as local communities were subjected to the influence of various global changes—even aside from technology—and took place in a social context that contained multiple variables, some of which were detrimental to the process. Because of this, the local population faced clear challenges even as the technology provided some unprecedented opportunities for improving their daily lives. Adding to their difficulties was the lack of enthusiasm among the state authorities, with the exception of the Nationalist government, for allowing steamboat business owners to use foreign technology. Regardless, the people of Zhenjiang rose to the challenge. Through relentless efforts, by relying on their own abilities, they successfully navigated the challenges and made the new technology a useful addition to daily life. Through intense negotiation, they made it possible for their local communities to join China's technological transformation.

◆

China underwent an unprecedented historical transition characterized by its local society's intense negotiation with the global changes after the arrival of industrialized countries hastened the interaction between Chinese local society and the global processes—namely, the rise of modern imperialism, the acceleration of economic integration, and the spread of mechanized technology. As the negotiation took place in a local society that carried a unique set of variables, many of which had roots in China's long history and tradition, it not only led to profound human suffering but also generated various challenges as well as opportunities for local communities. Still, the people of China survived these changes. By successfully navigating the challenges posed by and seizing the opportunities afforded by global changes, they effected local changes that helped place China on its own path to modernity. As the result of the negotiation, global and local processes merged, enabling the global and the local to become a continuum.

NOTES

ARCHIVES AND PRIMARY SOURCES

INDEX

NOTES

INTRODUCTION

1. See similar discussion in Paul A. Cohen, *Discovering History in China: American Historical Writing on the Recent Chinese Past* (New York: Columbia University Press, 2010), xiii.

2. Frederic E. Wakeman, *Strangers at the Gate: Social Disorder in South China, 1839–1861* (Berkeley: University of California Press, 1966).

3. Lynn Hunt, *Writing History in the Global Era* (New York: W. W. Norton, 2014), 40.

4. Lea H. Wakeman, "Chinese Archives and American Scholarship on Modern Chinese History," in *Telling Chinese History: A Selection of Essays*, ed. Lea H. Wakeman (Berkeley: University of California Press, 2009), 315–329. The only book on the war in this period was James M. Polachek, *The Inner Opium War* (Cambridge, MA: Council on East-Asian Studies, Harvard University, 1992). Polachek did his work in the 1970s, studying the war with an emphasis on social history.

5. For a discussion of the growing interest in cultural studies, see the introduction by Timothy Brook and Bob Tadashi Wakabayashi in *Opium Regimes: China, Britain, and Japan, 1839–1952*, ed. Timothy Brook, Patrick Carr, and Maria Kefalas (Berkeley: University of California Press, 2000), 1–30; Carl A. Trocki, ed., *Opium, Empire, and the Global Political Economy: A Study of the Asian Opium Trade, 1750–950* (New York: Routledge, 1999); Yangwen Zheng, "The Social Life of Opium in China," *Modern Asian Studies* 37, no. 1 (2003): 1–39; Yangwen Zheng, *The Social Life of Opium in China* (Cambridge: Cambridge University Press, 2005).

6. See J. Y. Wong, *Deadly Dreams: Opium, Imperialism, and the Arrow War (1856–1860) in China*, Cambridge Studies in Chinese History, Literature, and Institutions (Cambridge: Cambridge University Press, 1998); Glenn Melancon, *Britain's China*

Policy and the Opium Crisis: Balancing Drugs, Violence, and National Honor, 1833–1840 (Burlington, VT: Ashgate, 2003); Harry Gregor Gelber, *Opium, Soldiers and Evangelicals: Britain's 1840–42 War with China, and Its Aftermath* (New York: Palgrave Macmillan, 2004).

7. James Louis Hevia, *English Lessons: The Pedagogy of Imperialism in Nineteenth-Century China* (Durham, NC: Duke University Press, 2003).

8. For the study of Qing officials' personal characters and morals, see Haijian Mao, *Qing Empire and the Opium War* (Cambridge: Cambridge University Press, 2016); for those who paid attention to cultural conflict, see Peter J. Kitson, *Forging Romantic China: Sino-British Cultural Exchange 1760–1840* (Cambridge: Cambridge University Press, 2013); Dennis Abrams, *The Treaty of Nanking* (New York: Chelsea House, 2011). See also Julia Lovell, *The Opium War: Drugs, Dreams and the Making of China* (London: Picador, 2011); Li Chen, *Chinese Law in Imperial Eyes: Sovereignty, Justice, and Transcultural Politics* (New York: Columbia University Press, 2016); Song-Chuan Chen, *Merchants of War and Peace British Knowledge of China in the Making of the Opium War* (Hong Kong: Hong Kong University Press, 2017); Stephen R. Platt, *Imperial Twilight: The Opium War and the End of China's Last Golden Age* (New York: Knopf Doubleday, 2018).

9. See Timothy Brook, *Collaboration: Japanese Agents and Local Elites in Wartime China* (Cambridge, MA: Harvard University Press, 2005); Diana Lary, *The Chinese People at War: Human Suffering and Social Transformation, 1937–1945* (Cambridge: Cambridge University Press, 2010); R. Keith Schoppa, *In a Sea of Bitterness: Refugees during the Sino-Japanese War* (Cambridge, MA: Harvard University Press, 2011); Sheila Miyoshi Jager and Rana Mitter, *Ruptured Histories: War, Memory, and the Post-Cold War in Asia* (Cambridge, MA: Harvard University Press, 2007).

10. G. William Skinner, "Marketing and Social Structure in Rural China, Part I," *Journal of Asian Studies* 24, no. 1 (1964): 3–40; William Skinner, "Marketing and Social Structure in Rural China, Part II," *Journal of Asian Studies* 24, no.2 (1965a): 195–228; William Skinner, "Marketing and Social Structure in Rural China, Part III," *Journal of Asian Studies* 24, no.3 (1965b): 363–399. See also G. William Skinner and Hugh D. R. Baker, *The City in Late Imperial China* (Stanford, CA: Stanford University Press, 1977), 211–218.

11. Carolyn Cartier finds Skinner's model lacking in attention to "human agency"; see Carolyn Cartier, "Origins and Evolution of a Geographical Idea: The Macroregion in China," *Modern China* 28, no. 1 (2002): 79–142. Those who questioned Skinner's model include Charles Patterson Giersch, "Cotton, Copper, and Caravans: Trade and the Transformation of Southwest China," in *Chinese Circulations: Capital, Commodities, and Networks in Southeast Asia,* ed. Eric Tagliacozzo and Wen-chin Chang (Durham, NC: Duke University Press, 2011), 39; Prasertkul Chiranan, *Yunnan Trade in the Nineteenth Century: Southwest China's Cross-Boundaries Functional System* (Bangkok: Chulalongkorn University Printing House, 1989). Those who criticized

Skinner include Barbara Sands and Ramon Myers, "The Spatial Approach to Chinese History: A Test," *Journal of Asian Studies* 45 (1986): 721–743; William T. Rowe, *Hankow: Commerce and Society in a Chinese City, 1796–1889* (Stanford, CA: Stanford University Press, 1984), 60–61. For Peng Zizhi's view, see Cartier, "Origins and Evolution of a Geographical Idea," 118. For Chinese scholars' views, see Kui Yingtao, *Zhongguo Jindai Butong Leixing Chengshi Zonghe Yanjiu* 中国近代不同类型城市综合研究 [Integrated study of different types of cities in modern China] (Chengdu: Sichuan daxue chubanshe, 1998), 4–5; Yeh-chien Wang, "Secular Trends in Rice Prices in the Yangzi Delta: 1638–1935," in *Chinese History in Economic Perspective*, ed. Thomas G. Rawski and Lillian M. Li (Berkeley: University of California Press, 1992), 35–68. For the new vision on locality, see Peter K. Bol, "地域史と後帝政國について –金華の場合" [Local history and Later Imperial China: The Jinhua case], *Chugoku-shakai to bunka* 中國-社會と文化 20 (2005): 6.

12. Joseph Esherick, "Harvard on China: The Apologetics of Imperialism," *Bulletin of Concerned Asian Scholars* 4, no. 4 (1972): 3–8, 9–16. On the other side of the debate, see Rhoads Murphey, "The Treaty Ports and China's Modernization," in *The Chinese City between Two Worlds*, ed. Mark Elvin and G. William Skinner (Stanford, CA: Stanford University Press, 1974), 17–72; Thomas G. Rawski, *Economic Growth in Prewar China* (Berkeley: University of California Press, 1989). For an example of a new study on treaty ports, see Pär Kristoffer Cassel, *Grounds of Judgment: Extraterritoriality and Imperial Power in Nineteenth-Century China and Japan* (Oxford: Oxford University Press, 2012).

13. Kaoru Sugihara, "The Resurgence of Intra-Asian Trade, 1800–1850," in *How India Clothed the World: The World of South Asian Textiles, 1500–1850*, ed. Giorgio Riello (Leiden: Brill, 2013), 139–168.

14. Takeshi Hamashita, "Tribute and Treaties: Maritime Asia and Treaty Port Network in the Era of Negotiations, 1800–1900," in *The Resurgence of East Asia: 500, 150 and 50 Year Perspectives*, ed. Giovanni Arrighi, Takeshi Hamashita, and Mark Selden (London: Routledge, 2003), 17–50.

15. As I see it, these facets are two integral parts of one system: a subsystem of transregional trade within the country operating within the entire system of China's long-distance trade that extended to all Asia, and from Asia to the rest of the world. Neither are they mutually exclusive nor separate from each other. It is this system in its entirety that directly tied northern borders with Southeast Asia, linked the southwestern region with neighboring states in east Asia, and allowed China to be connected, directly and indirectly, with other parts of the globe before the mid-nineteenth century.

16. A brief list of the works on major cities includes Hanchao Lu, *Beyond the Neon Lights: Everyday Shanghai in the Early Twentieth Century* (Berkeley: University of California Press, 1999); Susan Naquin, *Peking: Temples and City Life, 1400–1900* (Berkeley: University of California Press, 2000); Steven B. Miles, *The Sea of Learning:*

Mobility and Identity in Nineteenth-Century Guangzhou (Cambridge, MA: Harvard University Asia Center, 2006); Zwia Lipkin, *Useless to the State: "Social Problems" and Social Engineering in Nationalist Nanjing, 1927–1937* (Cambridge, MA: Harvard University Asia Center, 2006); David Bordwell, *Planet Hong Kong: Popular Cinema and the Art of Entertainment* (Cambridge, MA: Harvard University Press, 2000); Ruth Rogaski, *Hygienic Modernity: Meanings of Health and Disease in Treaty-Port China* (Berkeley: University of California Press, 2004); Cathryn H. Clayton, *Sovereignty at the Edge: Macau and the Question of Chineseness* (Cambridge, MA: Harvard University Asia Center, 2009).

17. Lu, *Beyond the Neon Lights;* Wen Hsin Yeh, *Shanghai Splendor: Economic Sentiments and the Making of Modern China, 1843–1949* (Berkeley: University of California Press, 2007); Bryna Goodman, *Native Place, City, and Nation: Regional Networks and Identities in Shanghai, 1853–1937* (Berkeley: University of California Press, 1995); Elizabeth J. Perry, *Shanghai on Strike: The Politics of Chinese Labor* (Stanford, CA: Stanford University Press, 1995); Yinjing Zhang, ed., *Cinema and Urban Culture in Shanghai, 1922–1943* (Stanford, CA: Stanford University Press, 1999); Gail Hershatter, *Dangerous Pleasures: Prostitution and Modernity in Twentieth-Century Shanghai* (Berkeley: University of California Press); Christian Henriot, *Prostitution and Sexuality in Shanghai: A Social History, 1849–1949* (New York: Cambridge University Press).

18. Qin Shao, *Culturing Modernity: The Nantong Model, 1890–1930* (Stanford, CA: Stanford University Press); Elisabeth Köll, *From Cotton Mill to Business Empire: The Emergence of Regional Enterprises in Modern China* (Cambridge, MA: Harvard University Asia Center, 2003); Hanchao Lu, "A Blessing in Disguise: Nanxun and China's Small Town Heritage," *Frontier of History in China* 8, no. 3 (2013): 434–454.

19. Mary Clabaugh Wright, *The Last Stand of Chinese Conservatism: The Tung-Chih Restoration, 1862–1874* (Stanford, CA: Stanford University Press, 1957); Joseph Richmond Levenson, *Confucian China and Its Modern Fate,* 3 vols. (Berkeley: University of California Press, 1958); Joseph Needham, *The Grand Titration: Science and Society in East and West* (London: Allen and Unwin, 1969), 190.

20. Wen-yuan Qian, *The Great Inertia: Scientific Stagnation in Traditional China* (London: Croom Helm, 1985); Jacques Gernet, *China and the Christian Impact: A Conflict of Cultures* (Cambridge: Cambridge University Press, 1985); Derk Bodde, *Chinese Thought, Society, and Science: The Intellectual and Social Background of Science and Technology in Pre-Modern China* (Honolulu: University of Hawai'i Press, 1991).

21. Francesca Bray, *Technology and Gender: Fabrics of Power in Late Imperial China* (Berkeley: University of California Press, 1997).

22. Benjamin A. Elman, *A Cultural History of Modern Science in China* (Cambridge, MA: Harvard University Press, 2006); Benjamin A. Elman, "'Universal Science' versus 'Chinese Science': The Changing Identity of Natural Studies in China, 1850–1930," *Historiography East and West* 1, no. 1 (2003): 68–116; Benjamin A. Elman, *On Their Own Terms: Science in China, 1550–1900* (Cambridge, MA: Harvard University Press, 2005).

23. Fa-ti Fan, *British Naturalists in Qing China: Science, Empire, and Cultural Encounter* (Cambridge, MA: Harvard University Press, 2004).

24. Jean-Claude Martzloff, *A History of Chinese Mathematics* (New York: Springer, 2006); Liam Matthew Brockey, *Journey to the East: The Jesuit Mission to China, 1579–1724* (Cambridge, MA: Belknap Press of Harvard University Press, 2007); Kent Deng, "Movers and Shakers of Knowledge in China during the Ming-Qing Period," in "Chinese Technological History: The Great Divergence," ed. Jerry Liu and Kent Deng, special issue, *History of Techonology* 29 (2009): 57–80; Jerry Liu, "Cultural Logics for the Regime of Useful Knowledge during the Ming and Early-Qing China *c.* 1400–1700," in Liu and Deng, "Chinese Technological History," 29–56.

25. Francesca Bray, *Technology and Society in Ming China, 1368–1644*, Historical Perspectives on Technology, Society, and Culture (Washington, DC: American Historical Association, 2000); Bray, *Technology and Gender*, 9n11; Francesca Bray, *Technology, Gender and History in Imperial China: Great Transformations Reconsidered, Asia's Transformations* (London: Routledge, 2013).

26. See Kwang-Ching Liu, *Anglo-American Steamship Rivalry in China, 1862–1874* (Cambridge, MA: Harvard University Press, 1962). A recent excellent study of railroads is Elisabeth Köll, *Railroads and the Transformation of China* (Cambridge, MA: Harvard University Press, 2019).

27. Anne Reinhardt, *Navigating Semi-Colonialism in China: Shipping, Sovereignty, and Nation-Building in China, 1860–1937* (Cambridge, MA: Harvard University Asia Center, 2018).

28. Ying Jia Tan, *Recharging China in War and Revolution, 1882–1955* (Ithaca, NY: Cornell University Press, 2021).

29. Martin Heijdra, "A Preliminary Note on Cultural Geography and Ming History," *Ming Studies* 34 (1995): 30–60. See a summary of Rowe's view in Linda Cooke Johnson, *Cities of Jiangnan in Late Imperial China* (Albany: State University of New York Press, 1993), 5; G. William Skinner, *The City in Late Imperial China* (Stanford, CA: Stanford University Press, 1977), 211, 16.

30. We usually consider the Opium War as two wars: 1839 to 1842 and 1856 to 1860. I am using the term "Opium War" to include both wars. For Wong's discussion of the definition, see J. Y. Wong, *Deadly Dreams: Opium, Imperialism, and the Arrow War (1856–1860) in China* (Cambridge: Cambridge University Press, 1998), 37. I believe the term "transregional trade" is more suitable than "interregional trade"; see Carolyn Cartier's use of the term in *Globalizing South China* (Oxford: Blackwell Publishers, 2001), 128.

31. For a discussion of neighborhoods, see Frederick W. Mote, *Imperial China, 900–1800* (Cambridge, MA: Harvard University Press, 1999), 762; Lu, *Beyond the Neon Lights*. For a discussion of similar residents in Changan, see John Friedmann,

"Reflections on Place and Place-Making in the Cities of China," *International Journal of Urban and Regional Research* 31, no. 2 (2007): 262–263. For a discussion of ethnic enclaves in Shanghai, see Goodman, *Native Place.* For Henri Lefebvre's term, see Henri Lefebvre, *The Production of Space* (Oxford: Blackwell, 1991). For a discussion of the teahouse in Sichuan, see Di Wang, *The Teahouse: Small Business, Everyday Culture, and Public Politics in Chengdu, 1900–1950* (Stanford: Stanford University Press, 2008). For a discussion on a similar vision on locality, see Peter K. Bol, "地域史," 6.

32. G. William Skinner, "Marketing."

33. C. A. Bayly, "Rallying around the Subaltern," in *Mapping Subaltern Studies and the Postcolonial,* ed. Vinayak Chaturvedi (London: Verso, 2012), 126.

34. Iriye's quotation comes from Bayly, "Rallying around the Subaltern," 126.

35. David Faure, "An Institutional View of Chinese Business," in *Chinese and Indian Business Historical Antecedents,* ed. Medha M. Kudaisya and Chin-Keong Ng (Leiden: Brill, 2009), 57.

36. For an exemplary work on Chinese state making, see Stephen R. Halsey, *Quest for Power: European Imperialism and the Making of Chinese Statecraft* (Cambridge, MA: Harvard University Press, 2015).

37. Clifford Geertz, *The Interpretation of Cultures: Selected Essays* (New York: Basic Books, 1973), 5–6, 9–10. Some good examples of such narrative history are R. Keith Schoppa, *Blood Road: The Mystery of Shen Dingyi in Revolutionary China* (Berkeley: University of California Press, 1998); William T. Rowe, *Crimson Rain: Seven Centuries of Violence in a Chinese County* (Stanford, CA: Stanford University Press, 2007); Jonathan D. Spence, *Return to Dragon Mountain: Memories of a Late Ming Man* (New York: Viking, 2007).

38. Quote from M. R. Somers and G. D. Gibson, "Reclaiming the Epistemological Other: Narrative and the Social Construction of Identity," in *Social Theory and the Politics of Identity,* ed. C. Calhooun (Oxford: Blackwell, 1994), 60–63. For discussion of "conceptual narrative" and "ontological narrative," see Margaret R. Somers, "Deconstructing and Reconstructing Class Formation Theory: Narrativity, Relational Analysis, and Social Theory," in *Reworking Class,* ed. John R. Hall (Ithaca, NY: Cornell University Press, 1997), 84.

39. Andre Gunder Frank thinks that a world system (or systems) emerged long before the sixteenth century; see Frank, *Reorient: Global Economy in the Asian Age.* Fernand Braudel believes that there were at least three world systems; see Fernand Braudel, *Civilization and Capitalism, 15th–18th Century,* 3 vols. (New York: Harper and Row, 1982), 24, 69. Ravi Arvind Palat and Immanuel Wallenstein also suggest that there existed multiple historical "world-systems"; see Ravi Arvind Palat and Immanual Wallerstein, "Of What World System Was Pre-1500 'India' a Part?," in *International Colloquium on "Merchants, Companies and Trade"* (Paris: Maison des

Sciences de l'homme, 1990). For a summary of Immanuel Wallenstein's main argument, see Bertrand Badie, Dirk Berg-Schlosser, and Leonardo Morlino (eds.), *International Encyclopedia of Political Science,* vol. 1 (Thousand Oaks, CA: Sage Publications, 2011), 2759.

40. Christopher I. Beckwith, *Empires of the Silk Road: A History of Central Eurasia from the Bronze Age to the Present* (Princeton, NJ: Princeton University Press, 2009); Susan Whitfield, *Life along the Silk Road* (Berkeley: University of California Press, 1999); Xinru Liu, *The Silk Road in World History* (Oxford: Oxford University Press, 2010); James A. Millward, *The Silk Road: A Very Short Introduction* (Oxford: Oxford University Press, 2013); Luce Boulnois, *Silk Road: Monks, Warriors and Merchants* (Hong Kong: Odyssey Books, 2004); Frances Wood, *The Silk Road: Two Thousand Years in the Heart of Asia* (Berkeley: University of California Press, 2002). For Chinese calling Rome (or Syria) Daqin, see Philip Jenkins, *The Lost History of Christianity: The Thousand-Year Golden Age of the Church in the Middle East, Africa, and Asia—and How It Died* (New York: Harper One, 2008), 64–68. For European experiences, see Jerry H. Bentley, *Old World Encounters: Cross-Cultural Contacts and Exchanges in Pre-Modern Times* (Oxford: Oxford University Press, 1993); John Prevas, *Envy of the Gods Alexander the Great's Ill-Fated Journey across Asia* (New York: Da Capo Press, 2004).

41. For the emergence of the maritime trade in the Indian Ocean, see K. N. Chaudhuri, *Trade and Civilisation in the Indian Ocean: An Economic History from the Rise of Islam to 1750* (Cambridge: Cambridge University Press, 1985), 34–62. For a discussion of China's economic prosperity during the Tang dynasty, see Kangying Li, *The Ming Maritime Trade Policy in Transition, 1368 to 1567* (Wiesbaden: Harrassowitz, 2010), 6.

42. Diana Lary, *Chinese Migrations: The Movement of People, Goods, and Ideas over Four Millennia* (Lanham, MD: Rowman and Littlefield, 2012), 53–56.

43. Li, *Ming Maritime Trade Policy,* 6.

44. Janet L. Abu-Lughod, *Before European Hegemony: The World System A.D. 1250–1350* (New York: Oxford University Press, 1989), 124–125; Martin Wolf, *Why Globalization Works* (New Haven, CT: Yale University Press, 2004), 100.

45. Anthony Reid, *Southeast Asia in the Age of Commerce 1450–1680: Expansion and Crisis,* vol. 2 (New Haven, CT: Yale University Press, 1993). For a study on the Muslim traders, see Ira M. Lapidus, *A History of Islamic Societies,* 3rd ed. (Cambridge: Cambridge University Press, 2014), 436.

46. José Eugenio Borao, *The Spanish Experience in Taiwan, 1626–1642: The Baroque Ending of a Renaissance Endeavor* (Hong Kong: Hong Kong University Press, 2009); Lapidus, *A History of Islamic Societies,* 438.

47. For McNeill's term "Magellan Exchange," see John McNeill, "From Magellan to Miti: Pacific Rim Economies and Pacific Island Ecologies since 1521," in *Pacific*

Centuries: Pacific and Pacific Rim Economic History since the Sixteenth Century, ed. Dennis O. Flynn, Lionel Frost, and A.J.H. Latham (London: Routledge, 1999). The quotation comes from Adam Smith, *The Wealth of Nations* (New York: Random House, 1937 [1776]), 590.

48. C. A. Bayly thinks this archaic phase was in place by the sixteenth century; the proto one was during the seventeenth and eighteenth centuries, and the modern one is since the nineteenth century. See C. A. Bayly, *The Birth of the Modern World, 1780–1914: Global Connections and Comparisons* (Malden, MA: Blackwell, 2004); A. G. Hopkins, *Globalization in World History* (New York: Norton, 2002), 1–10, 11–46.

49. Geoffrey C. Gunn, *First Globalization: The Eurasian Exchange, 1500 to 1800* (Lanham, MD: Rowman and Littlefield, 2003); Dennis O. Flynn and Arturo Giráldez, "Globalization Began in 1571," in *Globalization and Global History*, ed. Barry K. Gills and William R. Thompson (London: Routledge, 2006).

50. Kevin H. O'Rourke and Jeffrey G. Williamson, "When Did Globalization Begin," *European Review of Economic History* 6, no. 1 (2002): 23–50.

51. Economic historian David Landes is one of those who held this opinion; see Landes, *The Wealth and Poverty of Nations: Why Some Are So Rich and Some So Poor* (New York: W. W. Norton, 1999), 335–349.

52. For a continuation of the assumption, see Peter N. Miller, *The Sea: Thalassography and Historiography* (Ann Arbor: University of Michigan Press, 2013), 190. For work that contradicts the assumption, see Joseph Fletcher, "China and Trans Caspia, 1368–1884," in *The Chinese World Order: Traditional China's Foreign Relations*, ed. John K. Fairbank (Cambridge, MA: Harvard University Press, 1968), 16–17, 207.

53. Millward's findings are based on a broader definition of "Silk Road"; see James A. Millward, *Eurasian Crossroads: A History of Xinjiang* (New York: Columbia University Press, 2007), 77. For the supporting study, see Carol Benedict, *Golden-Silk Smoke: A History of Tobacco in China, 1550–2010* (Berkeley: University of California Press, 2011), 26.

54. John King Fairbank and S. Y. Teng, "On the Ch'ing Tributary System," *Harvard Journal of Asiatic Studies* 6, no. 2 (1941), 135–246. For the study that shows the Qing dynasty used various methods, see Peter C. Perdue, *China Marches West: The Qing Conquest of Central Eurasia* (Cambridge, MA: Harvard University Press, 2005). For a discussion of the emerging awareness, see Laura Newby, *The Empire and the Khanate: A Political History of Qing Relations with Khoqand c. 1760–1860* (Leiden: Brill, 2005), 6–10.

55. C. Guillot, Denys Lombard, and Roderich Ptak, *From the Mediterranean to the China Sea: Miscellaneous Notes* (Wiesbaden: Harrassowitz, 1998); Gang Deng, *Maritime Sector, Institutions, and Sea Power of Premodern China* (Westport, CT: Greenwood Press, 1999); Murray A. Rubinstein, *Taiwan: A New History* (Armonk, NY: M. E. Sharpe, 1998), 45–106.

56. John E. Wills, "Maritime Asia, 1500–1800: The Interactive Emergence of European Domination," *American Historical Review* 98, no. 1 (1993): 83; Gungwu Wang, "Merchants without Empire: The Hokkien Sojourning Communities," in *The Rise of Merchant Empires: Long-Distance Trade in the Early Modern World, 1350–1750*, ed. James D. Tracy (Cambridge: Cambridge University Press, 1990); Leonard Blussé, *Strange Company: Chinese Settlers, Mestizo Women, and the Dutch in Voc Batavia* (Dordrecht: Foris Publications, 1986).

57. Nakami Tatsuo, "Russian Diplomats and Mongol Independence, 1911–1915," in *Mongolia in the Twentieth Century: Landlocked Cosmopolitan*, ed. Stephen Kotkin and Bruce A. Elleman (Armonk, NY: M. E. Sharpe, 1999), 70.

58. For a discussion of Asian trade networks being based on the Chinese tributary system, see Takeshi Hamashita, "The Tribute Trade System and Modern Asia," in *Japanese Industrialization and the Asian Economy*, ed. A. J. H. Latham and Heita Kawakatsu (London: Routledge, 1994), 91–107; Hamashita, "Tribute and Treaties."

59. Frank Dikötter, *Exotic Commodities: Modern Objects and Everyday Life in China* (New York: Columbia University Press, 2006), 32.

60. Adam Smith, *Wealth of Nations*, 38–39.

61. Zhaojin Ji, *A History of Modern Shanghai Banking: The Rise and Decline of China's Finance Capitalism* (Armonk, NY: M. E. Sharpe, 2003), 28.

62. Dennis O. Flynn and Arturo Giráldez, "Money and Growth without Development: The Case of Ming China," in *Asia Pacific Dynamism, 1550–2000*, ed. Heita Kawakatsu and A. J. H. Latham (London: Routledge, 2000), 215; Dennis O. Flynn, "Precious Metals and Money, 1200–1800," in *Handbook of Key Global Financial Markets, Institutions and Infrastructure*, ed. Gerard Caprio, Douglas W. Arner, and Thorsten Beck (Boston: Academic Press, 2012), 221–234.

63. Takeshi Hamashita, *China, East Asia and the Global Economy: Regional and Historical Perspectives*, ed. Linda Grove and Mark Selden (London: Routledge, 2008), 39–56.

64. See similar discussion in Geoffrey Parker, "Crisis and Catastrophe: The Global Crisis of the Seventeenth Century Reconsidered (Ahr Forum)," *American Historical Review* 113, no. 4 (2008): 1053–1079. See also discussion in John Brooke, "Ecology," in *A Companion to Colonial America*, ed. Daniel Vickers (Malden, MA: Blackwell, 2003), 50.

65. David Brophy has recently cast doubt on Uyghur being a group in the eighteenth and the nineteenth centuries. See David John Brophy, *Uyghur Nation: Reform and Revolution on the Russia-China Frontier* (Cambridge, MA: Harvard University Press, 2016). For the dynasty's reliance on skillful rulership, see Evelyn Sakakida Rawski, *The Last Emperors: A Social History of Qing Imperial Institutions* (Berkeley: University of California Press, 1998). For the dynasty promoting empire building in Central Asia and Xinjiang, see James A. Millward, *Beyond the Pass: Economy, Ethnicity,*

and Empire in Qing Central Asia, 1759–1864 (Stanford, CA: Stanford University Press, 1998). For research on the Qianlong emperor, see Pamela Kyle Crossley, *A Translucent Mirror: History and Identity in Qing Imperial Ideology* (Berkeley: University of California Press, 1999). For a study of China under Qianlong, see Mark C. Elliott, *Emperor Qianlong: Son of Heaven, Man of the World* (New York: Longman, 2009).

66. Quotation comes from William Rowe, *China's Last Empire: The Great Qing* (Cambridge, MA: Harvard University Press), 287. For the Qing dynasty's competition against Muscovite Russia and Mongolian Zunghars, see Perdue, *China Marches West,* 1, 10. For a study of the Qing's dealing with "British" India, see Matthew W. Mosca, *From Frontier Policy to Foreign Policy: The Question of India and the Transformation of Geopolitics in Qing China* (Stanford, CA: Stanford University Press, 2013), 2–3.

67. For the Qing dynasty's immediate restoration of China's trading relations, see David C. Kang, *East Asia before the West: Five Centuries of Trade and Tribute* (New York: Columbia University Press, 2010), 119. For the Qing taking an "open door" approach, see Yangwen Zheng, *China on the Sea: How the Maritime World Shaped Modern China* (Leiden: Brill, 2012).

PART I • WAR AS A NEGATIVE FORM OF LIAISON

1. Halvard Buhaug and Nils P. Gleditsch, "The Death of Distance? The Globalization of Armed Conflict," in *Territoriality and Conflict in an Era of Globalization,* ed. Miles Kahler and Barbara F. Walter (Cambridge: Cambridge University Press, 2006), 187; Tarak Barkawi, *Globalization and War* (Lanham, MD: Rowman & Littlefield, 2006), xiii; Tarak Barkawi, "Connection and Constitution: Locating War and Culture in Globalization Studies," in *Globalization and Violence,* vol. 3, *Globalization War and Intervention,* ed. Paul James and Jonathan Friedman (London: Sage Publications, 2006), 28.

1 • PLACE, HISTORY, AND PEOPLE

1. Although Yangzhou was not on the river per se, it is usually considered a city along the Yangtze River, given its proximity and convenient access through the Grand Canal.

2. Changjiangliuyuguihuaban, *Jin Ri Chang Jiang* 今日长江 [Today's Yangtze River] (Beijing: Shuili dianli chubanshe, 1985), 2.

3. Robert M. Hartwell, "Demographic, Political, and Social Transformations of China, 750–1550," *Harvard Journal of Asiatic Studies* 42, no. 2 (1982): 365–442. Quotation comes from Gilbert Rozman, *Urban Networks in Ch'ing China and Tokugawa Japan* (Princeton, NJ: Princeton University Press, 1974), 217. See similar discussion in Bruce J. Jacobs, "Uneven Development: Prosperity and Poverty in Jiangsu," in *The Political Economy of China's Provinces: Comparative and Competitive Advantage,* ed. Hans J. Hendrischke and Chongyi Feng (London: Routledge, 1999), 114.

4. Zhang Hua, Yang Xiu, and Ji Shijia, eds., *Qing Dai Jiangsu Shi Gai* 清代江苏史概 [General history of Jiangsu during the Qing dynasty] (Nanjing: Nanjing University Press, 1990), 40–41; Dengao Long, *Jiangnan Shichang Shi: Shiyi Zhi Shijiu Shiji De Bianqian* 江南市场史: 十一至十九世纪的变迁 [History of Jiangnan market: 11th–19th-century transition] (Beijing: Qinghua University Press, 2003), 2.

5. Xu Boming, ed., *Wu Wenhua Gaiguan* 吴文化概观 [A survey of Wu culture] (Nanjing: Nanjing University Press, 1996), 6–7, 17; Zhenhe Zhou, *Zhongguo Lishi-wenhua Quyu Yanjiu* 中国历史文化区域研究 [Studies of Chinese regions of historical culture] (Shanghai: Fudan University Press, 1997), 29.

6. Fan Ran and Zhang Li, eds., *Jianghe Yaojin* 江河要津 [Rivers and streams at strategic points] (Nanjing: Jiangsu renmin chuban she, 2004), 6–7.

7. Yan Qilin, *Zhenjiang Shishu* 镇江史述 [Zhenjiang: A historical narrative] (Changchun: Jilin wenshi chubanshe, 2006), 14–22; Fan and Zhang, *Jianghe Yaojin,* 23–24, 56.

8. Yan, *Zhenjiang Shishu,* 69, 88, 91–92.

9. Yan, *Zhenjiang Shishu,* 91–93.

10. Fan and Zhang, *Jianghe Yaojin,* 45, 59–60; Yan, *Zhenjiang Shishu,* 99–108.

11. Fan and Zhang, *Jianghe Yaojin,* 42–47;Yan, *Zhenjiang Shishu,* 124–125.

12. Fan and Zhang, *Jianghe Yaojin,* 36; Yan, *Zhenjiang Shishu,* 131.

13. Fan and Zhang, *Jianghe Yaojin,* 76–78.

14. R. S. Cohen, *Chinese Studies in the History and Philosophy of Science and Technology,* trans. Kathleen Dugan and Jiang Mingshan (Dordrecht: Kluwer Academic Publishers, 1996), 305–306.

15. Fan and Zhang, *Jianghe Yaojin,* 77–78.

16. Yan, *Zhenjiang Shishu,* 197–198, 215–223.

17. Yan, *Zhenjiang Shishu,* 195–197.

18. Richard John Lufrano, *Honorable Merchants: Commerce and Self-Cultivation in Late Imperial China* (Honolulu: University of Hawai'i Press, 1997), 25; Leo Kwok-yueh Shin, *The Making of the Chinese State: Ethnicity and Expansion on the Ming Borderlands* (Cambridge: Cambridge University Press, 2006), 171; James Tong, *Disorder under Heaven: Collective Violence in the Ming Dynasty* (Stanford, CA: Stanford University Press, 1991), 143; William T. Rowe, *Hankow: Commerce and Society in a Chinese City, 1796–1889* (Stanford, CA: Stanford University Press, 1984), 52.

19. James Gerber and Lei Guang, *Agriculture and Rural Connections in the Pacific, 1500–1900* (Aldershot: Ashgate, 2006), 200; Susan Naquin and Evelyn Sakakida

Rawski, *Chinese Society in the Eighteenth Century* (New Haven, CT: Yale University Press, 1987), 143.

20. Wan Shengnan, ed., *Zhongguo Changjiang Liuyu Kaifa Shi* 中国长江流域开发史 [History of the development of the Yangtze valley in China] (Hefei: Huangshan shushe, 1997), 181–182; Linda Cooke Johnson, *Cities of Jiangnan in Late Imperial China,* SUNY Series in Chinese Local Studies (Albany: State University of New York Press, 1993), 172.

21. According to Philip Huang, "no one in China wore cotton fabric" in 1350; however, by 1850 "almost every peasant did"; see Philip C. Huang, *The Peasant Family and Rural Development in the Yangzi Delta, 1350–1988* (Stanford, CA: Stanford University Press, 1990), 47–48. Also, in Huang's estimation, 45 percent of households engaged in cloth weaving but 100 percent in Songjiang wove cloth by the mid-nineteenth century; see Huang, *Peasant Family,* 44–47; Robert C. Allen, Tommy Bengtsson, and Martin Dribe, *Living Standards in the Past: New Perspectives on Well-Being in Asia and Europe* (Oxford: Oxford University Press, 2005), 59.

22. Wan, *Changjiang Liuyu,* 359.

23. Yiqi and Li Weiqiao Pao, eds., *Wuhu Gangshi* 芜湖港史 [History of Wuhu port] (Hankou: Wuhan chubanshe, 1989), 26; Xu Zhengyuan, Xu Hongsheng, Wang Yimin, and Hu Minyi, *Wuhu Mishi Shulue* 芜湖米市述略 [Brief history of Wuhu rice market] (Beijing: Zhongguo zhanwang chuban she, 1988), 2–7; Wan, *Changjiang Liuyu,* 359.

24. Yan, *Zhenjiang Shishu,* 201; Fan and Zhang, *Jianghe Yaojin,* 80–82.

25. Paul J. Smith, *Taxing Heaven's Storehouse: Horses, Bureaucrats, and the Destruction of the Sichuan Tea Industry, 1074–1224* (Cambridge, MA: Council on East Asian Studies Harvard University, 1991); Di Wang, *Kua Chu Fengbi De Shijie: Changjiang Shangyou Quyu Shehui Yanjiu (1644–1911)* 跨出封闭的世界: 长江上游区域城市研究 [Striding out of an enclosed world: A study of society in the upper Yangtze region, 1644–1911] (Beijing: Zhonghua shuju, 2001), 36, 40–41, 250–253.

26. The quotation comes from Naquin and Rawski, *Chinese Society,* 194; see also Naquin and Rawski, *Chinese Society,* 194, 96, 215; Wang, *Kua Chu Fengbi De Shijie,* 199.

27. Wan, *Changjiang Liuyu,* 202, 74; Naquin and Rawski, *Chinese Society,* 86, 159.

28. Wan, *Changjiang Liuyu,* 363; Naquin and Rawski, *Chinese Society,* 62, 159.

29. Yan, *Zhenjiang Shishu,* 201; Fan and Zhang, *Jianghe Yaojin,* 81–83.

30. "Zhenjiang Shangye Shiliao 镇江商业史料" [Historical materials of Zhenjiang trade], in *Government Document no. 850000041* (Zhenjiang: Zhenjiang Municipal Government, unpublished), 4–5, 10–11.

31. Yan, *Zhenjiang Shishu,* 80–81, 98, 129–130, 203.

32. Yan, *Zhenjiang Shishu,* 237.

33. Yan, *Zhenjiang Shishu,* 80–81, 98, 129–130, 203.

34. Zhejiangdifangzhiban, ed., *Zhenjiang Shizhi 镇江市志* [History of Zhenjiang City] (Shanghai: Shanghai shehuikexue chubanshe, 1993), 1:587.

35. Yan, *Zhenjiang Shishu,* 152–154.

36. Zhejiangdifangzhiban, *Zhenjiang Shizhi,* 587.

37. For comparison, see Cao Shuji, "Qingdai Jiangsu chengshi renkou yanjiu 清代江苏城市人口研究" [On the city population of Jiangsu in the Qing dynasty], *Hangzhou shifan xueyuan xuebao (shehui kexue ban) 杭州师范学院学报(社会科学版)* [Journal of Hangzhou Teacher's College (social sciences edition)] 4, no. 4 (2002), 50–57; Yan, *Zhenjiang Shishu,* 72–73, 132–134.

38. Yan, *Zhenjiang Shishu,* 232–237.

39. Fan and Zhang, *Jianghe Yaojin,* 88–89.

40. Peter Ward Fay, *The Opium War, 1840–1842: Barbarians in the Celestial Empire in the Early Part of the Nineteenth Century and the War by Which They Forced Her Gates Ajar* (Chapel Hill: University of North Carolina Press, 1997), 55; David Bello, "Opium in Xinjiang and Beyond," in *Opium Regimes: China, Britain, and Japan, 1839–1952,* ed. Timothy Brook, Patrick Carr, and Maria Kefalas (Berkeley: University of California Press, 2000), 127–151; Iltudus Thomas Prichard, *The Administration of India from 1859–1868: The First Ten Years of Administration under the Crown* (London: Macmillan, 1869), 2:207.

41. Yangwen Zheng, *The Social Life of Opium in China* (Cambridge: Cambridge University Press, 2005), 90. However, Richard Von Glahn doubts that the impact of opium trade alone was the cause for silver drain; see Richard Von Glahn, *Fountain of ortune: Money and Monetary Policy in China, 1000–1700* (Berkeley: University of California Press, 1996), 246–257.

42. Mao Haijian, *Tian Chao Di Beng Kui 天朝的崩溃* [The Qing Empire and the Opium War] (Beijing: Sanlian shudian, 1995), 89–125.

43. For the Warlike Party, see Song-Chuan Chen, *Merchants of War and Peace: British Knowledge of China in the Making of the Opium War* (Hong Kong: Hong Kong University Press, 2017). For the public perception of the British, see Peter J. Kitson, *Forging Romantic China: Sino-British Cultural Exchange 1760–1840* (Cambridge: Cambridge University Press, 2013). For cultural clashes, see Robert A. Bickers, *The Scramble for China: Foreign Devils in the Qing Empire, 1832–1914* (London: Penguin, 2012). For the British public having mixed opinions toward the opium trade, see Stephen R. Platt, *Imperial Twilight: The Opium War and the End of China's Last Golden Age* (New York: Knopf Doubleday, 2018), 315.

44. Julia Lovell, *The Opium War: Drugs, Dreams and the Making of China* (London: Picador, 2011), 87; Harry Gregor Gelber, *Opium, Soldiers and Evangelicals: Britain's 1840–42 War with China, and Its Aftermath* (New York: Palgrave Macmillan, 2004), 102.

45. Jessie Gregory Lutz, *Opening China: Karl F. A. Gützlaff and Sino-Western Relations, 1827–1852* (Grand Rapids, MI: William B. Eerdmans Publishing Company, 2008), 104–108.

46. Immanuel Chung-yueh Hsèu, *The Rise of Modern China,* 4th ed. (Oxford: Oxford University Press, 1990), 185–188.

47. Gelber, *Opium, Soldiers and Evangelicals,* 125–127; Hsèu, *Rise of Modern China,* 185–188.

48. Gelber, *Opium, Soldiers and Evangelicals,* 126–127; Hsèu, *Rise of Modern China,* 189.

49. Wei Yuan, *Chinese Account of the Opium War,* trans. Edward Harper Parker (Shanghai: Kelly and Walsh, 1888), 66. Quoted from George Pottinger, *Sir Henry Pottinger: First Governor of Hong Kong* (New York: St. Martin's Press, 1997), 91.

2 • THE BATTLE OF ZHENJIANG

1. The quotation comes from Charles R. Low, *Soldiers of the Victorian Age* (London: Chapman and Hall, 1880), 1:242.

2. "Daoguang Renyin Bingshi Guanshu Huichao 道光壬寅兵事官书汇钞" [Collection of official memorials related to war in 1842 during the Daoguang reign], in *Licheng juan zhi er* 里乘卷之二 [Collection of documents] (Zhenjiang: Jiangsu shengli guoxue tushuguan, 1934–1937), 72, 75; "Renyin Bingshi Xuchao 壬寅兵事续钞" [Collection of writings related to war in 1842], in *Licheng juan zhi er,* 91, 96.

3. Low, *Soldiers of the Victorian Age,* 1:242.

4. "Daoguang Renyin Bingshi Guanshu," 49.

5. Qi Sihe, Lin Shuhui, and Shou Jiyu, *Ya Pian Zhan Zheng* 鸦片战争 [The Opium War] (Shanghai: Shengzhou guoguangshe, 1954), 6:373; "Daoguang Renyin Bingshi Guanshu," 50–51.

6. "Daoguang Renyin Bingshi Guanshu," 49–51.

7. "Daoguang Renyin Bingshi Guanshu," 52.

8. Qi et al., *Ya Pian Zhan Zheng,* 4:692; "Daoguang Renyin Bingshi Guanshu," 55–56.

9. "Daoguang Renyin Bingshi Guanshu," 57–58.

10. "Daoguang Renyin Bingshi Guanshu," 57–58.

11. "Daoguang Renyin Bingshi Guanshu," 57–58.

12. Qi et al., *Ya Pian Zhan Zheng,* 4:692; "Daoguang Renyin Bingshi Guanshu," 55–56.

13. "Daoguang Renyin Bingshi Guanshu," 63–64.

14. "Daoguang Renyin Bingshi Guanshu," 64–65.

15. W. D. Bernard and W. H. Hall, *Narrative of the Voyages and Services of the* Nemesis *from 1840 to 1843 and of the Combined Naval and Military Operations in China: Comprising a Complete Account of the Colony of Hong-Kong, and Remarks on the Character and Habits of the Chinese* (London: H. Colburn, 1845), 410–411.

16. Chen Qingnian, "Daoguang Yingjian Po Zhenjiang Ji 道光英舰破镇江记" [History of the British warship invading Zhenjiang], in *Document no. 850000175* (Zhenjiang: Zhenjiang Municipal Government, unpublished), 3–4; Fa Zhirui "Jingkou Fen Cheng Lu 京口偾城录" [Assault on Jingkou City] (repr., Taipei: Wenhai chubanshe, n.d.), 8–9.

17. Chen, "Daoguang Yingjian Po Zhenjiang Ji," 3–4; Fa, "Jingkou Fen Cheng Lu," 8–9.

18. Chen, "Daoguang Yingjian Po Zhenjiang Ji," 3–4; Fa, "Jingkou Fen Cheng Lu," 8–9.

19. Chen, "Daoguang Yingjian Po Zhenjiang Ji," 3–4; Fa, "Jingkou Fen Cheng Lu," 8–9.

20. Xia Xie and Gao Hongzhi, "Zhong Xi Ji Shi 中西纪事" [China and the West] (repr., Changsha: Yuelu shushe, n.d.).

21. "Daoguang Renyin Bingshi Guanshu," 47.

22. Chen, "Daoguang Yingjian Po Zhenjiang Ji," 3–4.

23. "Daoguang Renyin Bingshi Guanshu," 54–55.

24. Wen Qing, ed., "Chouban Yiwu Shimo, Daoguan Chao 筹办夷务始末, 道光朝" [Complete records on managing foreign affairs: Daoguang reign] (repr., Taipei: Wenhai chubanshe, n.d.); Chen, "Daoguang Yingjian Po Zhenjiang Ji," 8–9; "Daoguang Renyin Bingshi Guanshu," 45–46.

25. Zhong Rui, "Jingkou Baqi Zhi 京口八旗志" [History of eight banners in Jingkou] (repr., New York: Columbia University, n.d.); "Daoguang Renyin Bingshi Guanshu," 61.

26. "Daoguang Renyin Bingshi Guanshu," 60.

27. Chen, "Daoguang Yingjian Po Zhenjiang Ji," 7; Zhong, "Jingkou Baqi Zhi."

28. *The Oxford Learner's Dictionary* defines "panic" as "a sudden feeling of great fear that cannot be controlled and prevents [people] from thinking clearly." *The Oxford Learner's Dictionary of Academic English* (Oxford: Oxford University Press, 2014), s.v. "panic."

29. Chen, "Daoguang Yingjian Po Zhenjiang Ji," 7; Zhong, "Jingkou Baqi Zhi"; Fa, "Jingkou Fen Cheng Lu," 11–12.

30. "Daoguang Renyin Bingshi Guanshu," 48, 85.

31. "Daoguang Renyin Bingshi Guanshu," 48, 85.

32. Chen, "Daoguang Yingjian Po Zhenjiang Ji," 6; Yang Qi, "Chu Wei Cheng Ji 出围城记" [Exodus from a besieged city] (repr., Taipei: Wenhai chubanshe, n.d.), 73–75.

33. Fa, "Jingkou Fen Cheng Lu," 28–30; Zhu Shiyun, "Caojian Riji 草间日记" [Thatch-hut diary] (repr., Taipei: Wenhai chubanshe, n.d.), 118–119.

34. Fa, "Jingkou Fen Cheng Lu," 28–30; Zhu, "Caojian Riji," 118–119.

35. John Ouchterlony, *The Chinese War: An Account of All the Operations of the British Forces from the Commencement to the Treaty of Nanking* (London: Saunders and Otley, 1844), 400–401.

36. Chen, "Daoguang Yingjian Po Zhenjiang Ji," 12–13; "Renyin Bingshi Xuchao," 93–94.

37. Yang, "Chu Wei Cheng Ji," 79.

38. Chen, "Daoguang Yingjian Po Zhenjiang Ji," 12–13; Yang, "Chu Wei Cheng Ji," 79.

39. Chen, "Daoguang Yingjian Po Zhenjiang Ji," 11–12; Fa, "Jingkou Fen Cheng Lu," 34.

40. Fa, "Jingkou Fen Cheng Lu," 34; Chen, "Daoguang Yingjian Po Zhenjiang Ji," 11–12; "Daoguang Renyin Bingshi Guanshu," 69.

41. Yang, "Chu Wei Cheng Ji," 78–79.

42. Chen, "Daoguang Yingjian Po Zhenjiang Ji," 9–10; Luo Zhirang, "Daoguang Renyin Yingbing Fancheng Shi 道光壬寅英兵犯城事" [A record of the British soldiers invading the city in 1842], in *Document no. 85000021* (Zhenjiang: Zhenjiang Municipal Government, unpublished).

43. For criticism from Wei Yuan (魏源), a contemporary Qing scholar of the Modern Text School of classical learning, see Wei Yuan, *Chinese Account of the Opium War*, trans. Edward Harper Parker (Shanghai: Kelly and Walsh, 1888), 65.

44. Arthur A. T. Cunynghame, *An Aide-de-Camp's Recollections of Service in China, a Residence in Hong-Kong, and Visits to Other Islands in the Chinese Seas* (London: Saunders and Otley, 1844), 82.

45. Bernard and Hall, *Narrative of the Voyages and Services*, 410–411; Wei Yuan, "Sheng Wu Ji 圣武记" [The record of the Majesty's expedition] (repr., Beijing: Zhonghua shuju, n.d.); Wei, *Chinese Account*, 66. Quoted from Ouchterlony, *Chinese War*, 410–411.

46. Quoted from Cunynghame, *Aide-de-Camp's Recollections*, 83.

47. Cunynghame, *Aide-de-Camp's Recollections*, 84–85.

48. Arthur Waley, *The Opium War through Chinese Eyes* (London: Allen and Unwin, 1958), 199.

49. Waley, *Opium War*, 199.

50. Fa, "Jingkou Fen Cheng Lu," 27–30.

51. Fa, "Jingkou Fen Cheng Lu," 27–30.

52. Chen, "Daoguang Yingjian Po Zhenjiang Ji," 8; Zhu, "Caojian Riji," 118–119; "Renyin Bingshi Xuchao," 94.

53. Edward H. Cree and Michael Levien, *Naval Surgeon: The Voyages of Dr. Edward H. Cree, Royal Navy, as Related in His Private Journals, 1837–1856* (New York: E. P. Dutton, 1982), 97; Ouchterlony, *Chinese War*, 347.

54. Cree and Levien, *Naval Surgeon*, 98; Ouchterlony, *Chinese War*, 349–350.

55. Cree and Levien, *Naval Surgeon*, 83–89.

56. Fa, "Jingkou Fen Cheng Lu," 27–30.

57. Both Deshubu and Zhou Suo reported this; see "Daoguang Renyin Bingshi Guanshu," 67–69.

58. This was confirmed by both British and Chinese eyewitness; see Granville G. Loch, *The Closing Events of the Campaign in China the Operations in the Yang-Tze-Kiang and Treaty of Nanking* (London: J. Murray, 1843), 104; "Renyin Bingshi Xuchao," 91.

59. Chen, "Daoguang Yingjian Po Zhenjiang Ji," 8; Ouchterlony, *Chinese War*, 343–344; Cree and Levien, *Naval Surgeon*, 98.

60. Michael Adas, *Machines as the Measure of Men: Science, Technology, and Ideologies of Western Dominance* (Ithaca, NY: Cornell University Press, 1989), 186; Liu Hongliang, "Di Yici Yapian Zhanzheng Shiqi Zhong Ying Shuangfang Huopao De Jishu Bijiao 第一次鸦片战争时期中英双方火炮的技术比较" [Performance

differences of Chinese and British cannons during the First Opium War], *Qingshi yanjiu* 清史研究 [Study of Qing history], no. 3 (2006), 3–31.

61. "Tatar" is one of the terms the Europeans used for the Mongols. Harry Gregor Gelber, *Opium, Soldiers and Evangelicals: Britain's 1840–1842 War with China, and Its Aftermath* (New York: Palgrave Macmillan, 2004), 134.

62. Liu Hongliang, "Ming Qing Wangchao Hongyi Dapao De Shengshuai Shi Jiqi Wenti Yanjiu 明清王朝红夷大炮的盛衰史及其问题研究" [A history of rise and decline of Dutch cannons in Ming and Qing dynasties], *Haerbin gongye daxue xuebao, shehui kexue ban* 哈尔滨工业大学学报, 社会科学版 [Journal of Harbin Institute of Technology, social sciences], no. 1 (2005), 1–5.

63. Liu, "Ming Qing Wangchao"; He Libo, "Yapian Zhanzheng Shi Zhong Ying Shuangfang Wuqi Zhi Bijiao 鸦片战争时中英双方武器之比较" [Comparing weapons used by the Chinese and the British during the Opium War], http://www.zisi.net/htm/ztlw2/zggds/2005-05-10-20645.htm.

64. Loch, *Closing Events,* 113–115.

65. Chen, "Daoguang Yingjian Po Zhenjiang Ji," 12–13; Yang, "Chu Wei Cheng Ji," 93–94.

66. Cree and Levien, *Naval Surgeon,* 98.

67. Waley, *Opium War,* 208; Cree and Levien, *Naval Surgeon,* 98; Ouchterlony, *Chinese War,* 358–360; "Daoguang Renyin Bingshi Guanshu," 66, 67, 72, 75, 77.

68. Cunynghame, *Aide-de-Camp's Recollections,* 97.

69. Cree and Levien, *Naval Surgeon,* 98; Ouchterlony, *Chinese War,* 349.

70. Cree and Levien, *Naval Surgeon,* 98; Waley, *Opium War,* 203; Chen, "Daoguang Yingjian Po Zhenjiang Ji," 12–13; Cunynghame, *Aide-de-Camp's Recollections,* 96.

71. Cree and Levien, *Naval Surgeon,* 100–101; Loch, *Closing Events,* 112–113.

72. Cree and Levien, *Naval Surgeon,* 100–101; Alexander Murray, *Doings in China. Being the Personal Narrative of an Officer Engaged in the Late Chinese Expedition, from the Recapture of Chusan in 1841, to the Peace of Nankin in 1842* (London: R. Bentley, 1943), 173–174.

73. Loch, *Closing Events,* 112–113; Chen, "Daoguang Yingjian Po Zhenjiang Ji," 13.

74. Yang, "Chu Wei Cheng Ji," 80–81.

75. Chen, "Daoguang Yingjian Po Zhenjiang Ji," 13, 18.

76. The first quotation comes from Cunynghame, *Aide-de-Camp's Recollections,* 99–100, 103–104.

77. Ouchterlony, *Chinese War,* 399–400.

78. Murray, *Doings in China,* 174–175; Wei, "Sheng Wu Ji," 65.

79. Fa, "Jingkou Fen Cheng Lu," 44–46; Chen, "Daoguang Yingjian Po Zhenjiang Ji," 13.

3 • THE INVADER AND THE INVADED

1. Gough quotation from Robert S. Rait, *The Life and Campaigns of Hugh, First Viscount Gough, Field-Marshal* (Westminster: A. Constable, 1903), 275.

2. Quotation from Andrew Holmes, *Carl Von Clausewitz's On War: A Modern-Day Interpretation of a Strategy Classic* (Oxford: Infinite Ideas, 2010), 71.

3. I have borrowed the term "everyday forms of resistance" from James Scott, *Weapons of the Weak: Everyday Forms of Peasant Resistance* (New Haven, CT: Yale University Press, 1985).

4. Armine S. H. Mountain, *Memoirs and Letters of the Late Colonel Armine S. H. Mountain, C.B., Aide-de-Camp to the Queen and Adjutant-General of Her Majesty's Forces in India* (London: Longman, Brown, Green, Longmans and Roberts, 1857), 209.

5. *The Last Year in China, to the Peace of Nanking as Sketched in Letters to His Friends* (London: Longman, Brown, Green, and Longmans, 1843), 177; Mountain, *Memoirs,* 208.

6. Granville G. Loch, *The Closing Events of the Campaign in China the Operations in the Yang-Tze-Kiang and Treaty of Nanking* (London: J. Murray, 1843), 107, 109–110.

7. Arthur A. T. Cunynghame, *An Aide-de-Camp's Recollections of Service in China, a Residence in Hong-Kong, and Visits to Other Islands in the Chinese Seas* (London: Saunders and Otley, 1844), 103.

8. Edward H. Cree and Michael Levien, *Naval Surgeon: The Voyages of Dr. Edward H. Cree, Royal Navy, as Related in His Private Journals, 1837–1856* (New York: E. P. Dutton, 1982), 105.

9. Cunynghame, *Aide-de-Camp's Recollections,* 104; Chen Qingnian, "Daoguang Yingjian Po Zhenjiang Ji Ji 道光英舰破镇江记" [History of the British warship invading Zhenjiang], in *Document no. 850000175* (Zhenjiang: Zhenjiang Municipal Government, unpublished), 13; Xunhe Zhao, "Dantu Zhanglu 丹徒掌录" [Anecdotal record of Dantu County] (Zhenjiang: Zhenjiang Municipal Archives, unpublished); "Daoguang Renyin Bingshi Guanshu Huichao 道光壬寅兵事官书汇钞" [Collection of official memorials related to war in 1842 during the Daoguang reign], in *Licheng juan zhi er 里乘卷之二* [Collection of documents] (Zhenjiang: Jiangsu shengli guoxue tushuguan, 1934–1937), 74.

10. Loch, *Closing Events,* 124.

11. Fa Zhirui, "Jingkou Fen Cheng Lu 京口偾城录" [Assault on Jingkou City] (repr., Taipei: Wenhai chubanshe, n.d.), 1; Chen, "Daoguang Yingjian Po Zhenjiang Ji," 17; Yang Qi, "Chu Wei Cheng Ji 出围城记" [Exodus from a besieged city] (repr., Taipei: Wenhai chubanshe, n.d.), 81–83.

12. Cree and Levien, *Naval Surgeon,* 102.

13. Mountain, *Memoirs,* 208; Cree and Levien, *Naval Surgeon,* 103–104; Duncan MacPherson, *The War in China. Narrative of the Chinese Expedition, from Its Formation in April, 1840, to the Treaty of Peace in August, 1842* (London: Saunders and Otley, 1843), 269.

14. MacPherson, *War in China,* 374–376; Rait, *Life and Campaigns,* 274–275; Cree and Levien, *Naval Surgeon,* 105.

15. John Francis Davis, *China, during the War and since the Peace* (London: Longman, Brown, Green, and Longmans, 1852), 1:248–249; MacPherson, *War in China,* 270; Mountain, *Memoirs,* 209.

16. Alexander Murray, *Doings in China: Being the Personal Narrative of an Officer Engaged in the Late Chinese Expedition, from the Recapture of Chusan in 1841, to the Peace of Nankin in 1842* (London: R. Bentley, 1843), 181–182; Davis, *China, during the War,* 248–249.

17. Cunynghame, *Aide-de-Camp's Recollections,* 105–106.

18. Cunynghame, *Aide-de-Camp's Recollections,* 103; MacPherson, *War in China,* 390–391.

19. Loch, *Closing Events,* 109–110.

20. Cunynghame, *Aide-de-Camp's Recollections,* 104; MacPherson, *War in China,* 404–405.

21. Cree and Levien, *Naval Surgeon,* 105; MacPherson, *War in China,* 394–395; "Daoguang Renyin Bingshi Guanshu," 72–73.

22. MacPherson, *War in China,* 394–395; Mountain, *Memoirs,* 205–207.

23. Cunynghame, *Aide-de-Camp's Recollections,* 106–107, 18; Mountain, *Memoirs,* 207.

24. Davis, *China, during the War,* 249; Cree and Levien, *Naval Surgeon,* 106.

25. For details of looting by British troops in Amoy, see Harry Gregor Gelber, *Opium, Soldiers and Evangelicals: Britain's 1840–42 War with China, and Its Aftermath* (New York: Palgrave Macmillan, 2004), 128. For details of looting by British troops in the Summer Palace in Beijing, see James Louis Hevia, *English Lessons: The Pedagogy of*

Imperialism in Nineteenth Century China (Durham, NC: Duke University Press, 2003), 76–82.

26. Cree and Levien call those looters the "most expert and desperate plunderers"; see Cree and Levien, *Naval Surgeon,* 104. Cunynghame considers them "the greatest thieves and the most disorderly of any in the world"; see Cunynghame, *Aide-de-Camp's Recollections,* 184–185; Loch, *Closing Events,* 116.

27. Loch, *Closing Events,* 120–121.

28. This was indicated by several memorials from local officials to Emperor Daoguang, as well as in the statement of a Chinese eyewitness. "Daoguang Renyin Bingshi Guanshu," 67, 69, 72, 75; "Renyin Bingshi Xuchao 壬寅兵事续钞" [Collection of writings related to war in 1842], in *Licheng juan zhi er* 里乘卷之二 [Collection of documents] (Zhenjiang: Jiangsu shengli guoxue tushuguan, 1934–1937), 96; Yang, "Chu Wei Cheng Ji," 84–86; Arthur Waley, *The Opium War through Chinese Eyes* (London: Allen and Unwin, 1958), 211.

29. Henry Keppel, *A Sailor's Life under Four Sovereigns* (London: Macmillan, 1899), 270; MacPherson, *War in China,* 420–421.

30. Chen, "Daoguang Yingjian Po Zhenjiang Ji," 18; MacPherson, *War in China,* 418–419;

31. Chen, "Daoguang Yingjian Po Zhenjiang Ji," 17; Yang, "Chu Wei Cheng Ji," 81–83; Murray, *Doings in China,* 183.

32. "Daoguang Renyin Bingshi Guanshu," 76; "Renyin Bingshi Xuchao," 98.

33. Cunynghame, *Aide-de-Camp's Recollections,* 110–111; "Daoguang Renyin Bingshi Guanshu," 89.

34. Waley, *Opium War,* 219–220.

35. Waley, *Opium War,* 216.

36. Fa, "Jingkou Fen Cheng Lu," 58–61.

37. Chen, "Daoguang Yingjian Po Zhenjiang Ji," 18; Zhu Shiyun, "Caojian Riji 草间日记" [Thatch-hut diary] (repr., Taipei: Wenhai chubanshe, n.d.), 141.

38. Waley, *Opium War,* 218; MacPherson, *War in China,* 269.

39. Cunynghame, *Aide-de-Camp's Recollections,* 109–110, 112–113.

40. Yang, "Chu Wei Cheng Ji," 96, 99.

41. Quoted from Fa, "Jingkou Fen Cheng Lu," 58–61.

42. Fa, "Jingkou Fen Cheng Lu," 58–61.

43. Cunynghame, *Aide-de-Camp's Recollections,* 109–110. The quotation comes from Mathew T. Brundage, "In Opposition to a Dark and Ignorant People: British Domestic Representations of He Chinese, 1834–1850" (master's thesis, Kent State University, 2007), 41–42.

44. Quote from Loch, *Closing Events,* 119–120.

45. Murray, *Doings in China,* 180, 86; Chen, "Daoguang Yingjian Po Zhenjiang Ji," 13.

46. Chen, "Daoguang Yingjian Po Zhenjiang Ji," 26.

47. Chen, "Daoguang Yingjian Po Zhenjiang Ji," 26; "Daoguang Renyin Bingshi Guanshu," 77.

48. Zhao Erxun, ed., "Qiying Zhuan 耆英传" [Biography of Qiying], in *Qing Shi Gao 清史稿* [Draft history of the Qing dynasty] (repr., Hongkong: Xianggang wenxue yanjiushe, 1960); Yang, "Chu Wei Cheng Ji," 96, 99.

49. Zhao, "Qiying Zhuan"; "Chen Huacheng Ji Hailing Zhuan 陈化成暨海龄传" [History of Chen Huacheng and Hailing], in *Qing Shi Gao* (repr., Hongkong: Xianggang wenxue yanjiushe, 1960).

50. Zhao, "Qiying Zhuan"; "Chen Huacheng Ji Hailing Zhuan."

51. "Chen Huacheng Ji Hailing Zhuan"; Diyilishidanganguan, *Ya Pian Zhan Zheng Dang an Shi Liao 鸦片战争档案史料* [Archival materials of the Opium War] (Shanghai: Shanghai renmin chubanshe, 1987), 5:31, 5:721; 6:56, 6:77, 6:90, 6:99, 6:250.

52. Chen, "Daoguang Yingjian Po Zhenjiang Ji," 26–28.

PART II • COMMERCIAL NETWORKS AND TRANSREGIONAL TRADE

1. For an estimation of Zhenjiang's economic activities, see "Sushu Caizheng Shuoming Shu 苏属财政说明书" [Manual of Jiangsu provincial finance] (Dalian Damiao Library, unpublished).

2. Kris James Mitchener and Hans-Joachim Voth, "Trading Silver for Gold: Nineteenth-Century Asian Exports and the Political Economy of Currency Unions," in *Costs and Benefits of Economic Integration in Asia,* ed. Robert J. Barro and Chong-hwa Yi (Oxford: Oxford University Press, 2010), 126–131; A. J. H. Latham and Heita Kawakatsu, *Intra-Asian Trade and the World Market* (London: Routledge, 2006), 1–3.

3. Sanjay Subramanyam, "Introduction," in *The Cambridge World History: The Construction of a Global World, 1400–1800 CE,* vol. 6, part I, *Foundations,* ed. Jerry H. Bentley, Sanjay Subramanyam, and Merry E. Wiesner-Hanks (Cambridge: Cambridge University Press, 2015), 1–26.

4 • THE NINETEENTH-CENTURY TRANSFORMATION

1. Immanuel C. Y. Hsü, *The Rise of Modern China*, 6th ed. (Oxford: Oxford University Press, 2000), 210–211.

2. Rhoads Murphey, *Shanghai, Key to Modern China* (Cambridge, MA: Harvard University Press, 1953), 70.

3. Jiang Tianfeng, ed., *Changjiang Hangyunshi: Jindai Bufen 长江航运史: 近代部分* [The history of shipping along the Yangtze River: Modern era] (Beijing: Renminjiaotong chubanshe, 1992), 60–61.

4. Wang Tieyai, *Zhongwai Jiuyuezhang Huibian 中外旧约章汇编* [Collections of the Sino–foreign treaties], vol. 3 (Beijing: Sanlian shudian, 1957), microform; Tōa Dōbunkai, *Shina ShōBetsu Zenshi* 支那省別全誌 [Chinese history classified by province] (Tokyo: Tōa Dōbunkai, 1917–1920), 15:22.

5. Tōa Dōbunkai, *Shina ShōBetsu Zenshi*, 15–22; Ming Guang, ed., *Zhenjiang Wenshi Ziliao, Wenhua Jiaoyu Zhuanji 镇江文史资料, 文化教育专辑* [Zhenjiang local history, culture and education edition], ed. Li Zhizhong and Ma Mingyi (Zhenjiang: Zhenjiang wenshi ziliao bianzuan weiyuanhui, 1990), 17: 242–246.

6. Fan Ran and Zhang Li, eds., *Jiang He Yao Jin 江河要津* [Rivers and streams at strategic points] (Nanjing: Jiangsu renmin chubanshe, 2004), 102–104.

7. Jiang, *Changjiang Hangyunshi*, 61–63; Dai Huizhen, ed., *Anhui Xiandaishi 安徽现代史* [A contemporary history of Anhui] (Hefei: Anhui renmin chubanshe, 1997), 16–17.

8. John W. Maclellan, *The Story of Shanghai from the Opening of the Port to Foreign Trade* (Shanghai: North-China Herald Office, 1889), 5–6; Rhoads Murphey, *The Treaty Ports and China's Modernization: What Went Wrong?* (Ann Arbor: University of Michigan Center for Chinese Studies, 1970), 40.

9. Murphey, *Shanghai*, 64–65.

10. Mao Jiaqi, ed., *Hengkanchenglin Cechengfeng, Changjiang Xiayiu Jindaiihua De Guiji 横看成林侧成峰, 长江下游城市近代化的轨迹* [Regards as forest when looking horizontally, regards as the peak of mountain when looking vertically: The path of urban modernization in the Lower Yangtze] (Nanjing: Jiangsu renmin chubanshe, 1993), 22–23.

11. After 1683, goods like Manchurian soybeans had already been transported on this sea route. However, more and more traders began to use the route after Shanghai became a major commercial center on the east coast. Yingtao Kui, *Zhongguo Jindai Butong Leixing Chengshi Zonghe Yanjiu 中国近代不同类型城市综合研究* [Integrated study of different types of cities in modern China] (Chengdu: Sichuan daxue chubanshe, 1998), 5.

12. Kui, *Zhongguo Jindai,* 5; Murphey, *Shanghai,* 100.

13. Kui Yingtao and Xie Fang, "Shanghai Kaibu Yu Changjiang Liuyu Chengshi Jindai Hua 上海开埠与长江流域城市近代化" [Opening of Shanghai port and urban modernity in the Yangtze valley] (Shanghai: Shanghai shehui kexueyuan, unpublished), 1, 9–11.

14. Hajime Kose, "Inter-Regional Trade in China: An Analysis of Chinese Maritime Customs Statistics," in *Intra-Asian Trade and Industrialization: Essays in Memory of Yasukichi Yasuba,* ed. A. J. H. Latham and Heita Kawakatsu (London: Routledge, 2009), 197–198.

15. See a similar discussion in Sherman Cochran, *Chinese Medicine Men: Consumer Culture in China and Southeast Asia* (Cambridge, MA: Harvard University Press, 2006), 4–8. See also Sherman Cochran, "Chinese and Overseas Chinese Business History: Three Challenges to the State of the Field," in *Chinese and Indian Business: Historical Antecedents,* ed. Medha M. Kudaisya and C. K. Ng (Leiden: Brill, 2009), 11–16.

16. G. William Skinner and Hugh D. R. Baker, *The City in Late Imperial China* (Stanford, CA: Stanford University Press, 1977), 211–218; William T. Rowe, *Hankow: Commerce and Society in a Chinese City, 1796–1889* (Stanford, CA: Stanford University Press, 1984), 12, 68, 76.

17. See a similar discussion in Lillian M. Li, *Fighting Famine in North China: State, Market, and Environmental Decline, 1690s–1990s* (Stanford, CA: Stanford University Press, 2007), 197; Rhoads Murphey, "The Treaty Ports and China's Modernization," in *The Chinese City between Two Worlds,* ed. Mark Elvin and G. William Skinner (Stanford, CA: Stanford University Press, 1974), 18; Wu Chengming, ed., *Zhongguo Zi Ben Zhu Yi Yu Guo Nei Shi Chang 中国资本主义和国内市场* [Chinese capitalism and domestic markets] (Xindian: Gufeng chubanshe, 1987), 265.

18. Takeshi Hamashita, Linda Grove, and Mark Selden, *China, East Asia and the Global Economy: Regional and Historical Perspectives* (London: Routledge, 2008), 12.

19. Takeshi Hamashita, "Tribute and Treaties: Maritime Asia and Treaty Port Networks in the Era of Negotiations, 1800–1900," in *The Resurgence of East Asia: 500, 150 and 50 Year Perspectives,* ed. Giovanni Arrighi, Takeshi Hamashita, and Mark Selden (London: Routledge, 2003), 19–20; Takeshi Hamashita, *Kindai Chūgoku No Kokusaiteki Keiki: Chō Kōbōeki Shisutemu to Kindai Ajia* [China-centered world order in modern times: Tribute trade system and modern Asia] (Tokyo: Tokyo University Press, 1990), 25–47l.

20. Hamashita, "Tribute and Treaties," 19–20.

21. Takeshi Hamashita, *Chōkō Shisutemu to Kindai Ajia* [Tribute system and modern Asia] (Tokyo: Iwanami Shoten, 1997), 23–24, 31; Takeshi Hamashita, "The Tribute Trade System and Modern Asia," in Hamashita, *China, East Asia and the*

Global Economy: Regional and Historical Perspectives, ed. Linda Grove and Mark Selden (London: Routledge, 2008), 12–26; Hamashita, "Tribute and Treaties," 19–20.

22. Quoted from Gary Hamilton, *Commerce and Capitalism in Chinese Societies* (London: Routledge, 2006), 116. For a discussion of Ishikawa Ryota's study, see Yu-ju Lin and Madeleine Zelin, *Merchant Communities in Asia, 1600–1980: Perspectives in Economic and Social History* (London: Pickering and Chatto, 2015), 95–108; Kazuko Furuta, "Kobe Seen as Part of the Shanghai Trading Network: The Role of Chinese Merchants in the Re-export of Cotton Manufactures to Japan," in *Japan, China, and the Growth of the Asian International Economy, 1850–1949,* ed. Kaoru Sugihara (Oxford: Oxford University Press, 2005), 40; Naosaku Uchida, *Nihon Kakyo Shakai No Kenkyu* [Studies in overseas Chinese communities in Japan] (Tokyo: Dobunkan, 1949); Michiaki Miyata, "Shinmatsu Ni Okeru Gaikoku Boekihin Ryutsu Kiko No Ichi Kosatsu: Girudo No Ryutsu Shihai O Chushin to Shite" [A study on the foreign trade organization in late Qing China with special reference to the control of distribution system by the Guild Organization], *Sundai Shigaku* 52 (1981), 73–102; Naoto Kagotani, *Ajia Kokusai Tsusho Chitsujo to Kindai Nihon* [The international commercial order of Asia and modern Japan] (Nagoya: Nagoya Daigaku Shuppankai, 2000).

23. Furuta, "Kobe Seen as Part of the Shanghai Trading Network," 40–41.

24. Hamashita, "Tribute and Treaties," 23; Takeshi Hamashita, "Overseas Chinese Financial Networks," in *The Chinese Overseas,* ed. Hong Liu. London (New York: Routledge, 2006), 167; Takeshi Hamashita, "Choko to Joyaku: Higashi Ajia Kaikojo O Meguru Kosho No Jidai, 1834–1894" [Tribute and treaties: Diplomatic negotiations and the open ports of East Asia, 1834–1894], *Ajia Kara Hangaeru 3, Shuhen Kara No Rekishi* [Asian perspectives 3: History from the periphery], ed. Mizoguchi Yuzo, Hiraishi Naoteru, and Miyajima Hiro (Tokyo: Daigaku Shuppankai, 1994). The quotation comes from Furuta, "Kobe Seen as Part of the Shanghai Trading Network," 42–43.

25. "Zhenjiang Shangye Shiliao 镇江商业史料" [Historical materials of Zhenjiang trade], in *Government Document no. 850000041* (Zhenjiang: Zhenjiang Municipal Government, unpublished), 6; House of Commons, "Reports of Journeys in China and Japan by Members of Her Majesty's Consular Service and Others, 1869–1892," in *Irish University Press Area Studies Series, British Parliamentary Papers: China* (Shannon: Irish University Press, 1971), 65.

26. "Zhenjiang Shangye Shiliao," 4–5.

27. "Zhenjiang Shangye Shiliao," 4–5.

28. The rhymes are Zhenjiang Nianyutao (镇江鲇鱼套), Guazhou liuqihao (瓜洲六七濠), and Yangzhou xiannu miao (扬州仙女庙). "Zhenjiang Shangye Shiliao," 6.

29. "Zhenjiang Shangye Shiliao," 66.

30. Here is a breakdown of each type of northern commodities that went to Japan and Southeast Asia: 2,080,000 *dan* (each *dan* equals 110 pounds) of bean cakes;

595,000 *dan* of sesame; 50,000 *dan* of peanut and sesame oil; and 80,000 *dan* of daylily. "Zhenjiang Shangye Shiliao," 24–26, 48.

31. Brown sugar was also known as the "greenish-colored sugar" (*qingtang* 青糖).

32. Luzon Island (吕宋岛) was part of the Philippines and a Spanish colony before 1898, and a colony of the United States from 1898 until 1946. Indonesia was a Dutch-controlled territory before World War II. Guo Xiaoyi, ed., *Jiangsu Hangyun Shi: Jindai Bufen 江苏航运史, 近代部分* [History of navigation and water transportation in Jiangsu: Modern period] (Beijing: Remin jiaotong chubanshe, 1990), 49–50; Zhengxiejiangsushengweiyuanhui, *Jiangsu Gongshang Jingji Shiliao 江苏工商经济史料* [Historical records on industries and commerce in Jiangsu] (Nanjing: Jiangsu wenshi ziliao bianjibu, 1989), 31:149; Zhenjiangshigongshanglian, "Zhenjiang Tang, Beiguo Ye De Bainian Xingshuai 镇江糖, 北货业的百年兴衰" [Rise and decline of the business of sugar and northern commodities in a hundred years], in *Zhenjiang Wenshi Ziliao 镇江文史资料* [Zhenjiang local history] (Zhenjiang: Zhenjiang shi zhengxie, 1989), 97–98.

33. Guo, *Jiangsu Hangyun Shi,* 47.

34. Guo, *Jiangsu Hangyun Shi,* 66–68.

35. Guo, *Jiangsu Hangyun Shi,* 50–51.

36. Guo, *Jiangsu Hangyun Shi,* 68. Zhengxiejiangsushengweiyuanhui, *Jiangsu Gongshang Jingji Shiliao,* 31, 153.

37. Zhejiangshidifangzhibangongshi, *Zhenjiang Yaolan 镇江要览* [General history of Zhenjiang] (Nanjing: Jiangsu guji chubanshe, 1989), 70–71.

38. Guo, *Jiangsu Hangyun Shi,* 24–26.

39. Guo, *Jiangsu Hangyun Shi,* 68. Zhengxiejiangsushengweiyuanhui, *Jiangsu Gongshang Jingji Shiliao,* 31, 153.

5 • BROKERING MULTIPLE COMMERCIAL NETWORKS

1. Granovetter, Mark, "Economic Action and Social Structure: The Problem of Embeddedness," in *The New Economic Sociology: A Reader,* ed. Frank Dobbin (Princeton, NJ: Princeton University Press, 2004), 245–274

2. On "shang" meaning "merchant," see John Lust, *Chinese Popular Prints* (Leiden: E. J. Brill, 1996), 309. On the adoption of the word "bang," see Peter J. Golas, "Early Ch'ing Guilds," in *The City in Late Imperial China,* ed. G. William Skinner (Stanford, CA: Stanford University Press, 1977), 555–580. On the range of meanings of "bang," see Bryna Goodman, *Native Place, City, and Nation: Regional Networks and Identities in Shanghai, 1853–1937* (Berkeley: University of California Press, 1995), 39.

3. For Peng Chang's view on merchants, see Carolyn Cartier, *Globalizing South China* (Oxford: Blackwell Publishers, 2001), 128; Wellington K. K. Chan, "Chinese Entrepreneurship since Its Late Imperial Period," in *The Invention of Enterprise: Entrepreneurship from Ancient Mesopotamia to Modern Times,* ed. D. S. Landes, Joel Mokyr, and William J. Baumol (Princeton, NJ: Princeton University Press, 2010), 484.

4. Chan, "Chinese Entrepreneurship," 484. For a discussion of Skinner's view, see Gary Hamilton, *Commerce and Capitalism in Chinese Societies* (London: Routledge, 2006), 59–63.

5. Yang Yongquan, ed., *Zhongguo Shi Da Shang Bang Tan Mi 中国十大商帮探秘* [Exploring the mystery of the ten largest merchant groups in China] (Beijing: Qiye guanli chubanshe, 2005).

6. During the second half of the nineteenth century, Shanxi merchants provided financial loans to local entrepreneurs. See Madeleine Zelin, *The Merchants of Zigong: Industrial Entrepreneurship in Early Modern China* (New York: Columbia University Press, 2005), 77–80. For a discussion of Shaanxi merchants, see Antonia Finnane, *Speaking of Yangzhou: A Chinese City, 1550–1850* (Cambridge, MA: Harvard University Asia Center, 2004), 52. Shanxicaijingdaxue, *Jinshang Yu Zhongguo Shangye Wenming 晋商与中国商业文明* [Shaanxi merchants and the Chinese business culture] (Beijing: Jingji guanli chubanshe, 2008).

7. Li Gang and Zhao Pei, *Dahua Shanshang 大话陕商* [Speaking of Shaanxi merchant group] (Xian: Shaanxi renmin chubanshe, 2007).

8. Zheng Jiajie and Gao Ling, *Mei Li Hui Shang: "Wu Hui Bu Cheng Shang" 魅力徽商: "无徽不成商"* [The charm of Huizhou merchants: "There is no business without the Huizhou merchants"] (Beijing: Beijing gongye daxue chubanshe, 2007).

9. For details, see Chen Xuewen, *Longyou Shangbang Yanjiu: Jinshi Zhongguo Zhuming Shangbang Zhiyi 龙游商帮研究: 近世中国著名商帮之一* [A study of the Zhejiang merchant group: One of the well-known merchant groups in modern China] (Hangzhou: Hangzhou chubanshe, 2004). See also Fan Jinmin and Xia Aijun, *Dongting Shangbang 洞庭商帮* [Suzhou merchant group] (Hefei: Huangshan shushe, 2005).

10. Zhiyuan Fang, *Jiangyou Shangbang 江右商帮* [Jiangxi merchant group] (Hong Kong: Zhonghua shuju, 1995). In Menchang County (Hubei), the merchant group were in control of most of the county's transport and marketing of commodities; see William T. Rowe, *Crimson Rain: Seven Centuries of Violence in a Chinese County* (Stanford, CA: Stanford University Press, 2007), 62.

11. Linsun Cheng, *Banking in Modern China: Entrepreneurs, Professional Managers and the Development of Chinese Banks, 1897–1937* (Cambridge: Cambridge University Press, 2003), 227–228; Susan Mann Jones, "The Ningpo Pang and Financial Power at Shanghai," in *The Chinese City between Two Worlds,* ed. Mark Elvin and G. William Skinner (Stanford, CA: Stanford University Press, 1974), 73–96; Kathy Le Mons Walker,

Chinese Modernity and the Peasant Path: Semi-Colonialism in the Northern Yangzi Delta (Stanford, CA: Stanford University Press, 1999), 92.

12. Li Xinsheng, *Lushang Wenhua Yu Zhongguo Shangbang Wenhua 鲁商文化与中国商帮文化* [The culture of Shandong merchants and Chinese trading blocs] (Jinan: Shandong renmin chubanshe, 2010).

13. Su Wenjing, *Minshang Wenhua Lun 闽商文化论* [On Fujian merchant culture] (Beijing: Zhonghua shuju, 2010); Tan Jiangwei, *Putianshi Wenshi Ziliao 莆田市文史资料* [Local history of Putian City], vol. 2 (Fuzhou: Fujian renmin chubanshe, 2003).

14. For Peng Chang's view, see Cartier, *Globalizing South China,* 128; cf. Hamilton, *Commerce and Capitalism,* 59–63.

15. William T. Rowe, *Hankow: Commerce and Society in a Chinese City, 1796–1889* (Stanford, CA: Stanford University Press, 1984), 71.

16. Michael Tsang-Woon Tsin, *Nation, Governance, and Modernity in China: Canton, 1900–1927* (Stanford, CA: Stanford University Press, 1999), 20. See discussion in Joseph Esherick and Mary B. Rankin, *Chinese Local Elites and Patterns of Dominance* (Berkeley: University of California Press, 1990), 333.

17. Carol Benedict, *Golden-Silk Smoke: A History of Tobacco in China, 1550–2010* (Berkeley: University of California Press, 2011), 54.

18. Cartier, *Globalizing South China,* 128–132.

19. See discussion in Cartier, *Globalizing South China,* 77; Sucheta Mazumdar, *Sugar and Society in China: Peasants, Technology, and the World Market* (Cambridge, MA: Harvard University Asia Center, 1998), 70–75.

20. Chin-Keong Ng, *Boundaries and Beyond: China's Maritime Southeast in Late Imperial Times* (Singapore: NUS Press, 2017); Steven B. Miles, *Upriver Journeys: Diaspora and Empire in Southern China, 1570–1850* (Cambridge, MA: Harvard University Asia Center, 2017).

21. Guo Xiaoyi, ed., *Jiangsu Hangyun Shi: Jindai Bufen 江苏航运史, 近代部分* [History of navigation and water transportation in Jiangsu: Modern period] (Beijing: Remin jiaotong chubanshe, 1990), 50–51.

22. Guo, *Jiangsu Hangyun Shi,* 50–51

23. Guo, *Jiangsu Hangyun Shi,* 57.

24. Guo, *Jiangsu Hangyun Shi,* 57.

25. Guo, *Jiangsu Hangyun Shi,* 58; Zhenjiangshigongshanglian, "Zhenjiang Tang, Beiguo Ye De Bainian Xingshuai 镇江糖, 北货业的百年兴衰" [Rise and decline of

the business of sugar and northern commodities in a hundred years], in *Zhenjiang Wenshi Ziliao* 镇江文史资料 [Zhenjiang local history] (Zhenjiang: Zhenjiang shi zhengxie, 1989), 121–122.

26. Guo, *Jiangsu Hangyun Shi,* 58.

27. Guo, *Jiangsu Hangyun Shi,* 58–59.

28. Guo, *Jiangsu Hangyun Shi,* 54–55.

29. The word *ya* (牙) became associated with them during the Sui and Tang dynasties, after their activities were sanctioned by the dynasties. Afterward, names such as *yakuai* (牙侩), *yaru* (牙入), *yaji* (牙纪), *yazi* (牙子), *yalang* (牙郎), and *yakuai* (牙侩), which all meant "broker," appeared in records. These middlemen continued to play an important role in long-distance trade, despite the changes in names over time in the ensuing dynasties of Song, Yuan, and Ming. For instance, they were called "common folks' guide" (*yinling baixing* 引领百姓), "manager" (*jingji* 经纪), and "broker" (*hanglao* 行老), before *yahang* was finally adopted in the Ming dynasty. Rajeswary Ampalavanar Brown, *Chinese Business Enterprise* (London: Routledge, 1996), 1: 445; Susan Mann, *Local Merchants and the Chinese Bureaucracy, 1750–1950* (Stanford, CA: Stanford University Press, 1987), 29–51; Rowe, *Hankow,* 70, 187–188.

30. The fee was called *yaqian* (牙钱). Mann, *Local Merchants,* 29–51; Rowe, *Hankow,* 70, 187–188.

31. "Qing Shengzu Shi Lu Xuan Ji 清圣祖实录选辑" [Selections of Emperor Kangxi's record], (repr., Tatong shuju, n.d.); Peng Zeyi and Wang Renyuan, *Zhongguo Yanye Shi Guoji Xueshu Taolun Hui Lunwen Ji* 中国盐业史国际学术讨论会论文集 [International symposium on Chinese salt industry] (Chengdu: Sichuan renmin chubanshe, 1991), 346.

32. Guo, *Jiangsu Hangyun Shi,* 7–8, 68; Zhengxiejiangsushengweiyuanhui, *Jiangsu Gong Shang Jing Ji Shi Liao* 江苏工商经济史料 [Historical records on industries and commerce in Jiangsu] (Nanjing: Jiangsu zhengxie, 1989), 31:153.

33. Zhengxiejiangsushengweiyuanhui, *Jiangsu Gong Shang,* 31:153.

34. Guo, *Jiangsu Hangyun Shi,* 56; Zhenjiangshigongshanglian, "Zhenjiang Tang, Beiguo Ye," 99.

35. Guo, *Jiangsu Hangyun Shi,* 70.

36. Guo, *Jiangsu Hangyun Shi,* 54–55.

37. Guo, *Jiangsu Hangyun Shi,* 69–70.

38. Guo, *Jiangsu Hangyun Shi,* 70–71.

39. Guo, *Jiangsu Hangyun Shi,* 71–72.

40. Guo, *Jiangsu Hangyun Shi,* 7–8.

41. This is similar to what happened in Hankou; see Rowe, *Hankow,* 70–71.

42. Guo, *Jiangsu Hangyun Shi,* 54–56, 60; Zhenjiangshigongshanglian, "Zhenjiang Tang, Beiguo Ye," 101–102.

43. Guo, *Jiangsu Hangyun Shi,* 60.

44. Guo, *Jiangsu Hangyun Shi,* 60–61.

45. Guo, *Jiangsu Hangyun Shi,* 59.

46. Guo, *Jiangsu Hangyun Shi,* 59.

47. Guo, *Jiangsu Hangyun Shi,* 54–55.

48. Guo, *Jiangsu Hangyun Shi,* 52–53; Zhenjiangshigongshanglian, "Zhenjiang Tang, Beiguo Ye," 99–100.

49. Guo, *Jiangsu Hangyun Shi,* 52–53.

50. Guo, *Jiangsu Hangyun Shi,* 59–62.

51. Guo, *Jiangsu Hangyun Shi,* 59–62.

52. Guo, *Jiangsu Hangyun Shi,* 62.

53. Guo, *Jiangsu Hangyun Shi,* 61.

54. Guo, *Jiangsu Hangyun Shi,* 63–64.

55. Guo, *Jiangsu Hangyun Shi,* 63–64.

56. Guo, *Jiangsu Hangyun Shi,* 64.

57. Guo, *Jiangsu Hangyun Shi,* 65.

58. Guo, *Jiangsu Hangyun Shi,* 65.

6 • THE SHANGHAI COMMERCIAL NETWORK

1. Takeshi Hamashita, *East Asia and the Global Economy: Regional and Historical Perspectives,* ed. Mark Selden and Linda Grove, trans. Frank Baldwin (New York: Routledge, 2008), 167.

2. Maria Fusaro, "Cooperating Mercantile Networks in the Early Modern Mediterranean," *Economic History Review* 65 (2012): 702.

3. The term "interfaces" is from David Carvajal de la Vega, "Merchant Networks in the Cities of the Crown of Castile," *Commercial Networks and European Cities: 1400–1800*, ed. Andrea Caracausi and Christof Jeggle (London: Pickering and Chatto, 2014), 2.

4. Jaruko Furuta, "Kobe Seen as Part of the Shanghai Trading Network: The Role of Chinese Merchants in the Re-export of Cotton Manufactures to Japan," in *Japan, China, and the Growth of the Asian International Economy, 1850–1949*, ed. Kaoru Sugihara (Oxford: Oxford University Press, 2005), 29–32.

5. Furuta, "Kobe Seen as Part of the Shanghai Trading Network," 29–31.

6. Shin ya Sugiyama and Linda Grove, *Commercial Networks in Modern Asia* (London: Routledge, 2013), 55. Quoted from Michiaki Miyata, "Shinmatsu Ni Okeru Gaikoku Boekihin Ryutsu Kiko No Ichi Kosatsu: Girudo No Ryutsu Shihai O Chushin to Shite" [A study on the foreign trade organization in late Qing China with special reference to the control of distribution system by the Guild Organization], *Sundai Shigaku* 52 (1981): 75.

7. For Furuta's view, see Furuta, "Kobe Seen as Part of the Shanghai Trading Network," 43; Takeshi Hamashita, *Chugoku Kindai Keizaishi Kenkyu* [Economic history of modern China] (Tokyo: Tokyo Daigaku Toyo Bunka Kenkyujo, 1989), 99.

8. Takeshi Hamashita, "Overseas Chinese Financial Networks and Korea," in *The Chinese Overseas*, ed. Hong Liu (London: Routledge, 2006), 218–223.

9. "Zhenjiang Shangye Shiliao 镇江商业史料" [Historical materials of Zhenjiang trade], in *Government Document no. 850000041* (Zhenjiang: Zhenjiang Municipal Government, unpublished), 9, 19; Alan Baumler, *The Chinese and Opium under the Republic: Worse Than Floods and Wild Beasts* (Albany: State University of New York Press, 2007), 14.

10. "Zhenjiang Shangye Shiliao," 9–10.

11. "Zhenjiang Shangye Shiliao," 9–10, 32–33.

12. Timothy Brook and Bob Tadashi Wakabayashi, *Opium Regimes: China, Britain, and Japan, 1839–1952* (Berkeley: University of California Press, 2000), 272; "Zhenjiang Shangye Shiliao," 32–33; Zhengxiejiangsushengweiyuanhui, *Jiangsu Gong Shang Jing Ji Shi Liao 江苏工商经济史料* [Historical records on industries and commerce in Jiangsu] (Nanjing: Jiangsu zhengxie, 1989), 148.

13. "Zhenjiang Shangye Shiliao," 33.

14. "Zhenjiang Shangye Shiliao," 32–33.

15. "Zhenjiang Shangye Shiliao," 34.

16. "Zhenjiang Shangye Shiliao," 35–36.

17. Yongming Zhou, *Anti-Drug Crusades in Twentieth-Century China: Nationalism, History, and State Building* (Lanham, MD: Rowman and Littlefield, 1999), 27; "Zhenjiang Shangye Shiliao," 36. European-style banking emerged in China roughly in 1897 but appeared in Zhenjiang around 1910; see discussion in Xinwei Peng, *A Monetary History of China* (Bellingham: Western Washington University Press, 1994), 2:831.

18. "Zhenjiang Shangye Shiliao," 36. For further discussion, see Linsun Cheng, *Banking in Modern China: Entrepreneurs, Professional Managers and the Development of Chinese Banks, 1897–1937* (New York: Cambridge University Press, 2003).

19. "Zhenjiang Shangye Shiliao," 36. For a description of *qianzhuang* in Hankou, see William T. Rowe, *Hankow: Commerce and Society in a Chinese City, 1796–1889* (Stanford, CA: Stanford University Press, 1984), 161.

20. Wang Shuhuai, *Zhongguo Xiandaihua De Quyu Yanjiu. Jiangsusheng, 1860–1916 中国现代化的区域研究, 江苏省* [Region studies of Chinese modernization, Jiangsu province, 1860–1916] (Nangang: Zhongyang yanjiuyuan, 1984), 48:326.

21. "Zhenjiang Shangye Shiliao," 36–37.

22. "Zhenjiang Shangye Shiliao," 36–37.

23. "Zhenjiang Shangye Shiliao," 37; Rowe, *Hankow,* 160.

24. "Zhenjiang Shangye Shiliao," 37.

25. "Zhenjiang Shangye Shiliao," 38.

26. "Zhenjiang Shangye Shiliao," 38; Peter J. Golas, "Early Ch'ing Guilds," in *The City in Late Imperial China* (Stanford, CA: Stanford University Press, 1977), 555–557. Cited from Zhang Yan, *Qingdai Shehui Jingjishi Yanjiu 清代社会经济史研究* [Social and economic history of the Qing dynasty] (Beijing: Beijing shifandaxue chubanshe, 2010), 997–1048.

27. For a discussion of Xu Dixin's and Wu Chenming's research, see Christine Moll-Murata, "Chinese Guilds from the Seventeenth to the Twentieth Centuries: An Overview," *International Review of Social History* 53, no. S16 (2008): 245–247.

28. For a discussion of the studies, see Xu Dixin and Wu Chengming, eds., *Chinese Capitalism, 1522–1840* (Basingstoke: Macmillan, 2000), 181–183. For Li Hua's estimation, see "Da Qing Shengzu Ren (Kangxi) Huangdi Shilu 大清圣祖仁（康熙）皇帝实录" [The veritable records of the reign of the Kangxi emperor] (repr., Taipei: Huawen Shuju, n.d.), 59–60. For a discussion of L. Eve Armentrout Ma's study, see Marjolein t'Hart and Dennis Bos, eds., *Humour and Social Protest* (Cambridge: Cambridge University Press, 2007), 20.

29. Quoted from Rowe, *Hankow,* 264.

30. Rowe, *Hankow,* 59, 61, 255.

31. The first quotation is from Xiaoqun Xu, *Chinese Professionals and the Republican State: The Rise of Professional Associations in Shanghai, 1912–1937* (Cambridge: Cambridge University Press, 2001), 83–86. The second quotation is from Bryna Goodman, *Native Place, City, and Nation: Regional Networks and Identities in Shanghai, 1853–1937* (Berkeley: University of California Press, 1995), 39.

32. Di Wang, *The Teahouse: Small Business, Everyday Culture, and Public Politics in Chengdu, 1900–1950* (Stanford: Stanford University Press, 2008), 59.

33. Wang, *The Teahouse*, 59.

34. Wang, *The Teahouse, 59;* "Zhenjiang Shangye Shiliao," 38–40.

35. Zhaojin Ji, *A History of Modern Shanghai Banking: The Rise and Decline of China's Finance Capitalism* (Armonk, NY: M. E. Sharpe, 2003), xxv; "Zhenjiang Shangye Shiliao," 42–43.

36. "Zhenjiang Shangye Shiliao," 42–46.

37. "Zhenjiang Shangye Shiliao," 42–43.

38. "Zhenjiang Shangye Shiliao," 38–40, 42–43.

39. Wei Jianyou, *Zhongguo Jindai Huobi Shi 中国近代货币史* [The history of China's modern currency] (Shanghai: Qunlian chubanshe, 1955), 29; Yang Duanliu, ed., *Qingdai Huobi Jinrong Shigao 清代货币金融史稿* [A draft history of money and finance under the Qing dynasty] (Beijing: Sanlian shudian, 1962), 74.

40. Each two-four ingot weighing 52 taels (each tael equals 50 grams) had a purity that qualified it for an added value of 2.5 taels (2 taels being equal to 5 coins), so it became 52.5 taels in value when assessed against fine silver (*wenyin* 纹银), the standard silver used by the Qing dynasty; each Zhenjiang two-seven ingot that weighed the same had a purity that would qualify it for an additional 2.7 taels of value when assessed against *wenyin.* "Zhenjiang Shangye Shiliao," 42–44; Wei, *Zhongguo Jindai Huobi Shi,* 29; Cheng Bin, "Anqing Jiuying 安庆旧影" [History of Anqing], (Anqing: Anqing Municipal Archives, unpublished), 143–144.

41. Zhongguorenminyinhang, *Zhonghua Minguo Huobishi Ziliao: 1912–1927 中华民国货币史资料: 1912–1927* [Materials on the monetary history of republican China: 1912–1927] (Shanghai: Shanghai renmin chubanshe, 1986), 1:689.

42. Wei, *Zhongguo Jindai Huobi Shi,* 29; Yang, *Qingdai Huobi,* 74.

43. "Zhenjiang Shangye Shiliao," 42–43.

44. The nickname for the Spanish silver dollar was *guiyuan* (规元). The conversion began by adding 2.7 taels of added value to each ingot from Zhenjiang that was worth 52 taels, to arrive at 54.7 taels. Then, 98 percent of that 54.7 taels was considered its actual value. "Zhenjiang Shangye Shiliao," 43–44.

45. Wei, *Zhongguo Jindai Huobi Shi,*" 29; Cheng, "Anqing Jiuying," 143–144.

46. "Zhenjiang Shangye Shiliao," 44.

47. Hong Jiaguan, Wang Xinxin, and Li Anding, *Shanghai Jinrong Zhi 上海金融志* [Shanghai Financial Chronicle] (Shanghai: Shanghai Academy of Social Sciences Press, 2003), 112–113.

48. "Zhenjiang Shangye Shiliao," 42–44.

49. "Zhenjiang Shangye Shiliao," 42–4

50. Zhengxiejiangsushengweiyuanhui, *Jiangsu Gong Shang Jing Ji Shi Liao 江苏工商经济史料* [Historical records on industries and commerce in Jiangsu] (Nanjing: Jiangsu zhengxie, 1989), 31:156–157.

51. Zhengxiejiangsushengweiyuanhui, *Jiangsu Gong Shang,* 31:155; "Zhenjiang Zhanqian Zhanhou Jiaotong Qingkuang 镇江战前战后交通情况" [Zhenjiang's transportation condition before and after the war], *Shiye xinbao 实业新报* [China enterprises daily news], January 10, 1939.

52. Zhengxiejiangsushengweiyuanhui, *Jiangsu Gong Shang,* 31:155–157.

53. Zhengxiejiangsushengweiyuanhui, *Jiangsu Gong Shang,* 5; "Zhenjiang Haiguan Maoyi Lunlue 镇江海关贸易论略" [General view of trade through Zhenjiang customs], *Zhenjiang Difangzhi Ziliao Xuanji 镇江地方志资料选辑* [Selected collection of Zhenjiang local history materials] (Zhenjiang: Zhenjiang difangzhi bangongshi, 1987), 35.

54. Kui Yingtao, *Zhongguo Jindai Butong Leixing Chengshi Zonghe Yanjiu 中国近代不同类型城市综合研究* [Integrated study of different types of cities in modern China] (Chengdu: Sichuan daxue chubanshe, 1998), 5; Yang, *Qingdai Huobi,* 73.

55. Yang, *Qingdai Huobi,* 28.

PART III • NEGOTIATING TECHNOLOGY

1. Quoted from Ritika Prasad, *Tracks of Change: Railways and Everyday Life in Colonial India,* (Daryaganj: Cambridge University Press, 2015), 3. For Claude S. Fischer's criticism of technological determinism, see Claude S. Fischer, *America Calling: A Social History of the Telephone to 1940* (Berkeley: University of California Press, 1992), 8. I use the term here to mean "physical objects and artifacts," such as steamships and railroads; see Wiebe E. Bijker, Thomas Parke Hughes, and T. J. Pinch, *The Social Construction of Technological Systems: New Directions in the Sociology and History of Technology* (Cambridge, MA: MIT Press, 2012), xli–xlii.

2. Prasad hints that such a negotiation is a global phenomenon; see Prasad, *Tracks of Change,* 20.

7 • STEAM NAVIGATION AS A MEANS OF DOMINANCE

1. A steamship could access the river's major tributaries to reach the rivers Gan, Han, Xiang, the Jialing, and Min. See Rhoads Murphey, *Shanghai, Key to Modern China* (Cambridge, MA: Harvard University Press, 1953), 93–94.

2. Jiang Tianfeng, ed., *Changjiang Hangyunshi: Jindai Bufen 长江航运史: 近代部分* [History of navigation and water transportation along the Yangtze River: Modern era] (Beijing: Renmin jiaotong chubanshe, 1992), 82–83; Kwang-Ching Liu, *Anglo-American Steamship Rivalry in China, 1862–1874* (Cambridge, MA: Harvard University Press, 1962), 9–10, 15.

3. Jiang, *Changjiang Hangyunshi,* 24, 29, 82–85.

4. Liu, *Anglo-American Steamship Rivalry,* 10, 112–113; Jiang, *Changjiang Hangyunshi,* 85–86.

5. Jiang, *Changjiang Hangyunshi,* 37–51.

6. Jiang, *Changjiang Hangyunshi,* 86–90.

7. Liu, *Anglo-American Steamship Rivalry,* 15; Albert Feuerwerker, *China's Early Industrialization: Sheng Hsuan-Huai (1844–1916) and Mandarin Enterprise* (Cambridge, MA: Harvard University Press, 1958), 281.

8. Jiang, *Changjiang Hangyunshi,* 62–63, 87, 163–165; Liu, *Anglo-American Steamship Rivalry,* 29–35, 113.

9. The chemist was Xu Shou (徐寿) and the mathematician was Hua Hengfang (华蘅芳). David Wright, *Translating Science: The Transmission of Western Chemistry into Late Imperial China, 1840–1900* (Leiden: Brill, 2000), 31–34.

10. Anhuiwenshiziliaobianjibu, *Jianghuai Gongshang 江淮工商* [Industry and commerce in Jiangsu and Anhui], vol. 28 of *Anhui Wenshi Ziliao 安徽文史资料* [Anhui local history] (Hefei: Anhui renmin chubanshe, 1988), 95–97.

11. Anhuiwenshiziliaobianjibu, *Jianghuai Gongshang,* 95–97; Anqingwenshiziliaobianjibu, "Anqing Wen Shi Ziliao 安庆文史资料" [Anqing local history] (Anqing: Anqing wenshi ziliao bianjibu, unpublished), 38–40.

12. Yi Li, *Chinese Bureaucratic Culture and Its Influence on the 19th-Century Steamship Operation, 1864–1885: The Bureau for Recruiting Merchants* (Lewiston, NY: E. Mellen Press, 2001), 15–16, 105; "Zhaoshang Ju 招商局" [China Merchants Group], *Zhonghua nianjian 中华年鉴* [The China yearbook] (Zhenjiang Municipal Government, 1948; repr., 860004853).

13. Jiang, *Changjiang Hangyunshi,* 146–149.

14. Jiang, *Changjiang Hangyunshi,* 146–149.

15. The dynasty stopped using the Grand Canal for this purpose in 1886; see "Zhaoshang Ju"; Guo Xiaoyi, ed., *Jiangsu Hangyun Shi: Jindai Bufen 江苏航运史, 近代部分* [History of navigation and water transportation in Jiangsu: Modern period] (Beijing: Remin jiaotong chubanshe, 1990), 20.

16. Guo, *Jiangsu Hangyun Shi,* 45–46.

17. "Ri Qing Lunchuan Gongsi Qingkuang 日清轮船公司情况" [Situation in Japan-China Steamboat Co.] (Zhenjiang: Zhenjiang Municipal Archives, unpublished), 2; Jiang, *Changjiang Hangyunshi,* 227–228.

18. Guo, *Jiangsu Hangyun Shi,* 45–46; "Ri Qing Lunchuan Gongsi," 1; "No Title," *Dongfang zazhi 东方杂志* [Eastern miscellany], July 8, 1904, 54 (Shanghai: Shangwu yinshuguan).

19. Gaimushōtsūshōkyoku, *Sokō Jijō 蘇杭事情* [General information on Suzhou and Hangzhou] (Tokyo: Japanese Government publication, 1921), 35; Zhang Li, *Zhenjiang Jiao Tong Shi 镇江交通史* [History of transportation in Zhenjiang] (Beijing: Renmin jiaotong chubanshe, 1989), 142.

20. Jiang, *Changjiang Hangyunshi,* 228–229.

21. Jiang, *Changjiang Hangyunshi,* 228–229.

22. Seiichi Asai, *Nisshin Kisen Kabushiki Kaisha SanjūNenshi Oyobi Tsuiho 日清汽船株式會社三十年史及追補* [Thirty-year history and reminiscence of the Japan-China Steamship Co.] (Tokyo: Nisshin Kisen Kabushiki Kaisha, 1941). For the Chinese official who received the letter, see Jinchang Gao, "Xu Dantu Xianzhi 续丹徒县志" [Enlarged local history of Dantu] (Zhenjiang: no publisher, 1930).

23. The company only started operating on the Yangtze River in 1896 by purchasing ships from McBain & Co. Guo, *Jiangsu Hangyun Shi,* 45–46.

24. Zhang, *Zhenjiang Jiao Tong Shi,* 142.

25. Jiang, *Changjiang Hangyunshi,* 233–234.

26. Guo, *Jiangsu Hangyun Shi,* 47.

27. John King Fairbank, Martha Henderson Coolidge, and Richard J. Smith, *H. B. Morse, Customs Commissioner and Historian of China* (Lexington: University Press of Kentucky, 1995); Jiang, *Changjiang Hangyunshi,* 128–129.

28. "Lunchuan Shixing Xuwen 轮船试行续闻" [Follow-up news about adopting steamship], *Shenbao 申报* [Shanghai news], July 15, 1882 (Shanghai: Shenbao Publishing House).

29. Guo, *Jiangsu Hangyun Shi,* 14; "No Title," *Shenbao,* October 27, 1890; "No Title," *Shenbao,* January 1, 1891.

30. The name of the governor-general of Liangjiang was Liu Kunyi (刘坤一); see Jiang, *Changjiang Hangyunshi,* 213–214; Liu Kunyi, *Liu Kunyi Yiji 刘坤一遗集* [Collected works of Liu Kunyi], ed. Zhongguo kexueyuan lishi yanjiusuo di san suo 中国科学院历史研究所第三所(Beijing: Zhonghua shuju, 1959), 2:681.

31. “No Title,” *Zilin xibao 字林西报* [North China daily news], January 30, 1887 (Shanghai); “No Title,” *Shenbao,* April 25, 1890.

8 • THE ROLE OF THE STEAMBOAT

1. Quoted from David Arnold, *Everyday Technology: Machines and the Making of India's Modernity* (Chicago: University of Chicago Press, 2013), 7. Quoted from Smritikumar Sarkar, *Technology and Rural Change in Eastern India,* 1830–1980 (New Delhi: Oxford University Press, 2014), 9.

2. Wu Bi, *Geming Yu Shengyi: Xinhai Geming Zhong De Shangye Yu Shangren Mingyun 革命与生意: 辛亥革命中的商业与商人命运* [Revolution and business: Commerce and businessmen's fate during the Republican Revolution] (Hangzhou: Zhejiang University Press, 2011); Guo Xiaoyi, ed., *Jiangsu Hangyun Shi: Jindai Bufen 江苏航运史, 近代部分* [History of navigation and water transportation in Jiangsu: Modern period] (Beijing: Remin jiaotong chubanshe, 1990), 51.

3. Guo, *Jiangsu Hangyun Shi,* 51.

4. Zhenjianggangshibianshenweiyuanhui, *Zhenjiang Gangshi 镇江港史* [History of Zhenjiang port] (Beijing: Renmin jiaotong chuban she, 1989), 65–66.

5. The name of the company is Gongmao Steamboat Co. (公茂轮船公司). Jiangsushengxingzhenggongshushiyesi, “Jiangsu Sheng Shiye Xingzheng Baogao Shu: Hangzheng 江苏省实业行政报告书 (航政)” [Report on the administration of industry in Jiangsu province: Administration of navigation] (Changshu: Changshu Municipal Library, Antiquarian Book Department, 1913), 8–11; Guo, *Jiangsu Hangyun Shi,* 51.

6. Jiangsushengxingzhenggongshushiyesi, “Jiangsu Sheng Shiye Xingzheng Baogao Shu,” 8–11; Guo, *Jiangsu Hangyun Shi,* 51.

7. Jiangsushengxingzhenggongshushiyesi, “Jiangsu Sheng Shiye Xingzheng Baogao Shu,” 8–11; Guo, *Jiangsu Hangyun Shi.*

8. Zhang Li, *Zhenjiang Jiao Tong Shi 镇江交通史* [History of transportation in Zhenjiang] (Beijing: Renmin jiaotong chubanshe, 1989), 149–150.

9. Qi was appointed by Duan Qirui's (段祺瑞) Beijing government. “Guazhoukou Xiaolun Shishi 瓜州口小轮失事” [Steamboat accident at Guazhoukou], *Minguo ribao,* March 24, 1917.

10. Guo, *Jiangsu Hangyun Shi,* 68.

11. Guo, *Jiangsu Hangyun Shi,* 68.

12. "Tongye Jingzheng, Xiaolun Diejia 同业竞争，小轮跌价" [Trade competition, small boat company lowering price], *Shenbao* 申报 [Shanghai news], June 29, 1912 (Shanghai: Shenbao Publishing House); TōaDōbunShoinDaigaku, *Shina Keizai Zensho* 支那經濟全書 [Compendium on the Chinese economy] (Tokyo: Tōa Dōbunkai, 1907–1908), 3:404–406.

13. Guo, *Jiangsu Hangyun Shi,* 52.

14. Zhang, *Zhenjiang Jiao Tong Shi,* 193–194.

15. Yan Xuexi and Ni Youchun, eds., *Lun Zhang Jian: Zhang Jian Guoji Xueshu Yantao Hui Lunwen Ji* 论张謇；张謇国际学术研讨会论文集 [On Zhang Jian: Working papers from the International Symposium on Zhang Jian] (Nanjing: Jiangsu renmin chuban she, 1993), 598.

16. Xiao Zhengde, ed., *Zhang Jian Suo Chuang Qishiye Gailan* 张謇所创企事业概览 [General view of the enterprises created by Zhang Jian] (Nantong: Nantong shi dangan guan, 2000), 143–144; Yangzhoudifangzhibiancuanweiyuanhui, *Yangzhou Shizhi* 扬州市志 [Gazetteer of Yangzhou City] (Shanghai: Zhongguo da baike quanshu chubanshe, 1997), 1:658–659.

17. Dashengzitongqiyeshi, ed., *Dasheng Xitong Qiye Shi* 大生系统企业史 [A history of the Dasheng System Enterprises] (Nanjing: Jiangsu guji chubanshe, 1990), 64, 65, 69l; Jiangsushengwenshiziliao, ed. *Jianghai Chunqiu* 江海春秋 [Spring and autumn of river and sea] (Nanjing: Jiangsu wenshiziliao bianjibu, 1998), 92–93.

18. Dashengzitongqiyeshi, *Dasheng Xitong Qiye,* 65, 69.

19. Guo, *Jiangsu Hangyun Shi,* 86; "Ri Qing Lunchuan Gongsi Qingkuang 日清轮船公司情况" [Situation in Japan-China Ss Co.] (Zhenjiang: Zhenjiang Municipal Archives, unpublished), 4–5.

20. For a discussion on the decrease of European goods in the world market, see Gerd Hardach, *The First World War, 1914–1918* (Berkeley: University of California Press, 1977), 263; "Zhanshi Changjiang Hangye Tan 战时长江航业谈" [Speaking of wartime transportation on Yangtze River], *Minguo ribao,* March 25, 1919.

21. "Ri Qing Lunchuan Gongsi," 4–5.

22. "Zhanshi Changjiang."

23. Zhu Jinru, ed., *Zhenjiang Zhinan* 镇江指南 [Guide to Zhenjiang] (Zhangjiang: Zhenjiang zhinan bianjishe, 1931), 32; Jiang Tianfeng, ed., *Changjiang Hangyunshi: Jindai Bufen* 长江航运史：近代部分 [History of navigation and water transportation along the Yangtze River: Modern era] (Beijing: Renmin jiaotong chubanshe, 1992), 243–244.

24. "Lunchuan Gongsi Liutong Cunhuo 轮船公司流通存货" [Distribution of inventory by steamship companies], *Minguo ribao,* July 20, 2020.

25. "Jiangsu Sheng Xingzheng Gongshu Xunling Di 887 Hao (Jiaotong Bu Ling Tiansong Jiangsu Sheng Shanglun Biao) 江苏省行政公署训令第887号 (交通部令填送江苏省商轮表)" [Instruction number 887 from the administrative office of Jiangsu province: Department of Transportation orders to submit the form listing the commercial ships in Jiangsu], *Jiangsu sheng gongbao 江苏省公报* [Jiangsu provincial gazette], 1914 (Changshu Municipal Library, Antiquarian Book Department).

26. "Xiaolun Gongsi Jingzheng 小轮公司竞争" [Competition among small steamship companies], *Shenbao,* July 6, 1913; "Ri Qing Lunchuan Gongsi," 4–5; Zhu, *Zhenjiang Zhinan,* 32.

27. Guo, *Jiangsu Hangyun Shi,* 110–111; "Ri Qing Lunchuan," 4–5.

28. For a discussion of widespread boycotts against Japanese products in Shanghai, see Bryna Goodman and David S. G. Goodman, *Twentieth Century Colonialism and China: Localities, the Everyday, and the World* (London: Routledge, 2012), 63.

29. "Jiangsu Zhengzhi Nianjian: Jiangtong 江苏政治年鉴: 交通" [Political yearbook of Jiangsu province: Transportation], in *Jiangsu zhengzhi nianjian 江苏政治年鉴* [Political yearbook of Jiangsu province] (Changshu Municipal Library, Antiquarian Book Department, 1921); "Xiaolun Yingye Mei Kuang Yu Xia 小轮营业每况愈下" [Steamboat business is in steady decline], *Minguo ribao,* June 27, 1922.

30. "Xiaolun Gonghui Zhi Qianxi 小轮公会之迁徙" [Steamboat business association is moving], *Minguo ribao,* August 14, 1923; "Jiangsu Shengzhang Gongshu Xunling Di 269 Hao 江苏省长公署训令第269号" [Order number 269 issued by the administrative office of the governor of Jiangsu], *Jiangsu sheng gongbao,* January 12, 1923.

31. "Xiaolun Tiankai Zhen-Qing Shuangban 小轮添开镇清双班" [Steamboats start Zhenjiang-Qingjiang double shift], *Minguo ribao,* May 29, 1924; Guo, *Jiangsu Hangyun Shi,* 110–111.

32. "Chengqing Jinling Guandao Xiangsong Zhangbing 呈请金陵关道详送章禀" [Detailed report submitted to the government office of Jinling Guan Prefecture], in *Changjiang Zhenjiang shangyou shangchuan gonghui bingding guize 长江镇江上游商船公会禀定规则* [Bylaws of the merchant shipping guild of the upper reaches of the Yangtze River from Zhenjiang] (Nanjing: Nanjing University Library, Antiquarian Book Department, unpublished); "Nong Gong Shang Bu Zha 农工商部札" [Correspondence of the Department of Agriculture, Industry, and Commerce], in *Changjiang Zhenjiang shangyou.*

33. "Zhenjiang Hangshang Dongshi Hui Dian 镇江航商董事会电" [Message from the board of directors of the shipping business association in Zhenjiang], *Shenbao,* September 27, 1912; "Chengqing Jinling Guandao Xiangsong Zhangbing."

34. "Jiangsu Sheng Gongbao Pi Di 560 Hao 江苏省公署批第560号" [Reply from the administrative office of the governor of Jiangsu on number 560], *Jiangsu sheng gongbao,* March 1922.

35. "Beibing Gongji Xiaolun 北兵攻击小轮" [Soldiers from the north attacked steamboat], *Minguo ribao,* September 18, 1916.

36. For the term "official-industrialist entrepreneur," see Peter J. Carroll, *Between Heaven and Modernity: Reconstructing Suzhou, 1895–1937* (Stanford, CA: Stanford University Press, 2006), 38; "Shouguan Xiao Lunju 收管小轮局" [Confiscate small steamship company], *Shenbao,* January 19, 1912.

37. "Jiangsu Xunanshi Gongshu Chi Di 3965 Hao (Baohu Shenji Lunchuan) 江苏巡按使公署饬第3965号" [Order number 3965 from the administrative office of the governor of Jiangsu], *Jiangsu sheng gongbao,* October 26, 1914.

38. "Hangye Fandui Hangzheng Ju Zhi Tongqi 航业反对航政局之通启" [Information on the shipping business community's opposition to the creation of Maritime Administration Bureau], *Minguo ribao,* October 27, 1923.

39. "Xiaolun Gonghui Zhi Qianxi 小轮公会之迁徙" [Steamboat business association is moving], *Minguo ribao,* December 23, 1921; "Xiaolun Yingye Mei Kuang Yu Xia."

40. At the time, the provincial government was under Governor Wang Hu (王瑚). "Jiangsu Shengzhang Gongshu Pi Di 1743 Hao: Chengqing Chi Chajinjin Chuanhuo Ji Tuochuan Ren Deng Zuzhi Gongsuo 江苏省长公署批第1743号: 呈请饬查禁船伙及拖船人等组织公所" [Reply from the administrative office of the governor of Jiangsu on number 1743: Requesting order to prohibit boatmen and tugboat workers from organizing guilds], *Jiangsu sheng gongbao,* June 6, 1921.

41. "Zhe Min Su Wan Gan Lianjun Zong Silingbu Jiangsu Shengzhang Gongshu Pi Di 1760 Hao 浙闽苏皖赣联军总司令部 江苏省长公署 批 第1760号" [Number 1760 reply from the general headquarters of allied military forces from Zhenjiang, Fujian, Jiangsu, Anhui, and Jiangxi per administrative office of Jiangsu provincial government], *Jiangsu sheng gongbao,* 1926.

42. Jiangsushengshekeyuan, "Jiang Hai Xue Kan 江海学刊" [Jianghai study journal] (Nanjing: Jianghai xuekan bianjibu, 1986), 81–82; Li Xiaojian, "Ji Zhenjiang Yidu Chuan 记镇江义渡船" [Memory of Zhenjiang's free ferry service], in *Zhenjiang Wenshi Ziliao 镇江文史资料* [Zhenjiang local history] (Zhenjiang: Zhenjiang wenshi ziliao weiyuanhui, 1987), 143–150.

43. Zhenjianggangshibianshenhui, *Zhenjiang Gangshi,* 67–69.

44. "Zhenjiang Haiguan Maoyi Lunlue 镇江海关贸易论略" [General view of trade through Zhenjiang maritime customs], in *Zhenjiang Difangzhi Ziliao Xuanji 镇江地方志资料选辑* [Selected collection of Zhenjiang local history materials] (Zhenjiang: Zhenjiang difangzhi bangongshi, 1987), 36.

45. "Zhen Shang Chuangshe Yili Shanglun Ju 镇商创设义立商轮局" [People in Zhenjiang founded a steamboat company named Yili], *Minguo ribao,* August 22, 1922.

46. "Renwu Ziliao Changbian 人物资料长编" [A chronological record of personalities] (Zhangjiang: Zhenjiang Municipal Government, unpublished).

47. "Zhen Shang Chuangshe."

48. "Jiangsu Shengzhang Gongshu Pi Di 1784 Hao: Chen Wei Chuanhuo Sizu Tuanti Yihai Wuqiong 江苏省长公署批第1784号: 呈为船伙私组团体贻害无穷" [Reply from the administrative office of the governor of Jiangsu on number 1784: Explaining the disastrous consequences that will result from the boatmen forming an organization privately], *Jiangsu sheng gongbao,* June 19, 1921; "Jiangsu Shengzhang Gongshu Pi Di 1743 Hao."

49. "Xiaolun Fenfen Tingban 小轮纷纷停班" [Steamboats canceling schedule sailing one after another], *Minguo ribao,* August 19, 1926; "Xiaolun Da Gongsi Gezi Danfang 小轮大公司各自单方" [Large steamboat companies going solo], *Minguo ribao,* February 22, 1926.

50. "Xiaolun Da Gongsi Gezi Danfang."

51. Ralph Schroeder, *Rethinking Science, Technology, and Social Change* (Stanford, CA: Stanford University Press, 2007), 99.

9 • FOREIGN TECHNOLOGY AND LOCAL SOCIETY

1. The "black box" analogy has been used by many historians of technology with different meanings. See Langdon Winner, "Social Constructivism: Opening the Black Box and Finding It Empty," in *Philosophy and Technology: The Technological Condition,* ed. R. C. Scharff and V. Dusek (Hoboken, NJ: Wiley-Blackwell, 2003), 233–243.

2. "Zhenjiang Haiguan Maoyi Lunlue 镇江海关贸易论略" [General view of trade through Zhenjiang customs], in *Zhenjiang Difangzhi Ziliao Xuanji* 镇江地方志资料选辑 [Selected collection of Zhenjiang local history materials] (Zhenjiang: Zhenjiang difangzhi bangongshi, 1987), 34.

3. "Jiangsu Xunanshi Gongshu Chi Di 3965 Hao (Baohu Shenji Lunchuan) 江苏巡按使公署饬第3965号" [Order number 3965 from the administrative office of the governor of Jiangsu], *Jiangsu sheng gongbao,* October 26, 1914.

4. "Beibing Gongji Xiaolun 北兵攻击小轮" [Soldiers from the North attacked steamboat], *Minguo ribao* 民国日报 [Republic daily, Shanghai], September 18, 1916. Nanjing Municipal Library, Department of Special Collections.

5. "Xiangmin Fenshao Tuochuan 乡民焚烧拖船" [Village people burned tugboat], *Minguo ribao,* August 19, 1916.

6. "Fenchuan Jiaoshe Xuwen 焚船交涉续闻" [More news on the boat-burning case], *Minguo ribao,* August 23, 1916.

7. "Jiaoshe an Yanshou Mimi 交涉案严守秘密" [Keeping secret of the case under negotiations], *Minguo ribao,* September 28, 1916; "Fenchuan Jiaoshe Zhi Jinkuang 焚船交涉之近况" [Recent development in negotiations concerning boat burning], *Minguo ribao,* September 18, 1916.

8. "Guazhoukou Xiaolun Shishi 瓜州口小轮失事" [Steamboat accident at Guazhoukou], *Minguo ribao,* March 24, 1917; "Guazhoukou Xiaolun Shishi: Xu 瓜州口小轮失事: 续" [Steamboat accident at Guazhoukou: Continued], *Minguo ribao,* March 25, 1917.

9. "Za Wen 杂闻" [Miscellaneous news], *Shenbao,* 1873; "Lunchuan Zhuangchen Dunchuan 轮船撞沉趸船" [Steamship sank land-stage boat], *Tuhua xinwen* 图画新闻 [Pictorial news], 1910 (Shanghai: Shanghai shishi bao).

10. "Lunchuan Xubei Jiuming Quan 轮船须备救命那个圈" [Steamship must provide ring buoy], *Tuhua xinwen,* 1907.

11. "Shang Shuo Liangtiao 商说两条" [Two business discussions], *Jiangnan shangwu bao* 江南商务报 [Jiangnan commercial news], 1900 (Nanjing: Jiangnan shangwu zongju Jiangsu shehui kexueyuan, jindaishi suo).

12. "Xiaolun Gonghui Zhi Qianxi 小轮公会之迁徙" [Steamboat business association is moving], *Minguo ribao,* December 23, 1921.

13. "Shang Shuo Liangtiao."

14. Chinese local society was in the midst of drastic changes in power structure; see Xin Zhang, *Social Transformation in Modern China: The State and Local Elites in Henan, 1900–1937* (Cambridge: Cambridge University Press, 2000).

15. Jiangsusheng jiaotongshizhi bianzuanweiyuanhui, *Jiangsu Gong Lu Jiao Tong Shi* 江苏公路交通史 [History of Public Road Transportation in Jiangsu] (Beijing: Renmin jiaotong chubanshe, 1989), 67, 78–82.

16. Jia Ziyi and Yu Leng, eds., *Jiangsu Shenghui Jiyao Muci* 江苏省会辑要目次 [Table of contents of document summary in Jiangsu provincial capital] (Zhenjiang: Zhenjiang jiangnan yinshu guan, 1936), 91–94, 181–183; Zhang Li, *Zhenjiang Jiao Tong Shi* 镇江交通史 [History of transportation in Zhenjiang] (Beijing: Ren min jiao tong chu ban she, 1989), 209–211.

17. Jia and Yu, *Jiangsu Shenghui Jiyao Muci,* 91–94, 181–183; Zhang, *Zhenjiang Jiao Tong Shi,* 209–211.

18. Wang Wenqing, ed., *Jiangsu Shi Gang: Jindai Juan* 江苏史纲: 近代卷 [Brief history of Jiangsu province: Modern period] (Nanjing: Jiangsu guji chubanshe, 1993), 415; Jiangsusheng jiaotongshizhi bianweihui, *Jiangsu Gong Lu Jiao Tong Shi,* 90–93.

19. Wang, *Jiangsu Shi Gang,* 415; Zhang, *Zhenjiang Jiao Tong Shi,* 174, 204; Jiangsu-sheng jiaotongshizhi bianweihui, *Jiangsu Gong Lu Jiao Tong Shi,* 90–93.

20. Zhang, *Zhenjiang Jiao Tong Shi,* 90–96, 115–118.

21. "Fei Jie San Lun, Sunshi Shu Wan Yuan 匪劫三轮, 损失数万元" [Plunderer seized three steamboats, loss in several tens of thousands], *Minguo ribao,* May 17, 1930.

22. "Jinyan Ju Fanchuan an 禁烟局翻船案" [Opium suppression bureau's boat accident], *Minguo ribao,* January 27, 1928.

23. "Hangye Gonghui Chengli 航业公会成立" [Shipping trade organization being formed], *Minguo ribao,* February 17, 1928.

24. "Hangye Gonghui Chengli."

25. "Zhenjiang Lunye Daizheng Junzhi Jiangyun Gongcheng Juan Zhangcheng 镇江轮业带征浚治江运工程捐章程" [Bylaws governing Zhenjiang steamship business community's management of levying surcharge for river dredging project], *Jiangsu sheng zhengfu gongbao 江苏省政府公报* [Jiangsu provincial government gazette], September 1928.

26. "Hangye Gonghui Chengli."

27. "Zhenjiang Lunye Daizheng Junzhi Jiangyun Gongcheng Juan Zhangcheng."

28. "Zhenjiang Lunye Daizheng Junzhi Jiangyun Gongcheng Juan Guanli Weiyuan Hui Zhangcheng 镇江轮业带征浚治江运工程捐管理委员会章程" [Bylaws of regulatory commission of Zhenjiang steamship business community's management of levying surcharge for river dredging project], *Jiangsu sheng zhengfu gongbao,* June 28, 1930.

29. "Shengfu Pi Zhenjiang Hangye Gonghui Changwu Zhuxi Lu Shiming Di 51 Hao 省府批 镇江航业公会常务主席卢世铭 第51号" [Provincial government's reply to the chief executive officer, Lu Shiming, of Zhenjiang Trade Association of Commercial Shipping in document number 51], *Jiangsu sheng zhengfu gongbao,* January 10, 1931.

30. "Pi Zhenjiang Hangye Gonghui Di 806 Hao 批 镇江航业公会 第806号" [Provincial government's reply to Zhenjiang Trade Association of Commercial Shipping in document number 806], *Jiangsu sheng zhengfu gongbao,* April 29, 1931.

31. "Ben Niu Canan Yu Shicheng Ying Fu Fuxu Yiwu 奔牛惨案俞世诚应负抚恤义务" [Yu Shicheng is responsible for paying reparations after the tragic accident involving *Benniu*], *Jiangsu sheng zhengfu gongbao,* September 27, 1929; Zhang Dechuan, "Jindai Zhenjiang Gangkou Liangqi Zhongda Canan 近代镇江港口两起重大惨案" [Two major tragedies in Zhenjiang in modern period], in *Zhenjiang Wenshi Ziliao 镇江文史资料* [Zhenjiang local history] (Zhenjiang: Zhenjiang shi zhengxie, 1989), 93–94.

32. "*Benniu* Lun Canan Jiashu Qingyuan 奔牛轮残案家属请愿" [Victim families of the tragic accident involving the steamboat named *Benniu* filed petition], *Minguo ribao,* July 31, 1929.

33. "Guanyu Ben Niu Xiaolun Canan Zhi Zhaoguo Shishi Ji Chuli Shanhou Jingguo 关于奔牛小轮惨案之肇祸事实及处理善后经过" [Concerning the facts about the cause of the tragic accident involving the steamboat named *Benniu* and the process of dealing with its aftermath], *Jiangsu sheng zhengfu gongbao,* September 3, 1929.

34. "Guanyu Ben Niu Xiaolun."

35. "Guanyu Ben Niu Xiaolun."

36. "Ben Niu Canan Yu Shicheng."

37. "Guanyu Ben Niu Xiaolun."

38. "Xiuzheng Fuxu Ben Niu Lun Canan 修正抚恤奔牛轮惨案" [Amendment to the method of compensation in the case of the tragic accident involving the steamboat named *Benniu*], *Jiangsu sheng zhengfu gongbao,* November 11, 1929.

39. On the "everyday state" concept, see Sheldon M. Garon, *Molding Japanese Minds: The State in Everyday Life* (Princeton, NJ: Princeton University Press, 1997); C. J. Fuller and Véronique Bénéï, *The Everyday State and Society in Modern India* (London: Hurst, 2001); René Véron, Stuart Corbridge, Glyn Williams, and Manoj Srivastava, "The Everyday State and Political Society in Eastern India: Structuring Access to the Employment Assurance Scheme," *Journal of Development Studies* 39, no. 5 (2003), 1–28; Salwa Ismail, *Political Life in Cairo's New Quarters: Encountering the Everyday State* (Minneapolis: University of Minnesota Press, 2006); Taylor C. Sherman, William Gould, and Sarah F. D. Ansari, eds., *From Subjects to Citizens: Society and the Everyday State in India and Pakistan, 1947–1970* (New York: Cambridge University Press, 2014).

40. Zhang, *Zhenjiang Jiao Tong Shi,* 178–181; Jiangsusheng jiaotongshizhi bianweihui, *Jiangsu Gong Lu Jiao Tong Shi,* 90–93.

CONCLUSION

1. On the role of the state, see H. Lyman Miller, "The Late Imperial Chinese State," in *The Modern Chinese State,* ed. David L. Shambaugh (Cambridge: Cambridge University Press, 2000), 15–41.

2. Frederic E. Wakeman, *Strangers at the Gate: Social Disorder in South China, 1839–1861* (Berkeley: University of California Press, 1966), 55.

3. Adding to the suspicion was the rumor that the British were demon-like. See Philip A. Kuhn, *Soulstealers: The Chinese Sorcery Scare of 1768* (Cambridge, MA: Harvard University Press, 1990).

4. Matthew Harvey Sommer, *Sex, Law, and Society in Late Imperial China* (Stanford, CA: Stanford University Press, 2000); Janet M. Theiss, *Disgraceful Matters: The Politics of Chastity in Eighteenth-Century China* (Berkeley: University of California Press, 2004); Jimmy Y. F. Yu, *Sanctity and Self-Inflicted Violence in Chinese Religions, 1500–1700* (Oxford: Oxford University Press, 2012); Paul S. Ropp, Paola Zamperini, and Harriet Thelma Zurndorfer, *Passionate Women: Female Suicide in Late Imperial China* (Leiden: Brill, 2001).

5. See Émile Durkheim, *On Suicide* (London: Penguin Books, 2006), 222–225.

6. Tony Castanha, *The Myth of Indigenous Caribbean Extinction: Continuity and Reclamation in Borikén (Puerto Rico)* (New York: Palgrave Mącmillan, 2011), 53.

7. Christian Goeschel, *Suicide in Nazi Germany* (Oxford: Oxford University Press, 2009), 149–166; Richard Bessel, Alf Lüdtke, and Bernd Weisbrod, *No Man's Land of Violence: Extreme Wars in the 20th Century* (Göttingen: Wallstein, 2006), 78–79; Kyle Ikeda, *Okinawan War Memory: Transgenerational Trauma and the War Fiction of Medoruma Shun* (New York: Routledge, 2014), 26, 49, 96, 116; Hayashi Hirofumi, "Unsettled State Violence in Japan: The Okinawa Incident," in *State Violence in East Asia,* ed. N. Ganesan and Sung Chull Kim (Lexington: University Press of Kentucky, 2013), 75–104; Bruce M. Petty, *Saipan: Oral Histories of the Pacific War* (Jefferson, NC: McFarland, 2002).

8. For Germany, see Goeschel, *Suicide in Nazi Germany,* 149–166; Bessel et al., *No Man's Land of Violence,* 78–79. For Japan, see Ikeda, *Okinawan War Memory,* 26, 49, 96, 116; Hirofumi, "Unsettled State Violence," 75–104.

9. R. Gary Tiedemann, "Daily Life in China during the Taiping and Nian Rebellions, 1850s–1860s," in *Daily Lives of Civilians in Wartime Asia: From the Taiping Rebellion to the Vietnam War,* ed. Stewart Lone (Westport, CT: Greenwood Press, 2007), 7. On the Chinese literati keeping wartime atrocities alive, see Edward McCord, "Burn, Kill, Rape, and Rob: Military Atrocities, Warlordism, and Anti-Warlordism in Republican China," in *The Scars of War: The Impact of Warfare on Modern China,* ed. Diana Lary and Stephen R. MacKinnon (Vancouver: University of British Columbia Press, 2001), 18–49.

10. Rush W. Dozier, *Fear Itself: The Origin and Nature of the Powerful Emotion That Shapes Our Lives and Our World* (New York: St. Martin's Press, 1998), 129.

11. Rukang Tian, *Male Anxiety and Female Chastity: A Comparative Study of Chinese Ethical Values in Ming-Ch'ing Times* (Leiden: Brill, 1988); Ikeda, *Okinawan War Memory,* 26, 49, 96, 116; Hirofumi, "Unsettled State Violence," 75–104.

12. Quoted from Castanha, *The Myth of Indigenous Caribbean Extinction,* 53.

13. Paul James, *Globalization and Violence* (London: Sage Publications, 2007), ix.

14. For Ronald Burt's conception of interest-directed action, see George Ritzer, ed., *Encyclopedia of Social Theory* (Thousand Oaks, CA: Sage Publications, 2005), 1: 537.

15. Harrison C. White, *Markets from Networks: Socioeconomic Models of Production* (Princeton, NJ: Princeton University Press, 2002).

16. K. Polanyi, "Our Obsolete Market Mentality," in *Primitive, Archaic and Modern Economies: Essays of Karl Polanyi*, ed. George Dalton (Boston: 1968), 70; Karl Polanyi, *Conrad Maynadier Arensberg, and Harry W. Pearson, Trade and Market in the Early Empires: Economies in History and Theory* (Glencoe, IL: Free Press, 1957), 70–71; Karl Polanyi, *Dahomey and the Slave Trade: An Analysis of an Archaic Economy* (Seattle: University of Washington Press, 1966), xvii.

17. Quoted from Ritzer, *Encyclopedia of Social Theory*, 1: 536.

18. See Gary Hamilton, *Commerce and Capitalism in Chinese Societies* (Abingdon: Routledge, 2006), 116–117.

19. For Sherman Cochran's and Loren Brandt's similar views, see Hamilton, *Commerce and Capitalism*, 93–126.

20. Peter Spufford, *How Rarely Did Medieval Merchants Use Coin?* (Utrecht: Geldmuseum, 2008); Craig Muldrew, *The Economy of Obligation: The Culture of Credit and Social Relations in Early Modern England* (New York: St. Martin's Press, 1998); Mark Granovetter, "Economic Action and Social Structure: The Problem of Embeddedness," in *The Sociology of Economic Life*, ed. Mark Granovetter and Richard Swedberg (Boulder, CO: Westview Press, 1992), 60.

21. Robert Gardella and Andrea McElderry, "Introduction," in *Chinese Business History: Interpretive Trends and Priorities for the Future*, ed. Robert Gardella, Jane Kate Leonard, and Andrea Lee McElderry (Armonk, NY: M. E. Sharpe, 1998), 74.

22. See Yuru Lin and Madeleine Zelin, *Merchant Communities in Asia, 1600–1980* (London: Pickering and Chatto, 2015), 6; for discussion of Man-hong Lin's study, see Gardella and McElderry, "Introduction," in *Chinese Business History*, 76.

23. I define the word "everyday" in the same way as Prasad. Ritika Prasad, *Tracks of Change: Railways and Everyday Life in Colonial India* (Daryaganj: Cambridge University Press, 2015), 3, 9–10.

24. Thomas Parke Hughes, *Human-Built World: How to Think about Technology and Culture* (Chicago: University of Chicago Press, 2004).

25. Edward Beatty, *Technology and the Search for Progress in Modern Mexico* (Oakland: University of California Press, 2015), 14.

26. Angela Dale and Jennifer Mason, *Understanding Social Research: Thinking Creatively about Method* (London: Sage, 2011), 121; Donald A. MacKenzie and Judy Wajcman, *The Social Shaping of Technology* (Buckingham: Open University Press, 1999), 23; Edward Beatty, *Technology and the Search for Progress in Modern Mexico* (Oakland: University of California Press, 2015), 14; David Arnold, *Everyday Technology:*

Machines and the Making of India's Modernity (Chicago: University of Chicago Press, 2013), 42–43.

27. See discussion of the term in Abdullah A. Mohamoud, *State Collapse and Post-Conflict Development in Africa: The Case of Somalia (1960–2001)* (West Lafayette, IN: Purdue University Press, 2006), 18.

28. Those believing in social constructivism tend to see that social context determines the development of technology and science; see discussion in Ralph Schroeder, *Rethinking Science, Technology, and Social Change* (Stanford, CA: Stanford University Press, 2007), 1, 4.

29. See David Edgerton, *The Shock of the Old: Technology and Global History since 1900* (Oxford: Oxford University Press, 2007), 43. For Raymond Williams's idea, see David Croteau, William W. Hoynes, and Stefania Milan, *Media/Society: Industries, Images, and Audiences* (Thousand Oaks, CA: Sage Publications, 2012), 290.

30. Prasad, *Tracks of Change*, 20.

31. Dagmar Schäfer suggests technological and practical endeavor was a local matter between the Song and Qing dynasties. Dagmar Schäfer, *Cultures of Knowledge: Technology in Chinese History* (Leiden: Brill, 2012), 12. See also Sheldon M. Garon, *Molding Japanese Minds: The State in Everyday Life* (Princeton, NJ: Princeton University Press, 1997).

32. C. J. Fuller and Véronique Bénéï, *The Everyday State and Society in Modern India* (London: Hurst, 2001), 1–2; Prasenjit Duara, *Culture, Power, and the State: Rural North China, 1900–1942* (Stanford, CA: Stanford University Press, 1988); Huaiyin Li, *Village Governance in North China, 1875–1936* (Stanford, CA: Stanford University Press, 2005); Xin Zhang, *Social Transformation in Modern China: The State and Local Elites in Henan, 1900–1937* (Cambridge: Cambridge University Press, 2000).

ARCHIVES AND PRIMARY SOURCES

UNPUBLISHED AND RARE MATERIALS

"Anqing Jiuying 安庆旧影" [History of Anqing]. Anqing: Anqing Municipal Archives, unpublished. Contains some rare information about Zhenjiang and its commercial relationship with Anqing. By an anonymous author in the early nineteenth century.

Chen, Qingnian. "Daoguang Yingjian Po Zhenjiang Ji 道光英舰破镇江记" [History of the British warship invading Zhenjiang]. In *Document No. 850000175*. Zhenjiang: Zhenjiang Municipal Government, unpublished. Detailed account of the British invasion of Zhenjiang, written by Chen Qingnian (陈庆年, 1862–1929), a Zhenjiang native and a degree holder.

"Daoguang Renyin Bingshi Guanshu Huichao 道光壬寅兵事官书汇钞" [Collection of official memorials related to war in 1842 during the Daoguang reign]. In *Licheng juan zhi er* 里乘卷之二 [Collection of documents]. Zhenjiang: Jiangsu shengli guoxue tushuguan, 1934–1937. Collection of memorials and letters between local officials and the Daoguang emperor pertaining to the British invasion of Zhenjiang. Self-printed by local literati in the 1930s.

Luo, Zhirang. "Daoguang Renyin Yingbing Fancheng Shi 道光壬寅英兵犯城事" [A record of the British soldiers invading the city in 1842]. In *Document no. 85000021*. Zhenjiang: Zhenjiang Municipal Government, unpublished. Detailed description of the British invasion of Zhenjiang, written by Luo Zhiran (罗志让), a Zhenjiang native and a degree holder who lived through the second half of the nineteenth century.

"Renwu Ziliao Changbian 人物资料长编" [A chronological record of personalities]. Zhangjiang: Zhenjiang Municipal Government, unpublished. Written by local historians in the late 1980s, this manuscript contains a great deal of valuable information unavailable elsewhere.

"Renyin Bingshi Xuchao 壬寅兵事续钞" [Collection of writings related to war in 1842]. In *Licheng juan zhi er* 里乘卷之二 [Collection of documents]. Zhenjiang: Jiangsu shengli guoxue tushuguan, 1934–1937. Collection of personal writings containing eyewitness accounts of events surrounding the British invasion. Self-printed by local literati in the 1930s.

Zhao, Xunhe. "Dantu Zhanglu 丹徒掌录" [Anecdotal record of Dantu County]. Zhenjiang: Zhenjiang Municipal Archives, unpublished. Collection of anecdotes written by Zhao Xunhe (赵勋禾), a Zhenjiang native and a member of the local literati who lived through the second half of the nineteenth century.

"Zhenjiang Shangye Shiliao 镇江商业史料" [Historical materials of Zhenjiang trade]. In *Government Document no. 850000041*. Zhenjiang: Zhenjiang Municipal Government, unpublished. A manuscript written or compiled in the late 1950s by an anonymous author.

PRIVATE JOURNALS, DIARIES, AND MEMOIRS

WRITTEN BY MEMBERS OF THE LOCAL LITERATI IN ZHENJIANG

Fa, Zhirui. "Jingkou Fen Cheng Lu 京口偾城录" [Assault on Jingkou City]. Reprint, Taipei: Wenhai chubanshe, n.d.

Yang, Qi. "Chu Wei Cheng Ji 出围城记" [Exodus from a besieged city]. Reprint, Taipei: Wenhai chubanshe, n.d.

Zhu, Shiyun. "Caojian Riji 草间日记" [Thatch-hut diary]. Reprint, Taipei: Wenhai chubanshe, n.d.

WRITTEN BY BRITISH OFFICERS WHO PARTICIPATED IN THE INVASION OF ZHENJIANG

Bernard, W. D., and W. H. Hall. *Narrative of the Voyages and Services of the* Nemesis *from 1840 to 1843 and of the Combined Naval and Military Operations in China: Comprising a Complete Account of the Colony of Hong-Kong, and Remarks on the Character and Habits of the Chinese*. London: H. Colburn, 1845.

Cunynghame, Arthur A. T. *An Aide-de-Camp's Recollections of Service in China, a Residence in Hong-Kong, and Visits to Other Islands in the Chinese Seas.* London: Saunders and Otley, 1844.

Davis, John Francis. *China, during the War and since the Peace.* Vol. 1. London: Longman, Brown, Green, and Longmans, 1852.

The Last Year in China, to the Peace of Nanking as Sketched in Letters to His Friends. London: Longman, Brown, Green, and Longmans, 1843.

Loch, Granville G. *The Closing Events of the Campaign in China the Operations in the Yang-Tze-Kiang and Treaty of Nanking.* London: J. Murray, 1843.

Low, Charles R. *Soldiers of the Victorian Age.* Vol. 1. London: Chapman and Hall, 1880.

Maclellan, John W. *The Story of Shanghai from the Opening of the Port to Foreign Trade.* Shanghai: North-China Herald Office, 1889.

MacPherson, Duncan. *The War in China. Narrative of the Chinese Expedition, from Its Formation in April, 1840, to the Treaty of Peace in August, 1842.* London: Saunders and Otley, 1843.

Mountain, Armine S. H. *Memoirs and Letters of the Late Colonel Armine S. H. Mountain, C.B., Aide-de-Camp to the Queen and Adjutant-General of Her Majesty's Forces in India.* London: Longman, Brown, Green, Longmans and Roberts, 1857.

Murray, Alexander. *Doings in China: Being the Personal Narrative of an Officer Engaged in the Late Chinese Expedition, from the Recapture of Chusan in 1841, to the Peace of Nankin in 1842.* London: R. Bentley, 1843.

Prichard, Iltudus Thomas. *The Administration of India from 1859–1868: The First Ten Years of Administration under the Crown.* Vol. 2. London: Macmillan, 1869.

Rait, Robert S. *The Life and Campaigns of Hugh, First Viscount Gough, Field-Marshal.* Westminster: A. Constable, 1903.

ARCHIVAL RECORDS

"Ben Niu Canan Yu Shicheng Ying Fu Fuxu Yiwu 奔牛惨案俞世诚应负抚恤义务" [Yu Shicheng is responsible for paying reparations after the tragic accident involving *Benniu*]. *Jiangsu sheng zhengfu gongbao* 江苏省政府公报

[Jiangsu provincial government gazette], September 27, 1929. Nanjing Municipal Library, Department of Special Collections.

"Chengqing Jinling Guandao Xiangsong Zhangbing 呈请金陵关道详送章禀" [Detailed report submitted to the government office of Jinling Guan Prefecture]. In *Changjiang Zhenjiang shangyou shangchuan gonghui bingding guize 长江镇江上游商船公会禀定规则* [Bylaws of the merchant shipping guild of the upper reaches of the Yangtze River from Zhenjiang]. Nanjing: Nanjing University Library, Antiquarian Book Department, unpublished.

"Guanyu Ben Niu Xiaolun Canan Zhi Zhaoguo Shishi Ji Chuli Shanhou Jingguo 关于奔牛小轮惨案之肇祸事实及处理善后经过" [Concerning the facts about the cause of the tragic accident involving the steamboat named *Benniu* and the process of dealing with its aftermath]. *Jiangsu sheng zhengfu gongbao 江苏省政府公报* [Jiangsu provincial government gazette], September 3, 1929. Nanjing Municipal Library, Department of Special Collections.

Jia, Ziyi, and Yu Leng, eds. *Jiangsu Shenghui Jiyao Muci 江苏省会辑要目次* [Table of contents of document summary in Jiangsu provincial capital]. Zhenjiang: Zhenjiang jiangnan yinshu guan, 1936.

"Jiangsu Sheng Gongbao Pi Di 560 Hao 江苏省公署批第560号" [Reply from the administrative office of the governor of Jiangsu on number 560]. *Jiangsu sheng gongbao 江苏省公报* [Jiangsu provincial gazette], March 1922. Changshu Municipal Library.

"Jiangsu Sheng Xingzheng Gongshu Xunling Di 887 Hao (Jiaotong Bu Ling Tiansong Jiangsu Sheng Shanglun Biao) 江苏省行政公署训令第887号(交通部令填送江苏省商轮表)" [Instruction number 887 from the Administrative Office of Jiangsu province: Department of Transportation orders to submit the form listing the commercial ships in Jiangsu]. *Jiangsu sheng gongbao 江苏省公报* [Jiangsu provincial gazette], 1914. Changshu Municipal Library, Antiquarian Book Department.

"Jiangsu Shengzhang Gongshu Pi Di 1784 Hao: Chen Wei Chuanhuo Sizu Tuanti Yihai Wuqiong 江苏省长公署批第1784号: 呈为船伙私组团体贻害无穷" [Reply from the administrative office of the governor of Jiangsu on number 1784: Explaining the disastrous consequences that will result from the boatmen forming an organization privately]. *Jiangsu sheng gongbao 江苏省公报* [Jiangsu provincial gazette], June 19, 1921. Zhenjiang Municipal Library.

"Jiangsu Shengzhang Gongshu Pi Di 1743 Hao: Chengqing Chi Chajinjin Chuanhuo Ji Tuochuan Ren Deng Zuzhi Gongsuo 江苏省长公署批第1743号: 呈请饬查禁船伙及拖船人等组织公所" [Reply from the administrative office of the governor of Jiangsu on number 1743: Requesting order to prohibit boatmen and tugboat workers from organizing guilds]. *Jiangsu sheng gongbao 江苏省公报* [Jiangsu provincial gazette], June 6, 1921. Zhenjiang Municipal Library.

"Jiangsu Shengzhang Gongshu Xunling Di 269 Hao 江苏省长公署训令第269号" [Order number 269 issued by the administrative office of the governor of Jiangsu]. *Jiangsu sheng gongbao 江苏省公报* [Jiangsu provincial gazette], January 12, 1923. Changshu Municipal Library.

"Jiangsu Xunanshi Gongshu Chi Di 3965 Hao (Baohu Shenji Lunchuan) 江苏巡按使公署饬第3965号" [Order number 3965 from the administrative office of the governor of Jiangsu]. *Jiangsu sheng gongbao 江苏省公报* [Jiangsu provincial gazette], October 26, 1914. Changshu Municipal Library, Antiquarian Book Department.

"Jiangsu Zhengzhi Nianjian: Jiangtong 江苏政治年鉴: 交通" [Political yearbook of Jiangsu province: Transportation]. In *Jiangsu zhengzhi nianjian 江苏政治年鉴* [Political yearbook of Jiangsu province]. Changshu Municipal Library, Antiquarian Book Department, 1921.

Jiangsushengxingzhenggongshushiyesi. "Jiangsu Sheng Shiye Xingzheng Baogao Shu: Hangzheng 江苏省实业行政报告书 (航政)" [Report on the administration of industry in Jiangsu province: Administration of navigation]. Changshu: Changshu Municipal Library, Antiquarian Book Department, 1913.

"Nong Gong Shang Bu Zha 农工商部札" [Correspondence of the Department of Agriculture, Industry, and Commerce]. In *Changjiang Zhenjiang shangyou shangchuan gonghui bingding guize 长江镇江上游商船公会禀定规则* [Bylaws of the merchant shipping guild of the upper reaches of the Yangtze River from Zhenjiang]. Nanjing: Nanjing University Library, Antiquarian Book Department, unpublished.

"Pi Zhenjiang Hangye Gonghui Di 806 Hao 批 镇江航业公会 第806号" [Provincial government's reply to Zhenjiang Trade Association of Commercial Shipping in document number 806]. *Jiangsu sheng zhengfu gongbao 江苏省政府公报* [Jiangsu provincial government gazette], April 29, 1931. Zhenjiang Municipal Library.

"Ri Qing Lunchuan Gongsi Qingkuang 日清轮船公司情况" [Situation in Japan-China Ss Co.] Zhenjiang: Zhenjiang Municipal Archives, unpublished.

"Shengfu Pi Zhenjiang Hangye Gonghui Changwu Zhuxi Lu Shiming Di 51 Hao 省府批 镇江航业公会常务主席卢世铭 第51号" [Provincial government's reply to the chief executive officer, Lu Shiming, of Zhenjiang Trade Association of Commercial Shipping in document number 51]. *Jiangsu sheng zhengfu gongbao 江苏省政府公报* [Jiangsu provincial government gazette], January 10, 1931. Zhenjiang Municipal Library.

"Sushu Caizheng Shuoming Shu 苏属财政说明书" [Manual of Jiangsu provincial finance]. Dalian Damiao Library, unpublished.

Wang, Tieyai. *Zhongwai Jiuyuezhang Huibian 中外旧约章汇编* [Collections of the Sino–foreign treaties]. Vol. 3. Beijing: Sanlian shudian, 1957. Microform, 2nd vol., 21 cm.

"Xiuzheng Fuxu Ben Niu Lun Canan 修正抚恤奔牛轮惨案" [Amendment to the method of compensation in the case of the tragic accident involving the steamboat named *Benniu*]. *Jiangsu sheng zhengfu gongbao 江苏省政府公报* [Jiangsu provincial government gazette], November 11, 1929. Nanjing Municipal Library, Department of Special Collections.

"Zhe Min Su Wan Gan Lianjun Zong Silingbu Jiangsu Shengzhang Gongshu Pi Di 1760 Hao 浙闽苏皖赣联军总司令部 江苏省长公署 批 第1760号" [Number 1760 reply from the general headquarters of allied military forces from Zhenjiang, Fujian, Jiangsu, Anhui, and Jiangxi per administrative office of Jiangsu provincial government]. *Jiangsu sheng gongbao 江苏省公报* [Jiangsu provincial gazette], 1926. Zhenjiang Municipal Library.

"Zhenjiang Lunye Daizheng Junzhi Jiangyun Gongcheng Juan Guanli Weiyuan Hui Zhangcheng 镇江轮业带征浚治江运工程捐管理委员会章程" [Bylaws of regulatory commission of Zhenjiang steamship business community's management of levying surcharge for river dredging project]. *Jiangsu sheng zhengfu gongbao 江苏省政府公报* [Jiangsu provincial government gazette], June 28, 1930. Nanjing Municipal Library, Department of Special Collections.

"Zhenjiang Lunye Daizheng Junzhi Jiangyun Gongcheng Juan Zhangcheng 镇江轮业带征浚治江运工程捐章程" [Bylaws governing Zhenjiang steamship business community's management of levying surcharge for river dredging project]. *Jiangsu sheng zhengfu gongbao 江苏省政府公报* [Jiangsu provincial government gazette], September 1928. Zhenjiang Municipal Library.

NEWSPAPERS, MAGAZINES, AND JOURNALS

"Beibing Gongji Xiaolun 北兵攻击小轮" [Soldiers from the north attacked steamboat]. *Minguo ribao 民国日报* [Republic daily, Shanghai], September 18, 1916. Nanjing Municipal Library, Department of Special Collections.

"Benniu Lun Canan Jiashu Qingyuan 奔牛轮残案家属请愿" [Victim families of the tragic accident involving the steamboat named *Benniu* filed petition]. *Minguo ribao 民国日报* [Republic daily, Shanghai], July 31, 1929. Nanjing Municipal Library, Department of Special Collections.

"Fei Jie San Lun, Sunshi Shu Wan Yuan 匪劫三轮, 损失数万元" [Plunderer seized three steamboats, loss in several tens of thousands]. *Minguo ribao 民国日报* [Republic daily, Shanghai], May 17, 1930. Nanjing Municipal Library, Department of Special Collections.

"Fenchuan Jiaoshe Xuwen 焚船交涉续闻" [More news on the boat-burning case]. *Minguo ribao 民国日报* [Republic daily, Shanghai], August 23, 1916. Nanjing Municipal Library, Department of Special Collections.

"Fenchuan Jiaoshe Zhi Jinkuang 焚船交涉之近况" [Recent development in negotiations concerning boat burning]. *Minguo ribao 民国日报* [Republic daily, Shanghai], September 18, 1916. Nanjing Municipal Library, Department of Special Collections.

"Guazhoukou Xiaolun Shishi 瓜州口小轮失事" [Steamboat accident at Guazhoukou]. *Minguo ribao 民国日报* [Republic daily, Shanghai], March 24, 1917. Nanjing Municipal Library, Department of Special Collections.

"Guazhoukou Xiaolun Shishi: Xu 瓜州口小轮失事: 续" [Steamboat accident at Guazhoukou: Continued]. *Minguo ribao 民国日报* [Republic daily, Shanghai], March 25, 1917. Nanjing Municipal Library, Department of Special Collections.

"Hangye Fandui Hangzheng Ju Zhi Tongqi 航业反对航政局之通启" [Information on the shipping business community's opposition to the creation of the Maritime Administration Bureau]. *Minguo ribao 民国日报* [Republic daily, Shanghai], October 27, 1923. Nanjing Municipal Library, Department of Special Collections.

"Hangye Gonghui Chengli 航业公会成立" [Shipping trade organization being formed]. *Minguo ribao 民国日报* [Republic daily, Shanghai], February 17, 1928. Nanjing Municipal Library, Department of Special Collections.

"Jiaoshe an Yanshou Mimi 交涉案严守秘密" [Keeping secret of the case under negotiations]. *Minguo ribao 民国日报* [Republic daily, Shanghai], September 28, 1916. Nanjing Municipal Library, Department of Special Collections.

"Jinyan Ju Fanchuan an 禁烟局翻船案" [Opium suppression bureau's boat accident]. *Minguo ribao 民国日报* [Republic daily, Shanghai], January 27, 1928. Nanjing Municipal Library, Department of Special Collections.

"Lunchuan Gongsi Liutong Cunhuo 轮船公司流通存货" [Distribution of inventory by steamship companies]. *Minguo ribao 民国日报* [Republic daily, Shanghai], July 20, 1920. Nanjing Municipal Library, Department of Special Collections.

"Lunchuan Shixing Xuwen 轮船试行续闻" [Follow-up news about adopting steamship]. *Shenbao 申报* [Shanghai news], July 15, 1882. Shanghai: Shenbao Publishing House. Zhenjiang Municipal Government.

"Lunchuan Xubei Jiuming Quan 轮船须备救命那个圈" [Steamship must provide ring buoy]. *Tuhua xinwen 图画新闻* [Pictorial news], 1907. Shanghai: Shanghai shishi bao. Zhenjiang Municipal Library.

"Lunchuan Zhuangchen Dunchuan 轮船撞沉趸船" [Steamship sank landstage boat]. *Tuhua xinwen 图画新闻* [Pictorial news], 1910. Shanghai: Shanghai shishi bao. Zhenjiang Municipal Library.

"No Title." *Dongfang zazhi 东方杂志* [Eastern miscellany], July 8, 1904. Shanghai: Shangwu yinshuguan. Zhenjiang Municipal Government.

"No Title." *Shenbao 申报* [Shanghai news], April 25, 1890. Shanghai: Shenbao Publishing House. Zhenjiang Municipal Government.

"No Title." *Shenbao* 申报 [Shanghai news], October 27, 1890. Shanghai: Shenbao Publishing House. Zhenjiang Municipal Government.

"No Title." *Shenbao* 申报 [Shanghai news], January 1, 1891. Shanghai: Shenbao Publishing House. Zhenjiang Municipal Government.

"No Title." *Zilin xibao* 字林西报 [North China daily news], January 30, 1887. Shanghai. Zhenjiang Municipal Government.

"Shang Shuo Liangtiao 商说两条" [Two business discussions]. *Jiangnan shangwu bao* 江南商务报 [Jiangnan commercial news], 1900. Nanjing: Jiangnan shangwu zongju Jiangsu shehui kexueyuan, jindaishi suo.

"Shouguan Xiao Lunju 收管小轮局" [Confiscate small steamship company]. *Shenbao* 申报 [Shanghai news], January 19, 1912. Shanghai: Shenbao Publishing House. Zhenjiang Municipal Government.

"Tongye Jingzheng, Xiaolun Diejia 同业竞争, 小轮跌价" [Trade competition, small boat company lowering price]. *Shenbao* 申报 [Shanghai news], June 29, 1912. Shanghai: Shenbao Publishing House. Zhenjiang Municipal Government.

"Xiangmin Fenshao Tuochuan 乡民焚烧拖船" [Village people burned tugboat]. *Minguo ribao* 民国日报 [Republic daily, Shanghai], August 19, 1916. Nanjing Municipal Library, Department of Special Collections.

"Xiaolun Da Gongsi Gezi Danfang 小轮大公司各自单方" [Large steamboat companies going solo]. *Minguo ribao* 民国日报 [Republic daily, Shanghai], February 22, 1926. Nanjing Municipal Library, Department of Special Collections.

"Xiaolun Fenfen Tingban 小轮纷纷停班" [Steamboats canceling schedule sailing one after another]. *Minguo ribao* 民国日报 [Republic daily, Shanghai], August 19, 1926. Nanjing Municipal Library, Department of Special Collections.

"Xiaolun Gonghui Zhi Qianxi 小轮公会之迁徙" [Steamboat business association is moving]. *Minguo ribao* 民国日报 [Republic daily, Shanghai], December 12, 1921. Nanjing Municipal Library, Department of Special Collections.

"Xiaolun Gonghui Zhi Qianxi 小轮公会之迁徙" [Steamboat business association is moving]. *Minguo ribao* 民国日报 [Republic daily, Shanghai],

August 14, 1923. Nanjing Municipal Library, Department of Special Collections.

"Xiaolun Gongsi Jingzheng 小轮公司竞争" [Competition among small steamship companies]. *Shenbao* 申报 [Shanghai news], July 6, 1913. Shanghai: Shenbao Publishing House. Zhenjiang Municipal Government.

"Xiaolun Tiankai Zhen-Qing Shuangban 小轮添开镇清双班" [Steamboats start Zhenjiang-Qingjiang double shift]. *Minguo ribao* 民国日报 [Republic daily, Shanghai], May 29, 1924. Nanjing Municipal Library, Department of Special Collections.

"Xiaolun Yingye Mei Kuang Yu Xia 小轮营业每况愈下" [Steamboat business is in steady decline]. *Minguo ribao* 民国日报 [Republic daily, Shanghai], June 27, 1922. Nanjing Municipal Library, Department of Special Collections.

"Za Wen 杂闻" [Miscellaneous news]. *Shenbao* 申报 [Shanghai news], 1873. Shanghai: Shenbao Publishing House. Zhenjiang Municipal Government.

"Zhanshi Changjiang Hangye Tan 战时长江航业谈" [Speaking of wartime transportation in Yangtze River]. *Minguo ribao* 民国日报 [Republic daily, Shanghai], March 25, 1919. Nanjing Municipal Library, Department of Special Collections.

"Zhaoshang Ju 招商局" [China Merchants Group]. In *Zhonghua nianjian* 中华年鉴 [The China yearbook]. Zhenjiang Municipal Government, 1948. Reprint, 860004853.

"Zhen Shang Chuangshe Yili Shanglun Ju 镇商创设义立商轮局" [People in Zhenjiang founded a steamboat company named Yili]. *Minguo ribao* 民国日报 [Republic daily, Shanghai], August 22, 1922. Nanjing Municipal Library, Department of Special Collections.

"Zhenjiang Hangshang Dongshi Hui Dian 镇江航商董事会电" [Message from the board of directors of the shipping business association in Zhenjiang]. *Shenbao* 申报 [Shanghai news], September 27, 1912. Shanghai: Shenbao Publishing House. Zhenjiang Municipal Government.

"Zhenjiang Zhanqian Zhanhou Jiaotong Qingkuang 镇江战前战后交通情况" [Zhenjiang's transportation condition before and after the war]. *Shiye xinbao* 实业新报 [China enterprises daily news], January 10, 1939.

QING DOCUMENTARY COLLECTIONS

"Da Qing Shengzu Ren (Kangxi) Huangdi Shilu 大清圣祖仁(康熙)皇帝实录" [The veritable records of the reign of the Kangxi emperor]. Reprint, Taipei: Huawen Shuju, n.d.

"Qing Shengzu Shi Lu Xuan Ji 清圣祖实录选辑" [Selections of Emperor Kangxi's record]. Reprint, Tatong shuju, n.d.

Wen, Qing, ed., "Chouban Yiwu Shimo, Daoguan Chao 筹办夷务始末, 道光朝" [Complete records on managing foreign affairs: Daoguang reign]. Reprint, Taipei: Wenhai chubanshe, n.d.

Xia, Xie, and Gao Hongzhi. "Zhong Xi Ji Shi 中西纪事" [China and the West]. Reprint, Changsha: Yuelu shushe, n.d.

MISCELLANEOUS PUBLISHED SOURCES

Anhuiwenshiziliaobianjibu, ed. *Jianghuai Gongshang 江淮工商* [Industry and commerce in Jiangsu and Anhui]. Vol. 28 of *Anhui Wenshi Ziliao 安徽文史资料* [Anhui local history]. Hefei: Anhui renmin chubanshe, 1988.

Anqingwenshiziliaobianjibu. "Anqing Wen Shi Ziliao 安庆文史资料" [Anqing local history]. Anqing: Anqing wenshi ziliao bianjibu, unpublished.

Asai, Seiichi. *Nisshin Kisen Kabushiki Kaisha SanjūNenshi Oyobi Tsuiho 日清汽船株式會社三十年史及追補* [Thirty-year history and reminiscence of the Japan-China Steamship Co.]. Tokyo: Nisshin Kisen Kabushiki Kaisha, 1941.

Diyilishidanganguan. *Ya Pian Zhan Zheng Dang an Shi Liao 鸦片战争档案史料* [Archival materials of the Opium War]. Shanghai: Shanghai renmin chubanshe, 1987.

Gaimushōtsūshōkyoku. *Sokō Jijō 蘇杭事情* [General information on Suzhou and Hangzhou]. Tokyo: Japanese Government publication, 1921.

Gao, Jinchang. "Xu Dantu Xianzhi 续丹徒县志" [Enlarged local history of Dantu]. Zhenjiang: no publisher, 1930.

Li, Xiaojian. "Ji Zhenjiang Yidu Chuan 记镇江义渡船" [Memory of Zhenjiang's free ferry service]. In *Zhenjiang Wenshi Ziliao 镇江文史资料* [Zhenjiang local history]. Zhenjiang: Zhenjiang wenshi ziliao weiyuanhui, 1987.

Liu, Kunyi. *Liu Kunyi Yiji 刘坤一遗集* [Collected works of Liu Kunyi]. Edited by Zhongguo kexueyuan lishi yanjiusuo di san suo 中国科学院历史研究所第三所. Vol. 2. Beijing: Zhonghua shuju, 1959.

Ming, Guang, at al. *Zhenjiang Wenshi Ziliao, Wenhua Jiaoyu Zhuanji 镇江文史资料, 文化教育专辑* [Zhenjiang local history, culture and education edition]. Edited by Li Zhizhong and Ma Mingyi. Vol. 17. Zhenjiang: Zhenjiang wenshi ziliao bianzuan weiyuanhui, 1990.

Tan, Jiang wei. *Putianshi Wenshi Ziliao 莆田市文史资料* [Local history of Putian City]. Vol. 2. Fuzhou: Fujian renmin chubanshe, 2003.

Wei, Yuan. *Chinese Account of the Opium War.* Translated by Edward Harper Parker. Shanghai: Kelly and Walsh, 1888.

———. "Sheng Wu Ji 聖武记" [The record of the Majesty's expedition]. Reprint, Beijing: Zhonghua shuju, n.d.

Xiao, Zhengde, ed. *Zhang Jian Suo Chuang Qishiye Gailan 张謇所创企事业概览* [General view of the enterprises created by Zhang Jian]. Nantong: Nantong shi dangan guan, 2000.

Zhengxiejiangsushengweiyuanhui. *Jiangsu Gong Shang Jing Ji Shi Liao 江苏工商经济史料* [Historical records on industries and commerce in Jiangsu]. Vol. 31. Nanjing: Jiangsu zhengxie, 1989.

"Zhenjiang Haiguan Maoyi Lunlue 镇江海关贸易论略" [General view of trade through Zhenjiang customs]. In *Zhenjiang Difangzhi Ziliao Xuanji 镇江地方志资料选辑* [Selected collection of Zhenjiang local history materials]. Zhenjiang: Zhenjiang difangzhi bangongshi, 1987.

Zhenjiangshigongshanglian. "Zhenjiang Tang, Beiguo Ye De Bainian Xingshuai 镇江糖, 北货业的百年兴衰" [Rise and decline of the business of sugar and northern commodities in a hundred years]. In *Zhenjiang Wenshi Ziliao 镇江文史资料* [Zhenjiang local history]. Zhenjiang: Zhenjiang shi zhengxie, 1989.

Zhong, Rui. "Jingkou Baqi Zhi 京口八旗志" [History of eight banners in Jingkou]. Reprint, New York: Columbia University, n.d.

Zhongguorenminyinhang. *Zhonghua Minguo Huobishi Ziliao: 1912–1927 中华民国货币史资料c: 1912–1927* [Materials on the monetary history of republican China: 1912–1927]. Vol. 1. Shanghai: Shanghai remmin chubanshe, 1986.

INDEX